The North Devon Line

Adams 460 class 4-4-0 No. E0473, with Drummond boiler and chimney, at Barnstaple Junction in the mid 1920s.

A. Halls courtesy National Railway Museum

Above: 'West Country' class 4-6-2 No. 34108 *Wincanton* passes Crediton on the North Devon Line with the 12 noon Ilfracombe - Waterloo express on 22nd August 1959.

S. C. Nash

Below: Three-car diesel multiple unit No. P804 waits at Eggesford station on 19th September 1974.

A. E. West

The North Devon Line

The Exeter to Barnstaple railway from inception to the present day

by John Nicholas

The LSWR Crest

Oxford Publishing Co.

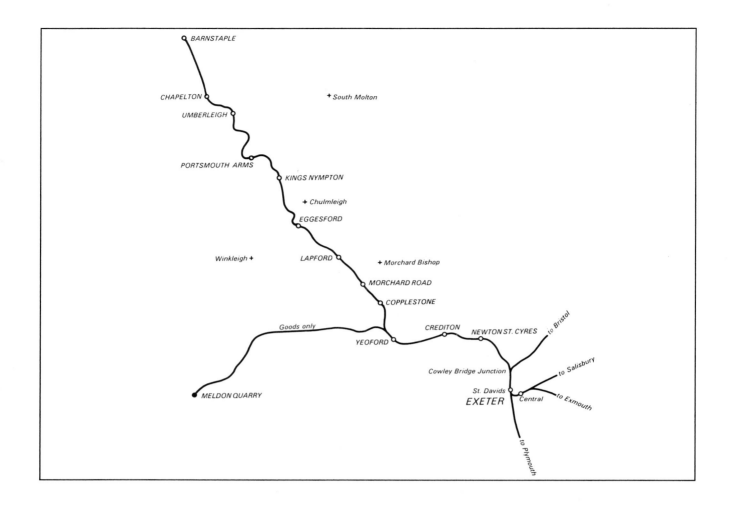

A catalogue record for this book is available from the British Library.

ISBN 0-86093-461-6

Library of congress catalog card number 92-64076

Oxford Publishing Co. is part of the
Haynes Publishing Group PLC
Sparkford, near Yeovil, Somerset, BA22 7JJ

Haynes Publications Inc.
861 Lawrence Drive, Newbury Park, California 91320, USA

Printed by: J. H. Haynes & Co. Ltd
Typset in Times Roman Medium

Note: Train times are as per SR/BR timetables, therefore the 24-hour clock has been used for 1964 and onwards.

Contents

Acknowledgements

This book would not have been written without the help of many people.

Numerous railwaymen have given generously of their time to provide a very detailed account of the operation of the line. These include Messrs K. Almond, E. Clapp, I. Dinmore, G. Facey, W. Keat, F. Kidwell, K. Ley, E McLaughlan, D Mantale, C. Nott, W. Passmore, D. Pearce, S. Pring, F. Sherwood, W. Southcombe and D. Vinsen. Men associated with businesses connected with the line have helped to widen the story, and these include Messrs A. Bussell, M. Maynard, F. Richards, W. Sutton and J. Parkman.

Considerable reference has been made to the standard works on the London & South Western Railway by Mr R. A. Williams, and on South Western and Southern locomotives by the late Mr D. L. Bradley, and both have assisted the author considerably by checking the manuscript and supplying additional information and advice. Mr H. Wilson, author of *T.P.O.*, has provided information on the sorting carriage workings, and Mr K. White has provided much information on broad gauge rolling stock. Reference has also been made to *Track Layout Diagrams of the Southern Railway Section 6* by Mr G. A. Pryer and Clinker's *Register of Closed Passenger Stations and Goods Depots.*

Generous assistance has also come from numerous photographers who have made a very large number of prints available to the author, those included in the book being individually credited. Additional help, support and advice has come from Messrs B. Hughes, D. Wroe, A. Kerr, R. E. Tustin and P. Swift who have also assisted in checking the manuscript. Mr A. Shelley kindly supplied copies of the Locomotive Duties and Carriage Working Notices. The author acknowledges the assistance of the staff of the Public Record Office at Kew, the British Library Newspaper Library at Colindale, the Devon Record Office and the House of Lords Record Office.

Reference has been made to Acts of Parliament, Board of Trade Inspecting Officers and Accident Reports, Minute Books of the North Devon, Exeter & Crediton, South Western and Southern Railways, Public and Working Timetables, South Western Signalling Instructions, the North Devon Journal, the North Devon Journal - Herald and Woolmers Exeter and Plymouth Gazette. Information on Ernest Bevin came from his biography by Mark Stevens, and the 1963 traffic survey was published in the North Devon Railway Report by David St John Thomas. Other sources used include the files of several magazines and periodicals including the South Western Railway Magazine, Southern Railway Magazine, The Locomotive, the Railway Magazine, Modern Railways, Rail, the South Western Circular, the Southern Railways Group Notebook and Newsletter of the North Devon Railway Line Development Group.

Introduction

The North Devon Line which runs from Exeter to Barnstaple is now the only surviving part of the once-extensive railway system that used to serve the region. It was no branch line but a secondary main line, double track for half its length. Local traffic was particularly heavy on Fridays with market traffic to both Exeter and Barnstaple, and during the summer months full length holiday express trains ran from Waterloo to the North Devon resorts. Passenger trains also conveyed parcels, newspapers and postal traffic, for some years a travelling sorting office running on the line. Freight traffic was often heavy with coal trains from Fremington, cattle traffic after the periodical auction markets held at almost every station, milk products from the Ambrosia factory at Lapford, timber from Chapleton and other sawmills, meat from local slaughterhouses, sweets from factories at Crediton, and much other merchandise. Incoming traffic included almost every necessity for local people and commerce such as food, clothing, coal, animal feedstuffs, fertilisers, stone, cement, bricks and steel.

In its 39 miles the North Devon Line, now marketed widely as the Tarka Line, serves only one intermediate town, Crediton, together with a number of villages. Running between Exmoor to the north and Dartmoor to the south along the Yeo and Taw valleys the line passes through unspoilt countryside of great beauty, if anything enhanced by many attractive stone railway structures. The distinctive stone three–arch bridges and station houses along the line have a charm of their own.

At the intermediate stations there was often an apparent lack of activity which might have misled the layman into thinking that little was going on. But in the signal boxes men were efficiently controlling the train service, no simple task on the single track section from Copplestone to Umberleigh on a busy summer Saturday, communicating with each other by bell or telephone and emerging only to exchange single line tablets with the drivers. After a quiet period, stations burst into life when 'up' and 'down' trains crossed at the passing loops, and at small stations, such as Portsmouth Arms or South Molton Road, for a few minutes there were three trains at the station, including a goods train shunted into the yard. Sometimes, the crossing loops were shorter than the trains, one of which then had to laboriously shunt back into a siding. In the booking office the station master or clerk was busy not only selling the occasional ticket but also attending to the extensive parcels and telegraph traffic, or preparing wagon labels for an important customer in the goods yard. Once a month, a livestock auction market was held in pens adjacent to almost every station, the local inn being open all day for the community to enjoy the important social and commercial occasion, whilst railwaymen loaded livestock into cattle trucks for onward transit to London or elsewhere. Each station also had its own permanent way ganger and platelayers who maintained their stretch of line. At night postmen from distant villages slept in bunkhouses at several stations between delivering mail to the 'up' evening mail train and collecting from the early morning 'down' mail. At the end of our line, Barnstaple Junction became an important railway centre employing hundreds of railwaymen. The motive power depot alone employed more than a hundred men, and in Victorian days, the workshops here were so well equipped and staffed that the South Western sent locomotives here for overhaul.

Although there have been many changes in the last thirty years of Western Region administration, it is still obvious that this was no Great Western line. Admittedly, both the Exeter & Crediton and the North Devon railways were opened on the broad gauge, but this was a short-term measure until the principal shareholder, the South Western, could get to Exeter. The station houses and three–arch bridges are North Devon Railway designs, the signal box at Crediton and many railway houses are pure South Western, and many standard Southern prefabricated concrete structures remain. For many, the North Devon Line is associated with Woolwich Moguls and 'West Country' class Pacifics hauling rakes of green Southern coaches, in particular, the "Atlantic Coast Express".

Both the Exeter & Crediton and the North Devon were born during the Railway Mania and had a turbulent early history - the tracks from Cowley Bridge Junction to Crediton were ready for traffic but lay rusting and unused for four years as a victim of railway politics. This skirmish in the Battle of the Gauges was won by the South Western over the broad gauge interests of the Bristol & Exeter Railway, by a combination of its own sharp practice and the naivity of its opponents, but the South Western then had to wait fifteen years to profit from its victory. After its arrival the LSWR did a great deal to modernise and develop the line until a traffic pooling agreement with the Great Western halted progress. Much later, the Beeching Report devastated the region's railways, the North Devon Line surviving only as a pale shadow of its former self, as a long branch line from Exeter with unstaffed stations and lifted goods yards. But now new life is being breathed into the line with an enthusiastic North Devon Railway Line Development Group working with local British Rail management to promote the use of the line.

This book describes fully the line from Cowley Bridge Junction, near Exeter, to Barnstaple. The author's first book, *Lines to Torrington* (OPC 1984), told the story of the line to Bideford, Torrington and Halwill Junction, whilst a third book will cover the Barnstaple to Ilfracombe line.

Chapter 1

The Line Described

Exeter Central

For more than a century trains to the North Devon line commenced their journey at Exeter Central station, 171 miles from Waterloo and the centre of the Southern network in the west country. Although North Devon line trains usually started their journey from here they often incorporated through coaches from Waterloo, brought down by an express train which was re-marshalled at Exeter Central, the restaurant cars being taken off, the through carriages to Plymouth, Padstow and Bude leaving first on the Plymouth train and the through carriages to Ilfracombe and Torrington following on the North Devon train. In Southern days the most famous of these trains was the "Atlantic Coast Express", the 11 o'clock from Waterloo, but the 1.10am, 9am, 1pm and 3pm expresses from Waterloo usually conveyed through coaches to North Devon, the corresponding 'up' services being the 10.30am, 12.30pm "Atlantic Coast Express", 2.30pm and 4.30pm, these being the times in the early 1960s. Freight services usually commenced a mile or so up the line at Exmouth Junction Sidings, adjacent to the extensive locomotive depot, carriage and wagon repair shops, and a concrete works which produced many items of standard lineside equipment to be found all over the Southern. The Southern also had extensive offices at Exeter Central, and much of the day to day management and control of the North Devon line was from here, with motive power controlled from Exmouth Junction depot.

A whole book could be written about Exeter Central station, its environs, and the work done here, but we will confine ourselves to the aspects of the station connected with the North Devon line. The station, as re-built by the Southern in the 1930s, consisted of four through tracks flanked by two platforms, each of which had an outer bay platform pointing east. Platforms Nos 1 and 4 were bays for the Exmouth branch service, No. 2 the 'down' through platform used for all 'down' departures, and No. 3 the 'up' through platform used for all 'up' arrivals and equipped with a scissors crossing midway to facilitate joining up portions of trains. Previously the South Western's Queen Street station had a similar layout with much shorter platforms, and overall train shed roof with a dark interior. Exeter Central station was very convenient for the city centre, far more so than St Davids, and dealt with heavy traffic including commuters, shoppers, travellers on business and market traffic on Fridays.

Southern Railway traffic statistics for 1928-36 show just how busy Exeter Central station was, with about a thousand tickets sold daily and two thousand collected. Freight traffic in the adjacent yard to the north was also heavy with some sixty loaded wagons forwarded and a hundred received every day. These figures account only for traffic originating or terminating here, but much more through traffic passed Exeter Central on journeys between Devon and Cornwall and the rest of the Southern system up to Waterloo.

Immediately after passing under Queen Street bridge trains ran slowly down the 1 in 37 gradient through the 184 yard St Davids Tunnel, and over an embankment to curve into the Great Western's Exeter St Davids station. Heavy 'up' trains required the assistance of banking engines from St Davids to Central, a practice now usually required only for ballast trains from Meldon Quarry to Salisbury.

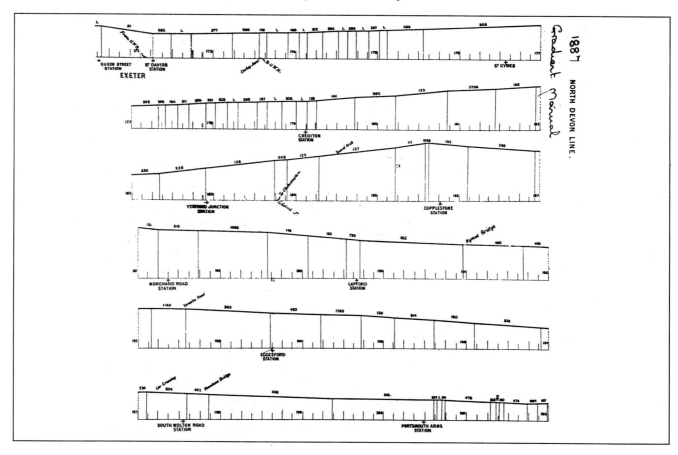

7

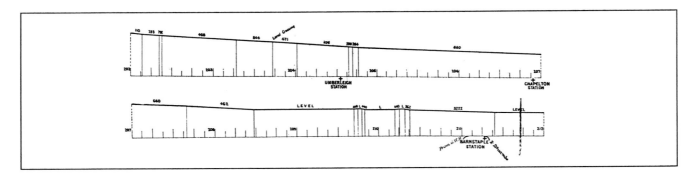

Exeter St Davids

Exeter St Davids has always been the busiest and most important station in the west country. Trains on the three main lines to Devon and Cornwall, from Bristol, Paddington and Waterloo all meet here, but while InterCity 125 trains on the first two routes now run through to Torbay, Plymouth and Cornwall the Waterloo trains now terminate here, although there are some through workings, making Exeter St Davids the focus of railway activity in the west country.

Again, our description is limited to that concerning North Devon line trains. After the re-building of 1912-14 the South Western trains have used the two faces of the middle island platform, Nos 3 and 4, all trains stopping here, and the practice continued until the 1985 changes. There has always been considerable interchange traffic between the Southern and Great Western lines, the South Western and Southern having their own booking office. During the period 1928-36 traffic statistics show up to 100 tickets a day sold here, many of these being passengers arriving on Great Western trains and re-booking to destinations on the Southern.

Leaving St Davids 'down' North Devon line trains ran up the Great Western main line past numerous signal boxes, sidings, goods sheds and the extensive Exeter Riverside yard until after about a mile they passed under a road bridge and arrived at Cowley Bridge Junction.

Cowley Bridge Junction
Chronology (North Devon Line only):

Crediton line completed	January 1847
Station constructed	1848
Crediton line opened	12th May 1851
Second viaduct into use	November 1858
Mixed gauge into use	1st February 1862
Cowley Loop and signal box into use	11th November 1874
Cowley Loop - St Cyres doubled	23rd February 1875
Cowley Junction - Cowley Loop doubled	2nd June 1875
Broad gauge abolished	20th May 1892
Signal box replaced by ground frame	26th March 1916
Ground Frame closed	1st August 1928
Single track over viaduct into use	28th November 1965
Third viaduct into use	15th January 1967
Crediton line singled	16th December 1984

Our detailed description of the North Devon line starts at Cowley Bridge Junction, the beginning of the Southern territory west of Exeter, sometimes known as the 'Withered Arm', of which the North Devon line was the original component. Cowley Bridge Junction was also a crucial battlefield of the 'War of the Gauges', lost by the broad gauge alliance to the South Western, which allowed the standard gauge into the west country. Had the result gone the other way, the South Western would not have

Cowley Bridge Junction in Southern days showing the layout before the 1943 extensions and resignalling. The South Western's viaduct of 1874 can be seen on the left.

LGRP

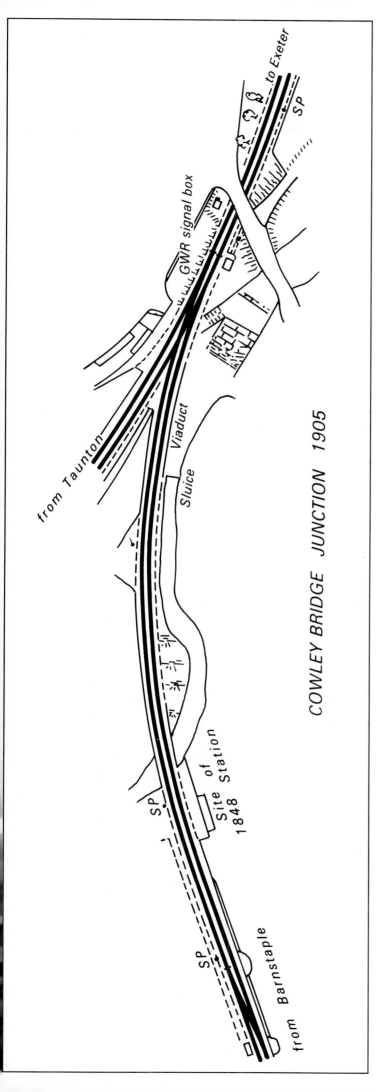

from Taunton

GWR signal box

Viaduct

Sluice

to Exeter

SP

SP

Site of Station 1848

SP

SP

from Barnstaple

COWLEY BRIDGE JUNCTION 1905

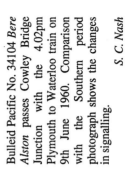

Bulleid Pacific No. 34104 *Bere Alston* passes Cowley Bridge Junction with the 4.02pm Plymouth to Waterloo train on 9th June 1960. Comparison with the Southern period photograph shows the changes in signalling.   *S. C. Nash*

9

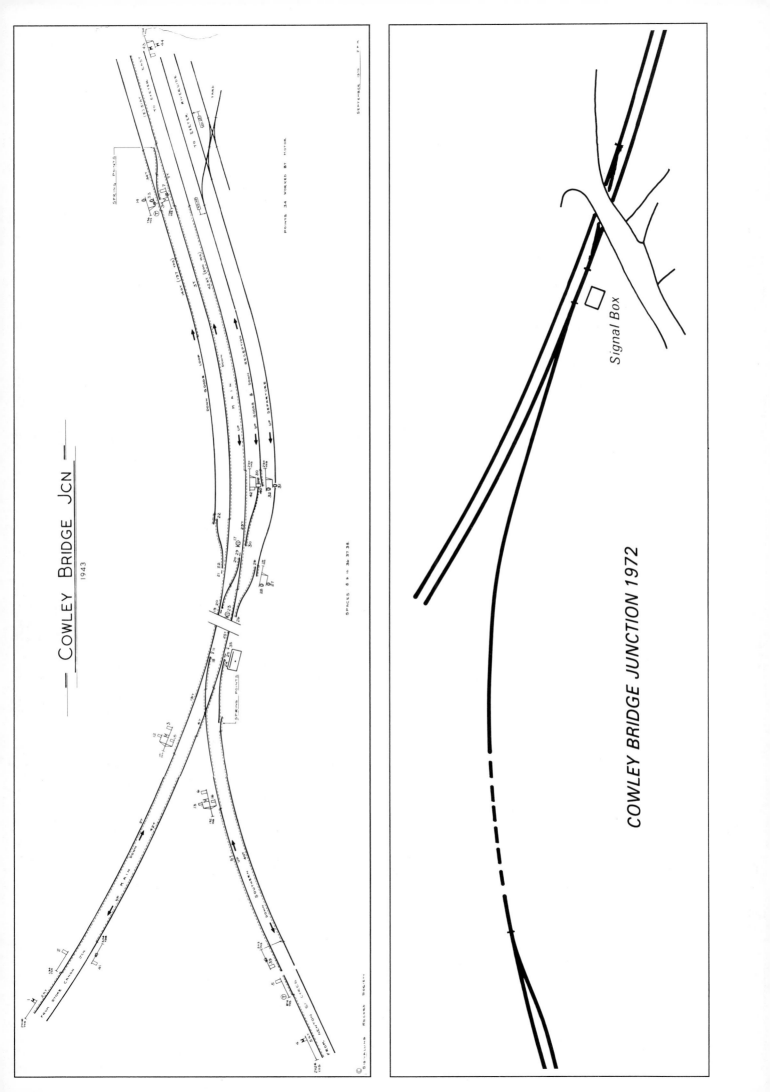

— COWLEY BRIDGE JCN —

1943

Signal Box

COWLEY BRIDGE JUNCTION 1972

Drummond T9 class 4-4-0 No. 30717 passes culvert No. 534A and the Cowley Bridge Junction 'up' home signals with the 2.33pm Plymouth to Waterloo train on 22nd August 1959. These signals were installed in 1943, and the train is signalled on to the Great Western 'down' main line.
S. C. Nash

The 12.50 train on 14th June 1982 from Exeter Central to Barnstaple passes a Class 33 with a ballast empties train in Exeter Riverside yard and approaches Cowley Bridge Junction. The trailing crossover is used by 'up' North Devon trains.
Author

On the same day, the 12.19 train from Barnstaple to Exeter St Davids approaches Cowley Bridge Junction over the single-track line on what were new bridges in the mid-1960s. The train joins the 'down' Western Region main line by using the crossover illustrated in the previous photograph.

Author

reached North Devon and beyond, and this might have weakened its resolve to build its main line from Salisbury to Exeter. Cowley Bridge Junction became a very well documented location, with no less than nine reports written by Inspecting Officers over a period of thirty years, as we see in Chapters 2 to 4.

After 1875, there was a conventional double–track junction at Cowley Bridge, complicated up to 1892 by mixed gauge on all lines. A photograph taken during this period shows the stone-built Great Western signal box adjacent to the curved South Western girder bridge, with the South Western signal box in the background, and both Great Western and South Western semaphore signalling. We will see in Chapter 4 some details of the South Western signalling, the box itself being a weatherboarded structure on a stone base similar to others of the period. Being somewhat remote, the signal box was supplied with stores, when required, by a passing goods train, in 1909 the 10.10am goods from Exmouth Junction to Barnstaple Junction. After its closure in 1916, all the signalling at Cowley Bridge was controlled by the brick-built Western signal box.

Up to 1943, the signalling was quite straightforward with 'up' home and outer home signals on the Southern line, the home just beyond the end of the first viaduct, No. 534 on the Southern system of numbering engineering structures. However, when the new Exeter Riverside yard was opened in 1943, the northern access to it was provided just to the south of Cowley Bridge Junction, and the area was re-signalled in a complex manner. There was considerable track circuiting but at the Southern 'up' outer

home signal there was a telephone to enable a driver to speak to the signalman in the event of delay. There was a speed restriction of 25mph for both 'up' and 'down' Southern trains, with catch points on the 'down' line. These were once required to derail a wagon which had run away from Yeoford during shunting operations, but subsequently catch points were also installed at Neopardy.

The Southern double-track line crossed the River Exe on a series of of three girder bridges. Between the second and third bridges, on an embankment, was the site of the 1848 station, built but never used, the original 1874 Cowley Loop and signal box, which later controlled a crossover and signals, and the ground frame which replaced it. In 1965-7 this part of the line was singled when the three viaducts of 1874-5 were replaced by modern steel structures, and the double junction at Cowley Bridge replaced by a crossover and a connection from the 'up' main line only. To the south of the A377 road bridge is Exeter Riverside yard, latterly starting point for all freight services on the line.

Having crossed the three bridges over the River Exe, the double-track Southern line then passed under the stone-built Pynes Bridge, which carried a minor road. Near here, between 1965 and 1984, the single track over the new viaducts opened up to double track. The Cowley Bridge Junction 'up' distant signal was passed and the line continued in a north westerly direction along the flat valley of the River Yeo, keeping to the north bank, until passing the 'down' distant signal for Newton St Cyres and running into the small rural station, 176¾ miles from Waterloo.

Newton St Cyres

Chronology:

Opened	12th May 1851
Mixed gauge into use	1st February 1862
Cowley Loop - St Cyres doubled and signal box opened	23rd February 1875
St Cyres - Crediton doubled	2nd June 1875
Broad gauge abolished	20th May 1892
First signal box closed and second box opened in booking office	17th August 1930
Goods yard closed	12th September 1960
Second signal box closed	31st July 1968
Line singled	16th December 1984

NEWTON ST CYRES

	1928	1930	1932	1934	1936
Passenger tickets issued	10,385	7,713	5,663,	5,356	5,608
Season tickets issued	33	25	20	16	18
Tickets collected	10,987	7,670	5,981	5,437	5,683
Parcels forwarded	266	289	195	175	182
Parcels received	448	439	503	637	526
Horses forwarded	1	–	1	1	8
Horses received	5	3	3	4	2
Milk forwarded (gal) (churns up to 1932)	–	–	–	2,668	–
Milk received (gal) (churns up to 1932)	–	–	–	–	–
Fish, meat, etc. forwarded (cwt)	76	38	13	21	5
Fish, meat etc. received (cwt)	–	–	16	–	–
General merchandise forwarded (tons)	466	441	348	315	128
General merchandise received (tons)	568	655	395	438	930
Coal forwarded (tons)	–	–	–	–	–
Coal received (tons)	272	358	350	291	237
Other minerals forwarded (tons)	–	–	–	16	–
Other minerals received (tons)	2,099	1,381	782	867	578
Livestock forwarded (trucks)	10	7	5	50	38
Livestock received (trucks)	15	8	6	17	7
Loaded wagons (not livestock) forwarded	130	117	77	95	45
Loaded wagons (not livestock) received	485	417	237	242	339

Nowadays most North Devon line trains speed through Newton St Cyres which supplies little traffic for the railway, but half a century ago it did provide a fair level of passenger traffic. This was the only intermediate station on the Exeter & Crediton Railway, but is situated a mile away from the village which is on the main road so that when bus services became established the railway patronage suffered. In South Western days it was called St Cyres, the Southern renaming it Newton St Cyres.

Newton St Cyres station was situated on the north side of the flat valley of the River Yeo at the small settlement of Sweetham, where there is a crossroads with the Railway Inn adjacent to the station approach on the north side of the line. Station Road crossed the line on an overbridge and ran south past Longbridge Cottages over the River Yeo on Long Bridge and so on to the village of Newton St Cyres. The station was situated to the east of the road bridge, with its two platforms wide apart, a legacy of the broad gauge inherited by all the stations on the line. Next to the bridge was the station house, a typical South Western brick building, now sold out of railway use and painted in white stucco. The main station buildings were on the 'up' platform, the small wooden structure incorporating the booking office, waiting room and, after 1930, the signal box as well. The original 1875 signal box was situated at the Exeter end of the 'up' platform, and although no photographs of it have come to light, it was probably of a similar design to that at Crediton and elsewhere. The 'down' platform boasted only a waiting shelter, again a small wooden building, although in later years this was replaced with a concrete structure. Both platforms had standard South Western iron fencing, platform seats and oil lamps, with Southern concrete nameboards, although electric lighting was installed in the late 1960s.

N class 2-6-0 No. 31832 pauses with a 'down' train at Newton St Cyres on 20th June 1959. There are no wagons in the small goods yard which closed the following year.

R. J. Sellick

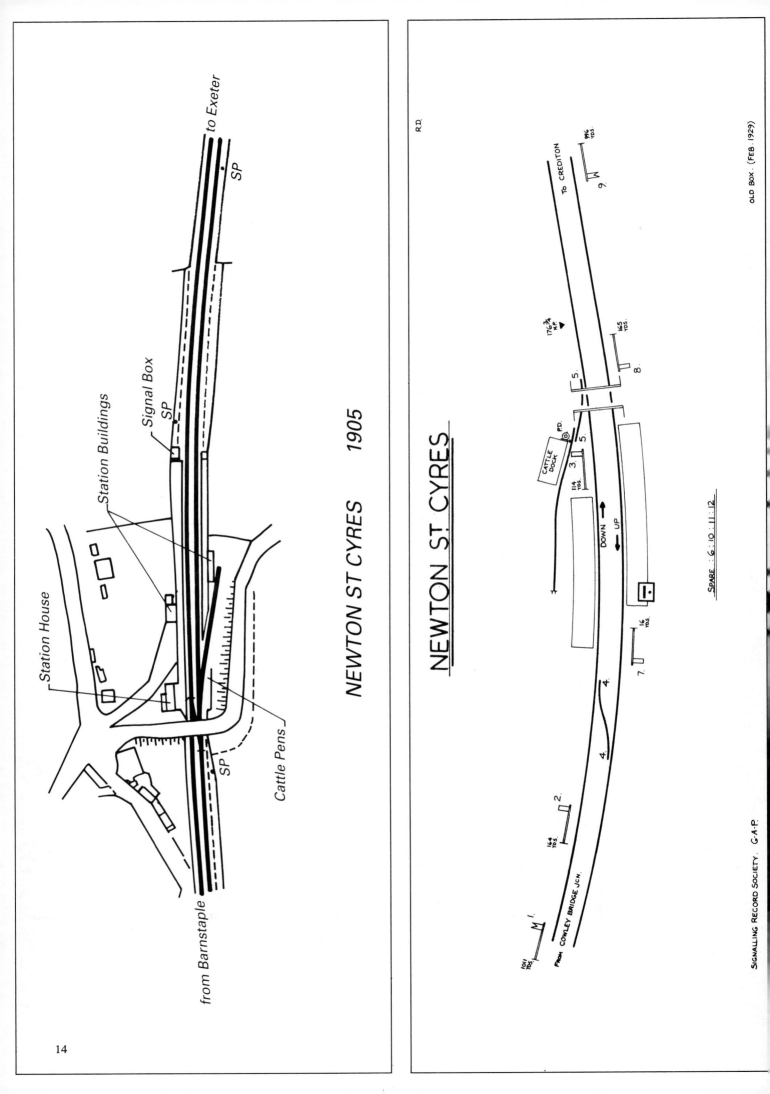

NEWTON ST CYRES   1905

Station House

Station Buildings

Signal Box

SP

to Exeter

SP

from Barnstaple

SP

Cattle Pens

14

NEWTON ST CYRES

R.D.

To CREDITON

996 YDS.

9.

176¾ M.P.

165 YDS.

8.

5.

CATTLE DOCK

P.D.

5.

3.

114 YDS.

DOWN

UP

16 YDS.

7.

4.

4.

2.

164 YDS.

1.

101 YDS.

FROM COWLEY BRIDGE JCN.

SPARE : 6 . 10 . 11 . 12

OLD BOX . (FEB. 1929)

SIGNALLING RECORD SOCIETY.   G·A·P.

Two views of Newton St Cyres on 3rd October 1964 showing the station house, buildings and fittings including many standard LSWR items. Comparison with the previous 1959 photograph shows that the siding in the yard has been lifted and the old wooden building on the 'down' platform replaced by a concrete structure.

C. L. Caddy

At the Crediton end, the 'down' platform was offset from the 'up' to facilitate a short siding into the tiny goods yard, which was provided only with a loading gauge and a loading dock with cattle pens. The only other pointwork was a crossover at the Exeter end of the station. The signalling was very simple, there being distant, home and starting signals in both directions, one crossover and one set of siding points, which left four levers spare in the twelve-lever frame in the booking office. Most signals were mounted on South Western lattice posts, but the 'up' starting signal was on a wooden post. As we shall see, the signal box was fitted with a through switch and was switched out for much of the time.

In the period 1928-36, the traffic returns show about one loaded wagon received per day and a couple forwarded in a week. There were a few hundred tons annually of general merchandise received and forwarded, a few hundred tons of coal and one or two thousand tons of minerals received, together with a small amount of cattle traffic. Passenger traffic fell off from an average of thirty tickets issued per day in 1928 to half that in 1936, about

the same number being collected, in addition to a few season tickets. There were a handful of telegrams and parcels dealt with in the booking office daily.

In 1910, the station master was Mr A. E. Hurst, but in later years, Newton St Cyres was supervised by the Crediton station master. The establishment was two porter signalmen who carried out all the duties of signalling, booking and goods clerks, and goods porters in the yard at this quiet station. In the 1930s, the two porter signalmen were Mr R. Wonnacott and Mr G. Beer, both of whom later went to Crediton, and the last two when the signal box closed in 1968 were Mr L. Purchase and Mr R Bailey.

Leaving St Cyres, the double track continued westwards along the Yeo valley, passing the St Cyres 'up' distant signal. After crossing the river and running on an embankment, the line ran into a cutting at Downes, the main earthworks on the Exeter & Crediton Railway, where it was crossed on an overbridge by the main A377 road at Codshead Bridge. Just beyond the end of the cutting the line ran on an embankment with a culvert for carrying away flood water, but was washed out in October 1960

Newton St Cyres 'up' starting signal in 1965, a concrete post structure.

A. E. West

16

Newton St Cyres station building on the 'up' platform in 1965. This was unusual in that the signal box was incorporated into part of the building, being moved there in 1930 as an economy measure and can be seen on the right hand side.

A. E. West

Newton St Cyres on 16th August 1984 showing the 12.28 train from Barnstaple to Exeter speeding through, most of the station structures now having been removed. Concrete troughing has been installed for cables in connection with resignalling and track singling later in in the year. The 'up' line is laid with a length of continuously-welded rail.

Author

after exceptionally heavy rain. The line then passed Crediton 'down' distant signal and ran past the yard into Crediton station, 179¼ miles from Waterloo.

Crediton
Chronology:

Line to Exeter completed	January 1847
Line to Exeter opened	12th May 1851
Line to Barnstaple opened	1st August 1854
Mixed gauge to Exeter into use	1st February 1862
Mixed gauge to Bideford into use	2nd March 1863
Crediton - St Cyres doubled and East and West signal boxes into use	2nd June 1875
Crediton - Yeoford doubled	1st June 1876
Broad gauge to Bideford taken out of use	30th April 1877
Footbridge constructed	1878
Broad gauge to Cowley Bridge out of use	20th May 1892
GWR freight service withdrawn	1903
East signal box reduced to ground frame	1916
Goods yard closed 4th December	1967
Resignalling as a junction into use	17th October 1971
Level crossing converted to lifting barriers	27th January 1974
Resignalling and singling to Cowley Bridge	16th December 1984

There can be few stations which can match the early history of that at Crediton. Ready for opening in 1847, it lay unused for four long years as a major casualty of the 'Battle of the Gauges'. The broad gauge faction wanted to open it, but the majority 'narrow' gauge faction refused to do so until the gauge was narrowed. But, when the gauge was narrowed, there was no station to go to at Exeter! When the line was eventually opened on the broad gauge there was an element of compromise, the second of the

Crediton station looking east from the footbridge, probably about 1960, showing the extensive goods yard on the 'up' side of the line and coaches stored in the 'down' sidings.

Lens of Sutton

two tracks remaining narrow. Crediton became an outpost of the broad gauge until its total demise in 1892. Here trains from Exeter were handed over from Bristol & Exeter to North Devon locomotives for onward transit to Bideford. Later, Crediton became an important standard gauge station on the South Western, and the major intermediate traffic centre between Exeter and Barnstaple. Recently, there has been a mixing of ancient and modern at Crediton, with the old 1875 signal box now equipped with a 1984 colourlight signalling panel.

CREDITON

	1928	1930	1932	1934	1936
Passenger tickets issued	19,788	14,541	11,150	10,474	8,724
Season tickets issued	101	85	59	54	112+
Tickets collected	22,448	19,912	17,767	14,014	12,898
Parcels forwarded	5,366	4,705	3,794	4,453	3,877
Parcels received	10,610	9,980	10,170	11,483	16,416
Horses forwarded	37	43	11	17	12
Horses received	58	42	23	21	22
Milk forwarded (gal) (churns up to 1932)	1,116	263	3,002	10,859	8,303
Milk received (gal) (churns up to 1932)	–	–	–	28	21
Fish, meat, etc. forwarded (cwt)	376	487	414	166	85
Fish, meat etc. received (cwt)	103	44	201	146	41
General merchandise forwarded (tons)	2,674	2,875	2,631	3,103	2,173
General merchandise received (tons)	6,339	7,462	7,384	9,249	10,465
Coal forwarded (tons)	–	–	18	18	–
Coal received (tons)	6,667	6,841	6,301	6,077	6,893
Other minerals forwarded (tons)	298	300	143	317	330
Other minerals received (tons)	8,763	5,741	4,438	4,791	4,195
Livestock forwarded (trucks)	409	346	229	342	364
Livestock received (trucks)	207	193	147	47	40
Loaded wagons (not livestock) forwarded	768	674	613	799	1,351
Loaded wagons (not livestock) received	2,946	3,305	3,769	4,084	4,462

(+ Factory girls from Exeter)

CREDITON

To YEOFORD

22.

21.

5.

UP SIDING NORTH

18y.

16.

17.

15.

16.

15.

14.

GATE LOCK - 1.

4.

DOWN
UP

13. 9.

12.

20.

12.

6y.

UP SIDING SOUTH.

7y. 13.

ELEC. REL. 15
11.

DOWN SIDINGS

SLOT 8.

7

10

GOODS

SLOT LIFTED BY
8 OR 5 REVERSE.

3.

6 17

5

3

5

4 Y

ELEC. REL. 14
10.

GROUND FRAME
A

NUMBERS THUS; 1

From NEWTON ST. CYRES.

2

19.

GAP
27.4.72

SIGNALLING RECORD SOCIETY

Crediton station looking west, about 1960, showing the gated level crossing and the 1874 signal box framed by the footbridge which has lost its overall roof.

Lens of Sutton

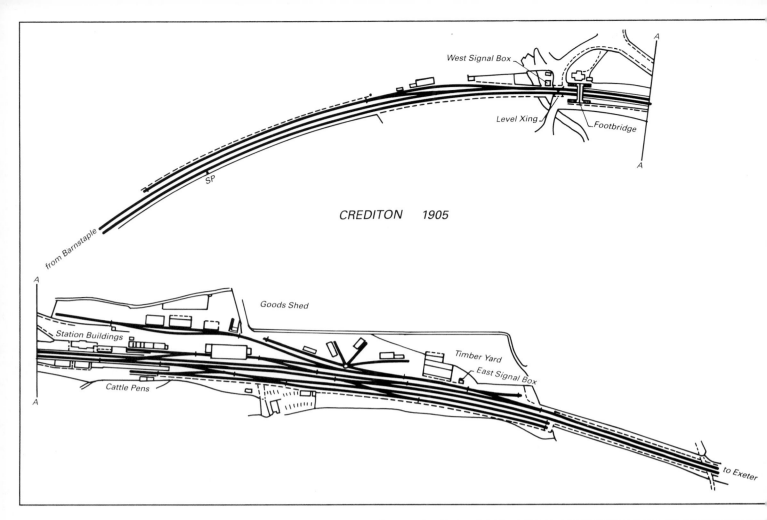

West Signal Box

Level Xing

Footbridge

CREDITON 1905

from Barnstaple

SP

A

Goods Shed

Station Buildings

Cattle Pens

A

Timber Yard

East Signal Box

to Exeter

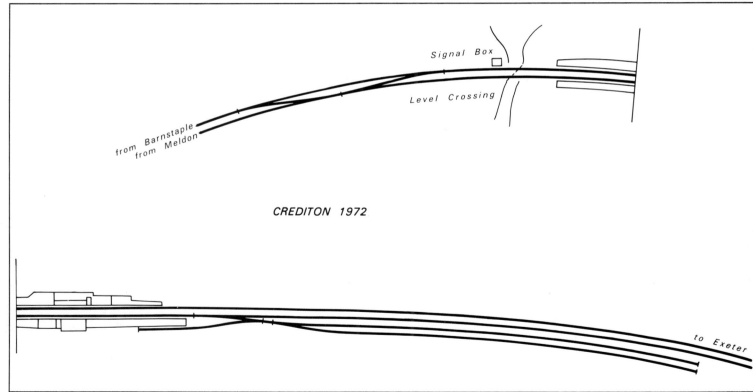

Signal Box

Level Crossing

from Barnstaple
from Meldon

CREDITON 1972

to Exeter

The town of Crediton stretches for almost two miles along the main Exeter to Barnstaple road, and the station was situated at Wellparks on the eastern end of the town. This was no disadvantage for many years, but as local bus services developed the passenger trains became less popular for local journeys. When the line opened in 1851 to the broad gauge terminus at Crediton, it must have looked like many other outposts of Brunel's broad gauge, except for the rusting 'narrow' gauge tracks. The station house which survives to this day was then described as very picturesque. The 1880 photograph with a 'down' train gives us an idea of its early appearance. The large wooden goods shed with its distinctive curved roof was used for the trans-shipment of goods between 'narrow'

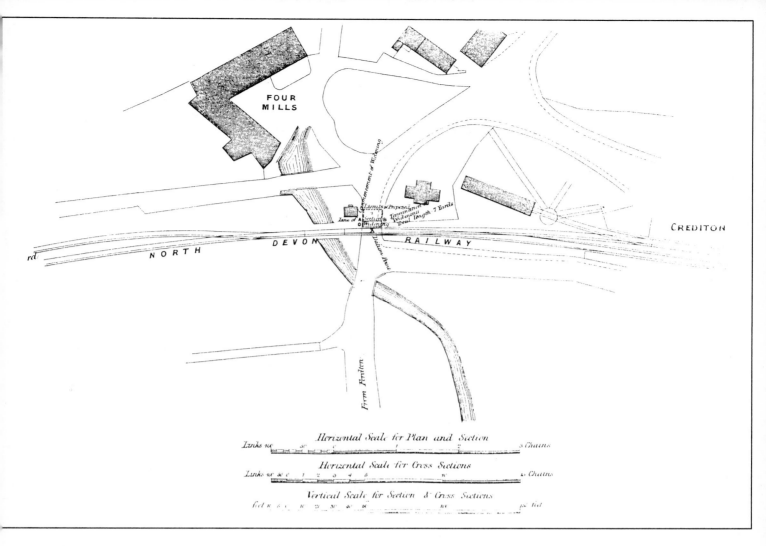

FOUR MILLS

CREDITON

NORTH DEVON RAILWAY

Horizontal Scale for Plan and Section

Horizontal Scale for Cross Sections

Vertical Scale for Section & Cross Sections

Crediton 1873. This plan, under the LSWR Various Powers Act, was drawn for the widening of Crediton Level Crossing. The mixed gauge track is clearly shown; the building to the right of the level crossing is the old North Devon locomotives shed used for stabling the broad gauge locomotive which worked the only broad gauge train of the day to Bideford and back. Later the platforms were extended over this area as far as the level crossing.

Courtesy Devon County Record Office

and broad gauge wagons. The North Devon had a small locomotive depot and turntable here also.

The station was situated on a long curve of double track, and approached from the Crediton to Fordton minor road which was crossed by a gated level crossing. This was controlled by the 1875 South Western signal box, Crediton West until 1916. Adjacent to the level crossing was the double footbridge, carrying a stone with the inscription "L&SWRY 1878", with one crossing for pedestrians for use when the crossing gates across the road were shut, and a second connecting the two platforms for the benefit of railway staff and passengers, the two being completely separated. The footbridge span consisted of a wooden floor on iron girders, supported on stone structures at each end. In South Western times the footbridge was protected from the elements by an arched roof, since removed.

The station approach was from this minor road, adjacent to the level crossing, opposite the Railway Hotel and next to a pair of South Western railway cottages. The small but elegant station house was constructed in brick and stone on the 'up' platform, and contained the station master's, booking and other offices. Adjacent to this was a waiting shelter, built to a typical South Western weather-boarded design. On the 'down' platform was another brick structure containing porters' and cloak rooms, and another wooden waiting shelter. The 1880 photograph shows a water column provided for locomotives at the end of the 'down' platform, before it was lengthened. This had

disappeared before the end of the South Western era, but it seems reasonable to suppose that other water columns were provided at that time. Water would probably have been pumped up by a steam engine from the stream which ran under the line near the signal box.

Entry to the goods yard was from the station approach. There was one very long siding forming a loop with trailing connections to both 'up' and 'down' main lines which ran through the goods shed, and another very long siding with a loop at the end ran along the back of the yard, there being several spur lines from these two. In South Western days three short spurs radiated from a wagon turntable, later replaced by two spurs served by points. The goods shed was of an unusual design with its large corrugated iron structure covered with a curved roof. Here was an office for the goods clerks, and inside a 2-ton crane for unloading heavy items. Outside in the yard was a 5-ton crane used for transferring containers between the road and rail vehicles. In South Western days there was a road vehicle weighbridge provided at the yard entrance, but this was removed by the Southern. There were cattle pens and an end-loading dock in the yard together with numerous outbuildings. In the 1950s, on a spur at the end of the 'up' platform, there was a fine old ex-GWR clerestory coach used by civil engineers staff, and in later years as a store for Silcocks animal feedstuffs.

Several buildings in the yard were occupied by the firm of Ward & Co., including an office at the yard entrance

Crediton station building - the original 1847 structure was little changed in 1963.

Author

and two stores near the goods shed. As we see in Chapter 8, Thomas Ward established his business here in 1851, and subsequently built up considerable trade in coal, fertilizers and animal feedstuffs. The firm of G. Symonds & Co., coal merchants and general hauliers, Copp & Co. and in Southern days, Martin & Co., all operated from the yard, Copp & Co. having its store on a siding beyond the signal box. Some buildings in the yard were used for a variety of purposes over the years. For example, adjacent to the old East signal box, was a large stone built structure with loading facilities on the loop siding. In 1921 this was described as a slaughterhouse, in the 1950s Mr Adams used it for processing chickens, eggs and vegetables, and later Shippams, the meat paste firm, took it over. There were various stores and one near the goods shed was formerly used as a stable for the shunting horse. Adjacent to the yard were cider mills and a timber yard. Apart from the goods yard, there were also two long 'down' sidings to

An N class 2-6-0 leaves Crediton with an 'up' train on 18th August 1954. The ex-GWR clerestory coach on the right was in use by the engineers department.

H. C. Casserley

A North British Type 2 diesel shunts mineral wagons across into the yard at Crediton from the 'down' main line on 28th August 1965.

A. E. West

The 13.11 train from Exeter to Barnstaple on 28th August 1981 at Crediton departs over the level crossing at Crediton, now equipped with lifting barriers operated from the signal box. The driver collects the single-line token for the section to Eggesford from signalman D. Vinsen. The junction for the two single lines to Meldon and Eggesford is formed by the two crossovers ahead of the train.

Author

On the wagon:

MARTIN
DIRECT COAL SUPPLY
25 CREDITON

Empty to
Tare 5-13-2

Load 8 Tons

COAL WAGON
14·5 × 6·11 × 3·1
Painted Dark Lead Color
Letters White
Shaded Red

GLOUCESTER RAILWAY
CARRIAGE & WAGON
COMPANY LIMITED
Sepᵗ 1903 Photo 2786

Private owner wagons on South Western lines in North Devon were rare. The firm of Martin no longer exists although several other companies survive in the station yard.

the south of the line used mainly for stabling rolling stock, although there was also a cattle dock here. To the west of the level crossing, there was also a long 'up' siding north which served Copp & Co.'s store.

Early signalling at Crediton was of the cross bar and disc variety, and the single line to Exeter was controlled by the staff and train ticket method. When the signalling was concentrated in the West signal box in 1916 a 22-lever, Stevens frame controlled distant, home, starting and advance starting signals in both directions, the level crossing and much of the pointwork. The ground frame in the old East signal box, interlocked with the signal box controlled the yard and other points at the east end of the station. The signals were all of South Western type on lattice posts.

In 1970 the redundant sidings in the closed yard were removed, although many firms remained in their premises, receiving all their deliveries by road. Only the two 'down' sidings were retained for the civil engineers, but as from 17th October 1971 considerable changes were made. A pair of crossovers to the west of the level crossing were installed to make Crediton a junction, the two lines east of Crediton, the 'up' and 'down' Exeter becoming two separate lines to the west, one each to Meldon and Barnstaple. New Great Western type signalling was installed with fixed distant, home and starting signals in each direction, although the two 'up' home signals were half a mile down the line. The level crossing gates were replaced by lifting barriers in 1974, but in 1984 the line to Exeter was singled, with a long crossing loop at Crediton, and re-signalled with colour light signals and points controlled from a new panel in the 1875 signal box, the new arrangements being brought into use on 16th December 1984.

Traffic figures recorded by the Southern Railway show Crediton to be the principal traffic centre for both passengers and freight between Exeter and Barnstaple. At this time an average of some fifty tickets a day were issued and slightly more collected. A footnote indicated that many of the season tickets issued in 1936 were purchased by girls commuting from Exeter to work in Authers' factory in Crediton. There were some twenty telegrams dealt with, twenty parcels forwarded and forty received, and twenty churns of milk forwarded on an average day in 1928, keeping the passenger station staff very busy. Goods forwarded from Crediton included livestock, meat, milk, confectionery from Bristows, Authers and Jacksons, meat products from Shippams and general merchandise. Goods received included coal for Ward & Co. and Symonds & Co., animal feedstuffs, fertilizers, livestock and general merchandise. At this time, Crediton goods forwarded six or seven loaded wagons and received between fifteen and twenty per day. In the yard a shunting horse was employed for many years, and at one time, was sent down the line to Eggesford on market days. The horse was loaded in a horsebox marshalled in a morning passenger train and unloaded onto the platform at Eggesford, and after a day's work shunting cattle trucks returned to Crediton in the same way.

The Crediton station master was responsible for a considerable staff. In 1910 the office was held by Mr J. Banks and in the early 1930s by Mr Clapp, whose brother and nephew were signalmen at Crediton and Coleford Junction respectively. Mr Clapp was followed by Mr S. H. Trett, who was there in 1937, and in 1947 it was Mr Warland. Later came Mr Platt who retired in the early 1960s to be succeeded by Mr H. Martin, the last station master at Crediton. For many years, the Crediton station master also supervised Newton St Cyres, paying a weekly visit to carry out these duties.

For many years, under the South Western and Southern, the Crediton signal box was very busy, handling some eighty trains a day, dealing with shunting operations and the level crossing. It was open twenty-four hours a day, seven days a week and was manned by three regular signalmen, together with rest day relief men. In 1947, one of the signalmen was Mr Clapp, in the early 1960s, Mr G. Osborne, Mr B. Horne and Mr R. Mills and in the early 1980s, Mr Knight, Mr N. Geeson and Mr D. Vinsen. Nowadays, the box is open from about 4am to 11pm, handling about thirty-six trains a day, but the signalmen work long shifts without rest day relief.

The passenger station was usually manned by two grade one porters, working alternate early and late turns. In 1947 they were Mr B. Copp and Miss S. Wheeler and in the 1960s Mr G. Vicary and Mr D. Leach, who was succeeded by Mr J. Elstone. Their duties included issuing tickets at the booking office, collecting tickets from passengers, dealing with the extensive parcels traffic, and so on. The staff was later augmented with a booking clerk, in the 1960s Mr J. Ridge and then Mr F. Sherwood.

The goods yard was a very busy place, employing numerous men in the depots of Ward & Co. and other firms, together with some ten railwaymen. For many years, up to the early 1960s, the Chief Clerk Mr Harris, was in charge of the goods yard. He had been there back in 1947, but sadly in the early 1960s, he was knocked down in the yard by a shunting engine, lost part of his heel and died a year or so later, being replaced by relief staff. In 1947, the goods staff working under Mr Harris comprised two clerks working in the goods office, Miss J. Baker and Mr D. Walker, a checker, Mr W. Pollard, a porter, Mr F. Sherwood, two porter shunters, Mr J. Parkhouse and Mr C. Braund and two delivery motor drivers, Mr C. Greenslade and Mr L. Cheriton. Mr Parkhouse and Mr T. Jones, both later transferred from porter shunter duties to motor drivers. By the early 1960s, the drivers were Mr Pollard, Mr Jones, Mr Cheriton and Mr Doidge, with Mr W. Edgworthy as checker. All the posts in the goods yard and passenger station were withdrawn in the mid 1960s, leaving only the signalmen and a mobile, permanent way gang, responsible for the southern half of the line.

Park Crossing
Leaving Crediton, over the level crossing and culvert No. 550 'down' trains commenced running over the former North Devon Railway, still in the valley of the River Yeo. After about half a mile was Park Crossing, where a minor track crossed the line. The gated crossing, normally closed to road traffic, was operated by the crossing keeper who lived in the adjacent house, built to a standard South Western design. The crossing gates were opened by the crossing keeper after gaining permission to do so from the Crediton signalman. Supplies for Park Crossing were brought by a porter from Crediton station. As an economy measure, the crossing was later closed to vehicles completely and converted to an unattended foot crossing, the crossing keeper's house being demolished.

A few hundred yards later the line cut into the hillside and passed under bridge No. 552, the first of the very attractive stone built North Devon Railway three-arch bridges. In 1971 the new Crediton 'up' home signals were sited here, being replaced by colour light signals CN 1 and CN 3 in 1984. The double track continued straight on to Salmon Pool crossing.

Salmon Pool Crossing
Salmon Pool Gates or Salmon Pool Crossing was provided for a narrow country lane leading to the small settlement of Uton. Near the crossing the road bridged the River Yeo at Yeoton Bridge, and some early railway documents

In August 1984 the two 1971 Crediton 'up' home signals, for the Eggesford line on the left, and Meldon on the right, continued to operate alongside their replacement colour light signals CN 1 and CN 3. The bridge, No. 552, was the first three-arch North Devon Railway overbridge west of Crediton.

Author

Salmon Pool Crossing in June 1982 where approaching trains automatically operate the flashing red lights to halt road traffic. Previously this was a manned, gated crossing, the crossing keeper residing in the cottage on the left, built to a standard South Western design.

Author

referred to Yeoton Crossing. There was a large pool in the River Yeo which formerly produced salmon, but in more recent times only good trout. The gated crossing was attended by a crossing keeper who resided in the adjacent crossing keeper's house. The gates were normally shut to road traffic, and when a road vehicle wished to cross the crossing keeper telephoned the signalmen at Crediton for permission. Supplies for Salmon Pool Crossing were sent from Crediton by a porter. The crossing was converted to automatic operation on 21st September 1980 and the then two posts of crossing keeper withdrawn, the approaching trains operating treadles which switch on the flashing red lights for road traffic. Occasionally, a long ballast train halted at the Crediton 'up' home signal causes the mechanism to continue operating after the train has passed. In July 1984 a passenger train collided with a car on the crossing, fortunately without injury to its driver.

Leaving Salmon Pool, the double track crossed a small stream and then the River Yeo on girder bridges, Nos 553 and 554 and continued westward along the valley. Later, the 1971 and 1984 colour light Crediton 'up' distant signals were installed along here. The line passed under three more three-arch bridges and over the River Yeo twice, until, after emerging from the third overbridge, it passed Neopardy cottages and the site of the former Neopardy signal box.

Neopardy Signal Box

Neopardy signal box was established to break the long section between Crediton and Yeoford when traffic was heavy or when shunting at Yeoford occupied the running lines. When it opened is not known, but is was mentioned in a South Western Instruction of 1890, which stated that Neopardy signal box was switched out at night and on Sundays. The signal box was situated to the south of the line, adjacent to the South Western cottages. It controlled distant, home and starting signals in each direction and possibly points to a siding. In later South Western days it

was switched out for most of the time, manned only at busy weekends by one of the Yeoford signalmen. It was closed on 7th April 1916 and no trace of it now remains. Later on catch points were put in on the 'down' main line here, and on one occasion a van which had run away from Yeoford during shunting, was derailed on the catch points, which were then situated 494 yards before the Yeoford 'down' home signal. Coal and other supplies for Neopardy were sent from Yeoford by trolley.

Leaving Neopardy, the line crossed a stream and the River Yeo twice, passing the Yeoford 'down' distant signal and the extensive 'down' yard to the south of the line before entering Yeoford station, 183 miles from Waterloo.

Yeoford
Chronology:

Opened	1st August 1854
Mixed gauge into use	2nd March 1863
Yeoford Junction - North Tawton opened	1st November 1865
Crediton - Yeoford Junction doubled and signal box opened	1st June 1876
Broad gauge take out of use	30th April 1877
Yeoford Junction - Coleford Junction doubled	16th May 1877
Goods yard closed	10th February 1964
Signal box closed	18th August 1968
Passenger service to Okehampton withdrawn	3rd June 1972

Standing today on the quiet platform of the unstaffed halt at Yeoford, it is perhaps difficult to envisage the bustle and volume of traffic handled at Yeoford Junction station in a byegone era. Yeoford Junction was the interchange station between the North Devon and Plymouth lines. Passengers travelling between the two lines changed trains here, although some who did not listen carefully to the station announcements, occasionally got on the wrong

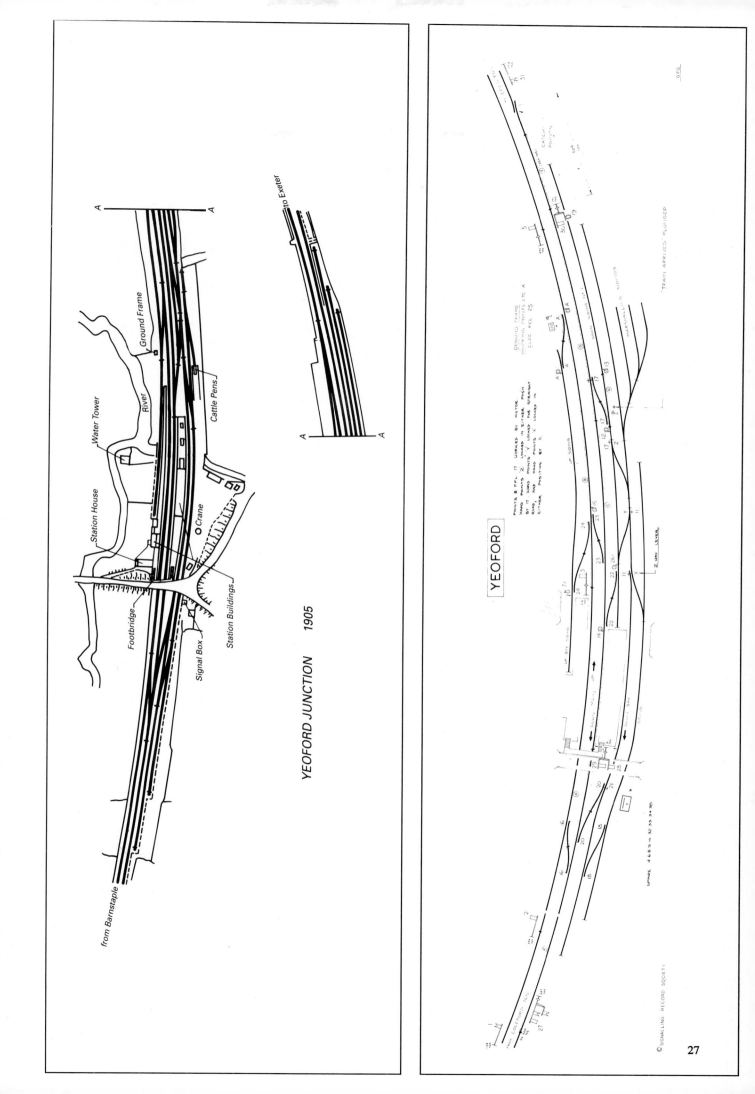

YEOFORD JUNCTION   1905

YEOFORD

© SIGNALLING RECORD SOCIETY

27

train and went back the way they had come! Refreshment rooms were provided on the 'down' island platform for passengers awaiting their next train. Occasionally the North Devon and Plymouth portions of trains were separated or joined up at Yeoford Junction instead of Exeter, and Yeoford was also a major marshalling yard for 'down' freight trains, with shunting continuing right around the clock with a break only on the sabbath.

The road from the small picturesque village of Yeoford to Cheriton Bishop crossed the line on bridge No. 569,

Looking east from the footbridge at Yeoford in June 1962 an 'up' passenger train departs whilst an 'up' goods is shunted in the bay siding, left. The extensive 'down' yard can be seen in the distance.

Author

Below: The view west from Yeoford 'up' platform showing the main station buildings in July 1964. The large structure on the 'down' island platform incorporated a refreshment room, and above it can be seen the roof of the signal box.

P. Swift

YEOFORD

	1928	1930	1932	1934	1936
Passenger tickets issued	12,807	10,977	9,706	9,182	7,842
Season tickets issued	30	18	15	11	20
Tickets collected	13,262	11,840	10,283	9,769	8,640
Parcels forwarded	538	498	399	364	360
Parcels received	894	914	635	736	640
Horses forwarded	15	14	6	1	4
Horses received	38	34	11	25	6
Milk forwarded (gal) (churns up to 1932)	2,080	855	9,793	21,689	15,458
Milk received (gal) (churns up to 1932)	–	–	–	–	–
Fish, meat, etc. forwarded (cwt)	17	99	12	29	71
Fish, meat etc. received (cwt)	–	–	–	–	–
General merchandise forwarded (tons)	859	644	495	469	477
General merchandise received (tons)	1,127	1,025	1,032	839	712
Coal forwarded (tons)	–	–	–	–	–
Coal received (tons)	262	223	212	213	258
Other minerals forwarded (tons)	–	64	–	82	23
Other minerals received (tons)	1,949	2,106	232	528	447
Livestock forwarded (trucks)	118	103	51	37	62
Livestock received (trucks)	70	35	10	4	11
Loaded wagons (not livestock) forwarded	212	238	153	338	199
Loaded wagons (not livestock) received	592	607	492	631	292
Wagons transferred (loaded & empty)	63,360	61,766	53,152	64,149	71,618

with both roads fully signalled, the 'down' bay also acting as the reception, shunting and departure road for the 'down' yard. This initially had three sidings, later extended to six much longer sidings in 1943. Next to the 'down' bay road was a loop siding catering for local goods traffic, served by a cattle dock, and a 5-ton crane. There was access from the Cheriton Bishop road and a number of wooden buildings used for various purposes, including stables and a slaughterhouse, and nowadays one of them is the Yeoford Post Office Stores. On the other side of the road bridge was the signal box, a squat weatherboarded structure on top of a tall stone column, giving the signalman a good view over the whole station.

originally a three-arched bridge later extended with a girder span over two more lines. From north to south, the station consisted of an 'up' bay siding, 'up' platform, 'up' and 'down' main tracks, a 'down' island platform, 'down' loop and a siding. All the station buildings were constructed in wooden weatherboarding on brick bases, a station master's house being provided behind the 'up'· platform. Access from the village was down a path from the road on to the 'up' platform, which had a booking office, waiting room and other offices. Passengers crossed the lines to the island platform using an open, iron footbridge, a barrow crossing being provided at the end of the platforms. The 'up' bay road incorporated a 30-ton wagon weighbridge which was used to check the loading of wagons, so 'up' freight trains were often held in the bay.

Bridge No. 568 carried the lines and platforms over the River Troney, which flowed beneath into the River Yeo, and near the 'up' bay was a pump house where water from the River Troney was pumped up to a tank. From there it gravitated down to taps on the station for non-drinking purposes and to the three LSWR-designed water columns, provided at the end of each platform for the locomotives. Years ago there was no supply of drinking water, so it was the duty of a porter to collect fresh water from a spring in the village and bring it to the station master's house and refreshment room.

The 'down' platform was an island

The tall, 1876 vintage signal box at Yeoford in 1964, mounted high up to give the signalman a good view of the yard on the other side of the road bridge.

P. Swift

The principal wooden buildings on the 'up' platform at Yeoford in 1965.

A. E. West

N class 2-6-0 No. 31847 arrives at Yeoford with an 'up' freight in the early BR period.

Lens of Sutton

Yeoford signal box was a very busy place indeed. Not only did the signalman have to look after the passing of some eighty trains a day, but he also had to fit in the large number of shunting operations. In the 35-lever box he had some help from track circuits, and also had a ground frame at the east end of the station, interlocked with the box, to operate points at that end of the station. When a long 'down' freight train arrived it was turned into the 'down' bay siding, but if the yard was full it was sometimes necessary to wait for the 'down' main line to to be clear so that it could be utilised for shunting purposes. 'Up' freight trains had to be reversed into the 'up' bay siding or 'up' siding. Yeoford signal box was continuously manned, twenty-four hours day, except on Sundays when it was

Yeoford water tower in 1965. Water was pumped from the adjacent River Troney into the large tank from where it gravitated for locomotive and station purposes.

A. E. West

switched out, the section being Crediton to Coleford Junction.

Yeoford yard was very important for the freight services west of Exeter. The Southern Region freight timetables included Salisbury to Plymouth, and Yeoford to Torrington and Ilfracombe, with several freight trains booked to start or finish here. 'Down' freight trains originating from Nine Elms, Salisbury and Templecombe passed through Exeter, collecting wagons at Exmouth Junction, Exeter Central, St Davids and Riverside, arriving at Yeoford Junction "rough" as the men called them. At Yeoford these wagons were shunted into the correct order for all stations to Barnstaple and Torrington with wagons for the Ilfracombe line, and also for freight trains running to Plymouth Friary, Bude and Wadebridge. Other wagons in transit between the North Devon and Plymouth lines were shunted into the appropriate train. Up to a dozen 'down' freight trains were booked to call at Yeoford, several staying for up to an hour. 'Up' freight trains were often reversed into the 'up' bay to weigh loads of hay, straw, clay and stone and to allow other trains to pass.

A South Western traffic return for March 1889 recorded 827 passenger tickets issued, and a similar picture emerges from the Southern Railway statistics for 1928-36. About thirty tickets were issued daily and about the same number collected, with a couple of parcels, some telegrams and a few churns of milk. About two loaded wagons were received per day and one forwarded, compared with about two hundred per day transferred in the yard. Local passengers went to Crediton, Exeter or destinations further afield. Goods traffic forwarded included timber for Yeoford Sawmills, meat, bone meal and hoof and horn from Tellams of Cheriton Bishop and some cattle. Opposite the Railway Hotel was the former site of cattle pens used for the auction market held many years ago, which produced considerable business for the railway. On one occasion a local farmer moved his entire farm stock

and equipment from Yeoford to Leicestershire by train. Another farmer regularly forwarded cider to Devonport.

Station staff at Yeoford were also kept very busy transferring parcels traffic between Plymouth and North Devon line trains. Parcels from Plymouth to North Devon included consignments from the Millbay dyeworks, pasties, pies and sausages from Millicans which were unloaded from the 'up' trains and forwarded on the 2.06am Mail and Freight train from Exeter to Torrington which left Yeoford at 3.45am. The Western Morning News was unloaded from the 1.25am from Plymouth and transferred to the overnight newspaper train from Waterloo which arrived just after 5am. Numerous mailbags and other parcels were transferred between the two lines, and three or four barrows were provided to assist the railwaymen with this heavy traffic.

There were a considerable number of railwaymen employed at Yeoford station. In 1889 a Sam Hoyle worked in the office, and in 1893 there was a Mr Capel. Mr Clapp senior, was a shunter here in the 1900s and in 1910 the station master was Mr S. Screttino. In the 1930s, the station master was Mr Whitford, followed by Mr Trigger, Mr Francis and Mr Leyman, who had been a driver on the Chagford bus, Mr H. Martin who went on to be the last station master at Bude, and Mr W. A. Short who was the last station master in the 1960s. With the station master was a staff including two porters, three signalmen, one porter signalman, six shunters and sometimes, a clerk also. The porter signalman had an interesting job of porters' duties at Yeoford for part of his shift, then walking to Coleford Junction to cover the middle of the day between the early turn and late turn signalman. Duties also included replacing signal lamps once a week for all the Coleford Junction signals. Mr Bill Keat became porter signalman at Yeoford in 1927, in 1938 shunter, 1939 signalman at Coleford Junction and 1944 signalman at Yeoford.

In the 1940s and 1950s, the Yeoford signalman included Messrs W. Keat, F. Phillips, H. Lang, A. Cleeve, C. Baker, W. Luxton and H. Holcombe. Shunters included Messrs P. Steer, A. Ellis, S. Taylor, S. Martin, J. Dallas (who later became a signalman here), B. Hunt, C. Bishop and H. Flitter. Mr Eddie Clapp became booking clerk in 1949 and in 1951 became signalman here. Mr F.A. Sherwood came in 1947 as a porter and together with the other porter, Mr Mills, working alternate shifts, issued tickets, dealt with parcels and goods accounts and in the absence of the station master, was responsible for trains leaving on time. After doing relief work, Mr Sherwood returned to Yeoford until 1961, when he moved on to Crediton and then Exeter St Davids, but has retained his link with the station, now living in the station house.

Mr Eddie Clapp started work at Yeoford as a shunter in 1946, working alternate shifts of 8am to 4pm and 7pm to 3am. He often worked with a head shunter who had such a remarkable memory that at the beginning of a shift he would walk round the sidings to make a few notes on the back of a wagon label and then, for the rest of the shift, call to his second man the number of wagons required from each siding. By the end of the shift, he had remarshalled the entire contents of the yard without going back into the sidings, and never made a false shunt. He eventually retired from St Davids yard as inspector. The very cold winter of 1947 brought very harsh conditions, with coal fires burning in braziers under the water columns to prevent them from freezing up, and railwaymen working in terrible conditions to keep the wheels rolling. At this time the yard was illuminated by Tilley lamps, the gas-oil lamps provided being without fuel after the gas-oil plant had blown up.

At the end of Yeoford 'up' platform there was a water crane and a South Western 'up' starting signal, the white diamond indicating track circuiting. Even as late as 28th June 1965 there was a large number of wagons in the 'down' yard beyond.

A. E. West

The 1pm Waterloo to Plymouth train departs from Yeoford on 7th May 1960 behind Bulleid Pacific No. 34057 *Biggin Hill*. The South Western extension to the original 1854 North Devon Railway three-arch bridge can be seen on the right.

S. C. Nash

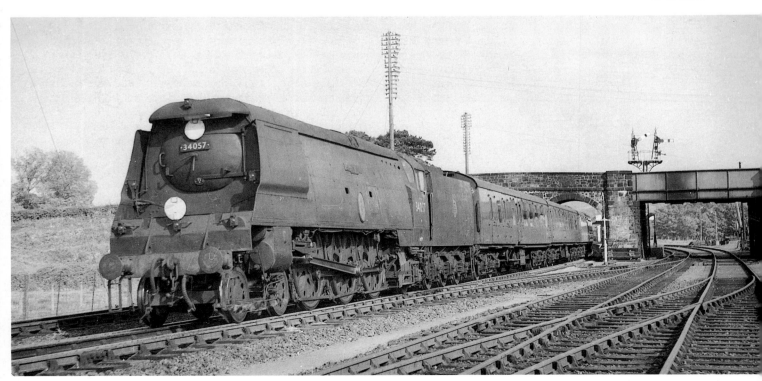

Mr Clapp's father had also worked at Yeoford as a shunter in the early 1900s and several stories of some of the activities of the shunters in those days have been handed down. The shunters at that time had a cabin in the yard which was provided with a fire, a very necessary provision for the men on a wet or cold winters' night. On one occasion, Mr Clapp senior, who lodged with a nearby gamekeeper, was provided with a pigeon pie for his meal. He and other shunters, had settled down for their meal break in the cabin, when somebody poured a bucket of paraffin down the chimney, causing flames to shoot out across the cabin, burning the pigeon pie and singeing the

men's' Edwardian moustaches. On another occasion a shunter arrived on duty very drunk and settled down to sleep it off in the cabin, but somebody put a sack over the top of the chimney. Fortunately, another shunter returned to the cabin just in time to prevent his asphyxiation. What other events occurred before or after these pranks are not recorded.

Leaving Yeoford station, the double-track line curved gradually round towards the north, following the River Yeo, crossing a stream and gaining elevation on an embankment, crossing over two minor roads. A few yards out from Yeoford was an interesting signal post, holding the Yeoford 'down' advanced starting signal, and splitting distant signals for Coleford Junction. The junction was reached about a mile north of Yeoford.

Coleford Junction

Chronology:

Signal Box and junction opened	16th May 1877
Coleford Junction - Copplestone doubled	4th November 1883
Signal box and junction closed	17th October 1971

Since the opening of the Devon & Cornwall Railway in 1865 there has been a divergence between the North Devon and Okehampton lines, with a physical junction for 94 years. Coleford Junction signal box was situated on the east side of the line, constructed as a weatherboarded cabin on a stone base. Adjacent to it was a corrugated iron lamp room. The frame held 13 levers to control the points and signals, the only points being for the normal double junction and a crossover used mainly when the engineers required possession of one line. Apart from the 'down' distant signals already described, there was a 'down' junction home signal, and in the 'up' direction distant and home signals on both Plymouth and North Devon lines, with an outer home on the Plymouth line. There was a speed restriction of 40mph, later reduced to 20mph, for Plymouth line trains round the sharp curve of 20 chains radius. Supplies for the signal box, including coal and water were sent from Yeoford by freight train, in 1932 the 6.18am from Exmouth Junction Sidings to Barnstaple.

Coleford Junction signal box was open when the North Devon line was open, it being switched out for several hours at night when the section was Yeoford to Okehampton. As with all the other signal boxes to Barnstaple, the establishment was two signalmen working early and late turns and a porter signalman working several hours in the middle of the day. During the Second

This wooden post carried signals for two signal boxes. There was the Yeoford 'down' advanced starting signal, together with the two splitting distants for Coleford Junction photographed in June 1965.
A. E. West

On 20th June 1959 a 'down' Plymouth train passes Coleford Junction, the signal box and points being hidden behind trees at the rear of the train. The North Devon line is visible in the background, passing over bridge No. 1.
R. J. Sellick

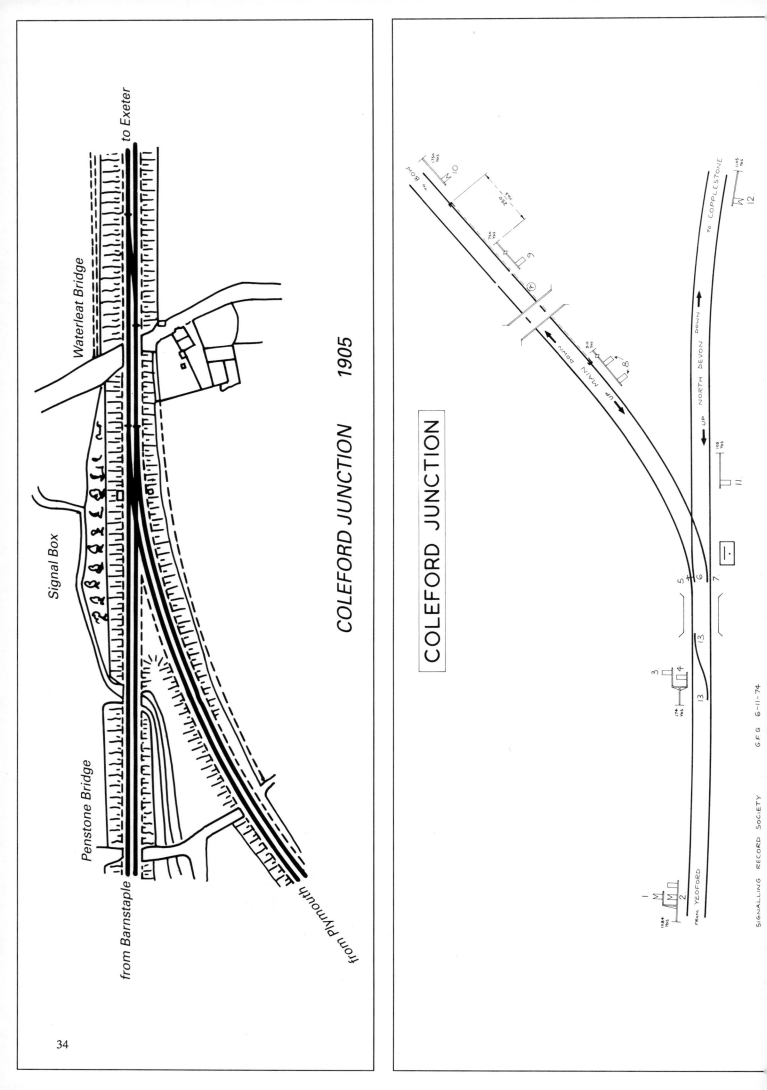

COLEFORD JUNCTION 1905

COLEFORD JUNCTION

to Exeter

Waterleat Bridge

Signal Box

Penstone Bridge

from Barnstaple

from Plymouth

SIGNALLING RECORD SOCIETY   G.F.G 6-11-74

World War, the two signalmen, Mr W. Keat and Mr M. Mathews had no porter signalmen and worked very long shifts. By 1951, the signalmen were Mr E. Clapp and Mr H. Mathews, with porter signalman, Mr N. Webber, and when the box closed in 1971, Mr E. Clapp was working with Mr S. Ponsford.

North Devon trains now headed north and passed over an underbridge, No. 1 on this section of line, and climbed over embankments and through cuttings under a road bridge at the village of Coleford, until it passed Copplestone 'down' distant signal and into the long cutting at the summit of the line, spanned by three bridges until entering Copplestone station, 186 miles from Waterloo.

Copplestone

Chronology:

Opened	1st August 1854
Mixed gauge into use	2nd March 1863
Signal box opened	1st October 1873
Broad gauge taken out of use	30th April 1877
Coleford Junction - Copplestone doubled	4th November 1883
Goods yard closed	6th September 1965
Copplestone - Crediton singled and signal box closed	17th October 1971

Copplestone station was the first on the North Devon line where drivers had to collect the single line token, or sometimes wait for a late running 'up' train to clear the single line section. This began several hundred yards to the north of the platforms, at the end of the goods yard on the 'down' side. This comprised two sidings connected to the 'up' and 'down' tracks by trailing connections, there also being a crossover at the Coleford Junction end of the station. On the 'down' platform was the main station house, a very attractive North Devon Railway standard design seen at five other stations which incorporated the booking office, waiting room and station house. On the 'up' platform was a waiting shelter only, the station being devoid of awnings, but both had Southern concrete nameboards and South Western oil lamps and seats. At the end of the 'up' platform was a water tower carrying a plate inscribed "L&SWR Wimbledon Works 1887", and underneath it was a flexible hose for watering

COPPLESTONE

	1928	1930	1932	1934	1936
Passenger tickets issued	4,224	3,908	3,338	2,997	2,377
Season tickets issued	8	8	5	15	10
Tickets collected	5,226	4,367	3,823	3,434	3,310
Parcels forwarded	371	349	342	372	504
Parcels received	1,171	1,237	1,109	1,041	1,083
Horses forwarded	–	5	2	–	1
Horses received	–	4	6	2	–
Milk forwarded (gal) (churns up to 1932)	20	433	2,225	–	308
Milk received (gal) (churns up to 1932)	–	–	–	–	–
Fish, meat, etc. forwarded (cwt)	8	79	64	60	80
Fish, meat etc. received (cwt)	–	–	–	–	–
General merchandise forwarded (tons)	1,784	1,161	868	584	558
General merchandise received (tons)	2,449	2,960	4,036	4,545	5,076
Coal forwarded (tons)	16	20	–	–	–
Coal received (tons)	465	402	322	298	321
Other minerals forwarded (tons)	–	179	6	793	804
Other minerals received (tons)	1,634	586	640	1,213	860
Livestock forwarded (trucks)	191	220	106	166	160
Livestock received (trucks)	73	108	41	4	12
Loaded wagons (not livestock) forwarded	738	577	544	353	446
Loaded wagons (not livestock) received	764	761	896	1,139	947

A non-stop train passes through Copplestone on 20th June 1959, the driver of No. 34058 *Sir Frederick Pile* collecting the single-line token from the signalman on the 'down' platform.

R. J. Sellick

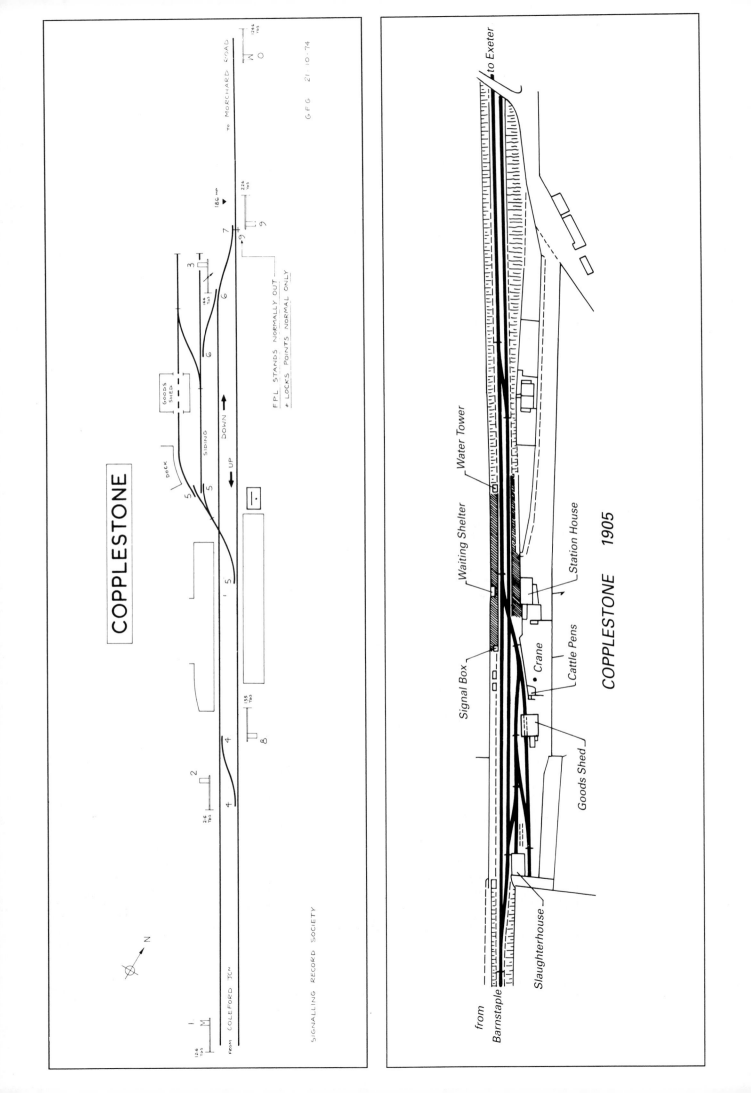

COPPLESTONE

N

126
YDS

1

M

216
YDS

2

4

4

135
YDS

8

5

5

DOCK

5

5

GOODS
SHED

SIDING

UP

DOWN

144
YDS

3

T

6

6

FPL STANDS NORMALLY OUT
+ LOCKS POINTS NORMAL ONLY

7

186 MP

9

9

226
YDS

1244
YDS

O

To MORCHARD ROAD

From COLEFORD JCN

SIGNALLING RECORD SOCIETY

G.F.G 21·10·74

COPPLESTONE 1905

from
Barnstaple

to Exeter

Signal Box

Waiting Shelter

Water Tower

Station House

Crane

Cattle Pens

Goods Shed

Slaughterhouse

Copplestone 'down' platform from a train on 25th July 1964.
P. Swift

locomotives. There was a standard South Western water column at the end of the 'down' platform. After the facility was withdrawn at South Molton Road, Copplestone station was the first after Barnstaple where 'up' trains could take water.

The signal box was on the 'up' side, opposite the yard and adjacent to the sleeper crossing between the platforms, there being no footbridge. The 1873 signal box was built in weatherboarding on a stone base, the ten levers in the box controlling the station completely. There were distant, home and starting signals in each direction, but some of the levers were unusual, such as No. 9 which operated both the 'up' home signal and the facing point lock for the loop points. The signal box controlled comparatively short sections of 2 miles 2 yards from Coleford Junction box

and 1 mile 1,146 yards from Morchard Road box, with running times of four and three minutes respectively for passenger trains.

In the yard the outer of the two sidings ran past a loading dock with a 5-ton crane and cattle loading pens, a store for fertilizers and animal feedstuffs and into the goods shed. This was a large wooden structure painted in a light colour which incorporated a loading platform, 2-ton crane and goods office. Both sidings terminated at buffer stops adjacent to another large wooden building, a slaughterhouse, and the sidings were connected by a crossover. In the goods yard were several more stores and offices together with a 7-ton cart weighbridge.

The Southern Railway traffic statistics show Copplestone station to be the least well patronised on the

The 1873 signal box at Copplestone in 1965. When it was demolished in 1971 many old LSWR documents were found here, several of which are illustrated in this book.

C. L. Caddy

Copplestone station looking north in January 1965 with meat containers in the yard beyond the goods shed.

C. L. Caddy

line for passenger traffic, with only a dozen or so tickets issued a day and a few more collected, local bus services being more convenient. However, there was a fair number of parcels and telegrams dealt with and some milk churn traffic. In the yard, three or four loaded wagons were received each day and two or three forwarded. The main customers were the local firm of W. A. Davey which received supplies of fertilizers and animal feedstuffs, and the slaughterhouse in the station yard. In the past, there was a periodical cattle auction market on a site now occupied by a garage and some houses, and this produced considerable traffic. A very early traffic was in copper ore mined near North Tawton, carted to Copplestone for rail transit to Fremington.

In Victorian times we know that William Shobrick was signalman in 1861 and that George Pope, Ernie Bevin's brother-in-law, worked here in the 1890s. In 1910, the station master was Mr R. W. Winter and in the 1920s it was Mr Drew, but later, the post was withdrawn and Copplestone station was supervised by the Lapford station master. The other railwaymen were the two signalmen and one porter signalman, in the 1920s these being Messrs H. Mearden, A. Roach and W. Mallet respectively, and in the 1940s, Messrs A. C. Taylor, W. J. Short and A. H. Harding. By the late 1960s, the signalmen were Messrs P. Turner, W. J. Beeves and B. Horne.

All the way from Copplestone to Umberleigh, the earthworks and bridges were ready for double track, leaving Copplestone the line followed gentle downhill gradients all the way to Barnstaple, passing over open countryside.

At the end of Copplestone 'up' platform was this water tank and hose. The tank bore a plate 'L&SWR Wimbledon Works 1887', it replacing an earlier North Devon Railway water crane. For many years this was the first water supply for 'up' trains since leaving Barnstaple. *A. E. West*

Copplestone goods shed and the adjacent store for fertilisers and animal feedstuffs in 1965.

A. E. West

Copplestone 'up' distant signal was passed and the line went under three bridges and over the odd embankment and culvert. Morchard Road 'down' distant signal was passed and under the third bridge, of three arches, the line ran into Morchard Road station, 187½ miles from Waterloo.

Morchard Road

Chronology:

Opened	1st August 1854
Mixed gauge into use	2nd March 1863
Signal box opened	1st October 1873
Broad gauge taken out of use	30th April 1877
Goods yard closed	30th December 1963
Signal box closed	6th March 1964

Morchard Road was a simple rural passing station on the line with a few sidings. The standard North Devon Railway station house was on the 'down' platform and opposite on the 'up' platform was a stone-built waiting shelter, both platforms having Southern concrete nameboards, and South Western oil lamps and seats. The signal box was on the 'up' side adjacent to the barrow and passenger crossing. A long Down Siding East ran from the end of the platform under the three-arch Morchard Road Bridge, where it served a loading dock from Mr A. Gunn's slaughterhouse. At the Lapford end of the station was the

MORCHARD ROAD

	1928	1930	1932	1934	1936
Passenger tickets issued	5,056	4,391	3,537	2,813	2,035
Season tickets issued	35	45	42	42	34
Tickets collected	5,785	4,821	3,919	3,094	2,528
Parcels forwarded	1,036	907	884	702	761
Parcels received	962	1,072	1,407	1,389	1,625
Horses forwarded	24	19	9	4	2
Horses received	29	17	3	2	3
Milk forwarded (gal) (churns up to 1932)	–	–	2,984	6,899	12
Milk received (gal) (churns up to 1932)	–	–	–	5	–
Fish, meat, etc. forwarded (cwt)	119	315	215	577	365
Fish, meat etc. received (cwt)	3	2	–	6	16
General merchandise forwarded (tons)	1,294	1,326	1,031	560	393
General merchandise received (tons)	1,295	1,111	1,002	688	841
Coal forwarded (tons)	–	–	–	–	–
Coal received (tons)	731	910	906	827	836
Other minerals forwarded (tons)	15	180	163	44	19
Other minerals received (tons)	2,288	1,361	3,127	1,497	2,333
Livestock forwarded (trucks)	52	77	56	64	161
Livestock received (trucks)	73	78	44	11	1
Loaded wagons (not livestock) forwarded	716	736	691	370	285
Loaded wagons (not livestock) received	612	668	697	442	574

On 20th June 1959 N class 2-6-0 No. 31840 arrives at Morchard Road with an 'up' train.

R. J. Sellick

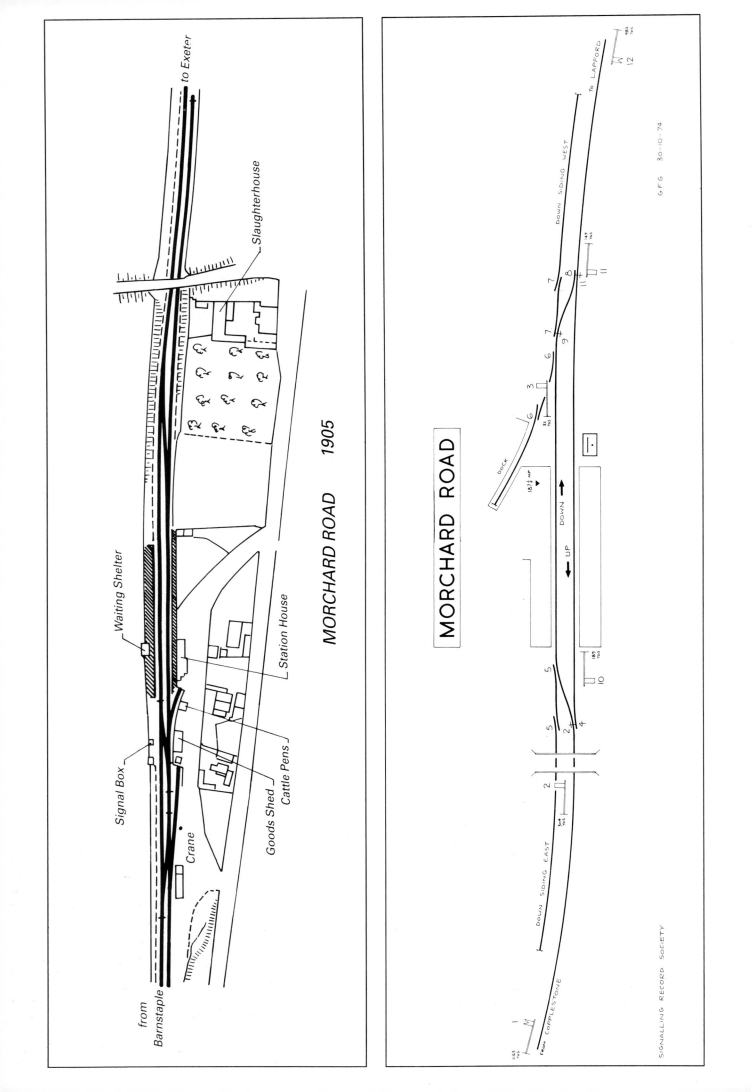

to Exeter

Slaughterhouse

MORCHARD ROAD *1905*

Waiting Shelter

Signal Box

Crane

Station House

Goods Shed

Cattle Pens

from Barnstaple

MORCHARD ROAD

DOCK

DOWN SIDING WEST

To LAPFORD

DOWN

UP

982 Yds

12

147 Yds

11

8

7

9

7

6

3

31 Yds

6

W

183¾ MP

DOWN SIDING EAST

From COPPLESTONE

1163 Yds

1

M

2

324 Yds

4

2

5

5

187 Yds

10

G F G 30-10-74

SIGNALLING RECORD SOCIETY

Morchard Road signal box in 1962.

P. Swift

Down Siding West with a couple of short spurs serving side and end-loading docks, cattle loading pens, a 5-ton crane and a wooden goods shed equipped with an interior 2-ton crane. Further down the yard was a large wooden store.

Opposite the station house were a number of buildings including three bungalows, occupied by the railwaymen and their families, together with a wooden building incorporating stables and a cabin for the postmen who lodged overnight here, as we see in Chapter 8. On the other side of the main A377 road were Brickyard Cottages

and several worked-out clay pits, apparently the site of the 1854 Morchard Road Brick and Tile Works. In the opposite direction, at the road junction, was the Sturt Arms Hotel and also the site of the periodic cattle auction market held here.

The 1873 signal box completely controlled the points and signals from the 12-lever frame. As at several other stations the home signal levers, Nos 2 and 11, also operated the facing point locks for the loop points. The crossing could accommodate a locomotive, thirty wagons and a brake van, and in the event of the 12.45am 'up'

A general view of Morchard Road station about 1960.

Lens of Sutton

The 13.00 train from Barnstaple to Exmouth passes Morchard Road on 23rd August 1980. The empty station house was for sale and there were practically no facilities for passengers.

Author

market goods from Torrington being too long to cross a 'down' passenger train the goods had to be shunted into a siding. However, the Morchard Road signalman had a real

problem on his hands with three trains in the station just after nine o'clock every morning. In South Western days the 5.50am goods from Barnstaple, 7.45am passenger from Torrington and 8.30am passenger from Exeter were all here at once, the goods being shunted into the yard to allow the two passenger trains to cross. In Southern days the three trains were the 4.25am freight from Barnstaple, 7.10am passenger from Torrington and 6.18am freight from Exmouth Junction.

Traffic figures recorded by the Southern Railway show that passenger traffic was light, only a dozen or so tickets being issued a day and slightly more collected. The booking office also dealt with a fair traffic in parcels, telegrams, churns of milk, horse boxes and coaching vehicles. The goods yard dealt with about three wagons a day in and three out. Several merchants used the yard for their businesses in coal, fertilizers and animal feedstuffs including Mr J. Gunn, licensee of the Sturt Arms Hotel, Mr Hole and Mr Bawdler, the Southern Railway agent who delivered to the villages in the district three days a week. Mr A. Gunn forwarded considerable traffic from his slaughterhouse, and cattle traffic was heavy after the periodic cattle auctions.

In the early 1900s the station master was Mr Labdon, and in 1910 Mr W. Lovell, but in Southern days Morchard Road was supervised by the Lapford station master. From the 1920s the staff consisted of two signalmen, one porter signalman and one porter, being Messrs Clapp senior, C. West, H. Osborne and H. Knight respectively. Later on, Mr Knight became signalman, and brothers B. Withers and K. Withers were porter and porter signalman. In the 1940s the staff were signalmen L. Short and K. Withers, porter signalman, W. King and porter D. Mantanle. When the signal box closed most of the men here were relief staff. The bungalows at the station were usually occupied by two signalmen, and the permanent way inspector, Mr Turner, who was responsible for the track between Coleford Junction and Umberleigh.

Leaving Morchard Road the line ran alongside the main A377 road, mainly on an embankment over several minor culverts and past the 'up' distant signal. After a couple of miles it entered the valley of the River Yeo, crossing and re-crossing the river and passing under three road bridges,

The exterior of Morchard Road station on the same day.

Author

Again on 23rd August 1980, the 13.45 train from Exeter St Davids to Barnstaple, consisting of Class 25 No. 25225 and eight coaches, speeds through Morchard Road.

Author

followed by the Lapford 'down' distant signal and arriving at Lapford station, 190 miles from Waterloo.

Lapford

Chronology:

Opened	1st August 1854
Mixed gauge into use	2nd March 1863
Signal box and 'down' platform opened	1st October 1873
Broad gauge taken out of use	30th April 1877
Ambrosia factory opened	April 1928
Goods yard closed for public traffic	4th December 1967
Signal box closed and replaced by ground frame	21st June 1970

For almost half a century Lapford station was synonymous with a household name - Ambrosia. Tucked at the back of the station yard was the extensive factory, with its name painted on the roof, "Ambrosia Ltd Dried Milk Works", which employed several hundred people and provided much traffic to the railway. The station itself was unusual, being cut in two by the main road bridge with one platform on either side, each with its own booking office.

Perhaps the most dominant and attractive feature at Lapford was the three-arch North Devon Railway stone bridge which took the A377 road over the line at an acute angle. On the west side was the 'up' platform with its South Western station house containing the booking office, waiting room and other facilities. Unusually, the

A view from Lapford village in the 1930s showing the then new Ambrosia factory, with the 'down' platform in front of it. To the left is the Yeo Vale Hotel and between the road and railway is the field used for periodic cattle auction markets.

Collection W. Sutton

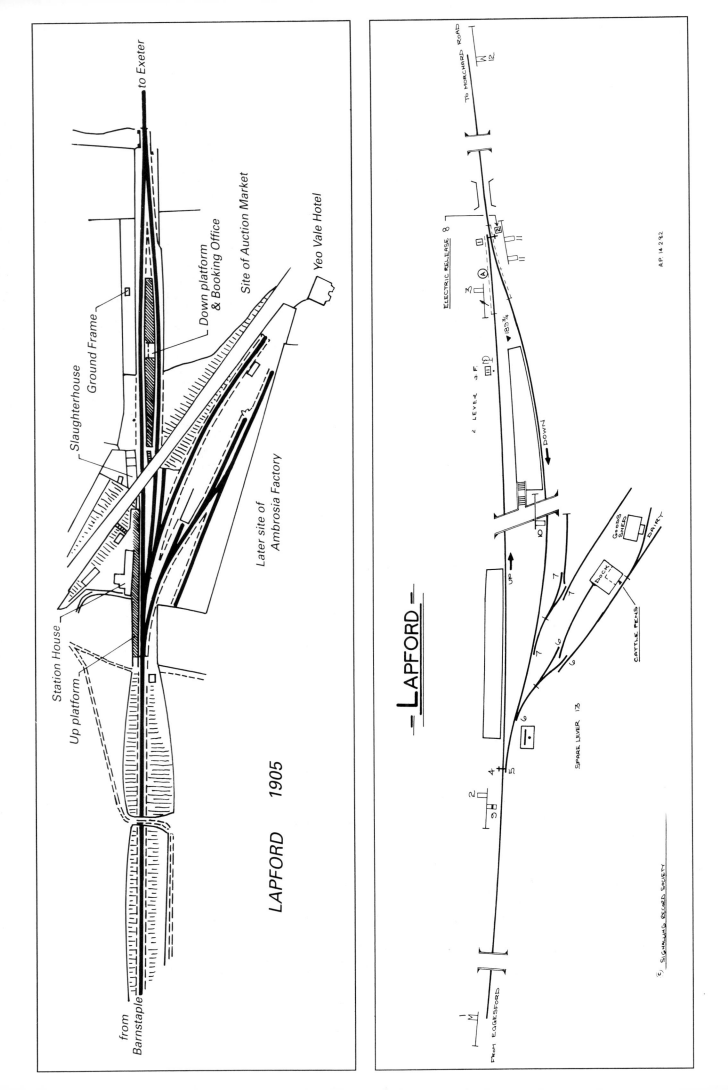

LAPFORD 1905

from
Barnstaple to Exeter

Slaughterhouse

Ground Frame

Down platform
& Booking Office

Site of Auction Market

Yeo Vale Hotel

Station House

Up platform

Later site of Ambrosia Factory

– LAPFORD –

To MORCHARD ROAD

W
12

ELECTRIC RELEASE 8

2 LEVER G.F.

18.3¾

DOWN

UP

7

7

7

7

6

6

6

SPARE LEVER 13

GOODS SHED

DAIRY

Dock

CATTLE PENS

4
5

2
3

FROM EGGESFORD

1
M

A.P. 14.2.82

© SIGNALLING RECORD SOCIETY

Inside the Ambrosia factory in the 1930s showing the roller drying of milk powder for use in infant food.

Collection W. Sutton

goods shed was also on the 'up' platform, and freight trains called here to load and unload parcels and other general merchandise. The 1873 signal box was opposite the end of the platform and controlled the entrance to the goods yard which contained five sidings, only two being of any length. The sidings served end and side-loading docks, a cattle dock and the Ambrosia factory. There was no crane provided, a travelling crane being sent when required, and there was a store built at the end of the yard for Silcocks animal feedstuffs. The large Ambrosia factory dominated the station, it being constructed in a mock-tudor style with black beams, with the manager's house and the social club constructed alongside.

When the South Western built the 'down' platform in 1873 there was no room for it opposite the 'up' platform so it was constructed on the other side of the road bridge, but fenced off from the 'up' line behind it. It was approached by steps from the road bridge, and by a sleeper crossing from the 'up' platform. On the 'down' platform was a waiting room which incorporated a booking office; after a 'down' passenger train had left Copplestone station the Morchard Road signalman asked Lapford for "Line Clear", and a handbell was rung from the signal box to alert the porter or clerk to go to the 'down' platform ticket office with a bag of change to sell tickets for stations below Lapford. The bell allowed about eight minutes before the train arrived, but on Friday mornings this was insufficient time for all passengers going to market at Barnstaple. In Southern days these tickets were printed *(D.O.) Lapford,* for Down Office. In front of the 'down' platform, was a field formerly used for the Lapford periodic cattle auctions, and beyond that, the main road and the Yeo Vale Hotel. The picturesque village of Lapford was spread out on the hill above the station.

LAPFORD

	1928	1930	1932	1934	1936
Passenger tickets issued	6,400	6,035	5,307	4,423	4,566
Season tickets issued	37	34	30	34	36
Tickets collected	7,448	7,084	6,220	5,605	5,389
Parcels forwarded	1,495	1,534	1,925	1,517	1,120
Parcels received	2,009	1,840	1,737	2,140	2,087
Horses forwarded	17	9	6	4	4
Horses received	10	7	6	17	18
Milk forwarded (gal) (churns up to 1932)	4,181	256	135,454	2,170	–
Milk received (gal) (churns up to 1932)	9,700	11,947	191,304	65,395	24,624
Fish, meat, etc. forwarded (cwt)	850	602	455	321	365
Fish, meat etc. received (cwt)	141	198	105	195	94
	1928	1930	1932	1934	1936
General merchandise forwarded (tons)	1,483	1,469	1,260	2,117	1,947
General merchandise received (tons)	2,135	1,847	2,023	2,500	3,059
Coal forwarded (tons)	–	–	–	52	9
Coal received (tons)	1,083	2,374	2,505	3,207	3,164
Other minerals forwarded (tons)	70	382	127	106	19
Other minerals received (tons)	1,575	1,833	2,487	2,628	2,000
Livestock forwarded (trucks)	186	135	112	101	165
Livestock received (trucks)	86	49	44	17	7
Loaded wagons (not livestock) forwarded	814	830	787	1,124	1,095
Loaded wagons (not livestock) received	1,077	1,420	1,456	1,604	1,631

The 1873 signal box controlled most of the station area from its 13-lever frame, but there was also a two-lever ground frame at the south end of the station to operate the loop points, this being interlocked with the signal box and operated by a porter. There were the usual distant, home and starting signals in both directions, and on the same

Lapford 'down' platform from a train on 25th July 1964. The waiting room incorporated a small booking office. The spare arch in the road bridge, with wooden additions, was at one time Mr Snell's slaughterhouse.

P. Swift

post were the 'up' home and 'down' advanced starting signals. The 'down' home signal was mounted on a tall post and had two co-acting arms. Several of the siding point levers also worked catch points to avoid wagons rolling out of the yard.

The Ambrosia factory was constructed in 1927 and started production of dried milk in April 1928, and tinned cream in July 1932. Other products included milk puddings, drinking chocolate, butter, clotted cream,

condensed milk and yeast extract. Initially, about half the milk used came from the Honiton area and half from local farms, but when the Milk Board was established in 1933, all the milk came from the Lapford area. A fleet of twenty lorries collected from local farms, but some churns also came by rail, in 1932 reaching a peak of 191,304 gallons. Churns were loaded in vans which were shunted directly into the Ambrosia siding. When the factory opened in 1928 it was managed by the landlord of the Yeo Vale

Looking south from Lapford 'up' platform in 1963.

Author

The view south from Lapford bridge, probably about 1960, showing the 'up' loop running behind the 'down' platform, and the ground frame controlling the loop points. The earthworks and bridges constructed for double track can be seen in the distance. Auction market pens are in the field on the right.

Lens of Sutton

Hotel, Mr Mannington, followed by a Mr Lavender, and from 1932 to 1966 by Mr William Sutton, who became a local magistrate. When the factory closed in 1970 the manager was Mr Horrell. Initially, about seventy people were employed here, rising to about two hundred during the war, and on closure there were about ninety. The other

Bulleid Pacific No. 34106 *Lydford* leaves Lapford with a 'down' train, passing the 'up' platform and the well-filled yard on 20th June 1959.

R. J. Sellick

Lapford in 1980. The Ambrosia factory right, is now used for other purposes but the loop and sidings are retained for occasional fertiliser traffic. Electric lighting and a modern shelter are provided for passengers.

Author

main customer at Lapford was Mr Snell who had his slaughterhouse in the spare arch of the road bridge.

In 1928-36 the Southern Railway traffic figures show that on average almost twenty tickets were issued per day and slightly more collected, with a few parcels and telegrams handled every day. The milk traffic became very extensive after the opening of the Ambrosia factory in 1928, and the number of loaded wagons forwarded increased for the same reason from about four to about six per day, with three or four received. The main traffic forwarded was milk products, cattle and meat, and traffic received included coal, fertilizers, animal feedstuffs, various supplies for Ambrosia, and bitumen for the nearby Bugford Quarry.

The Lapford station master was, at times, responsible not only for his own station but also for Copplestone, Morchard Road and Eggesford stations. In 1910, the station master was Mr F. Fishley, in 1928 Mr F. Cawsey and then Mr E. E. Northcott. In 1937 it was Mr W. J. Grayer, followed by Mr Reaves up to 1948 and Mr E. H. Harding until 1958. His staff at Lapford comprised two signalmen, one porter signalman and a clerk, in 1928 being Messrs T. Littlejohns, A. Withers, F. Southcombe and F. Whitworth respectively. In the early 1940s the same two signalmen had been joined by porter signalment Mr P. Bradford, who became signalman on the retirement of Mr T. Littlejohns in 1953, and clerk Mr Soper, then Mr Snelling, then Mr N. Mantanle until 1956. Later, signalmen were Messrs A. Rookes and J. Trigger, who was responsible for the most attractive floral displays at the station in later years. The last staff in the late 1960s were station master Mr C. H. Darke, clerk Mr D. Pearce and signalmen Messrs P. Bradford, A. Rookes and W. Butt.

Leaving Lapford station, the line wound along the valley of the River Yeo, between the river and the main road, until just after passing under Nymet Bridge the Yeo flowed into the River Taw. From here to Barnstaple, the railway and road kept close company alongside the river in the beautiful wooded valley. A mile or so after Nymet Bridge the line reached Chenson Crossing.

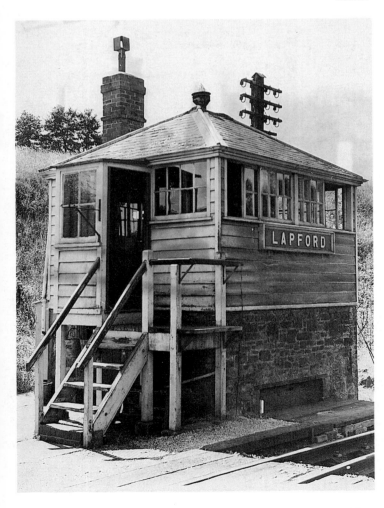

Lapford signal box in 1965.

A. E. West

48

Chenson Crossing in 1984, showing the crossing keeper's cottage and a variety of old and new railway notices.

Author

Chenson Crossing

Chenson Crossing was provided for a track which ran from the main A377 road to woodlands on the south side of the Taw valley, and was mainly used by farmers and forestry workers. The crossing keeper, for many years Mrs Wooldridge, lived in the adjacent house and normally kept the gates shut against road traffic. When a vehicle required to cross she ascertained the traffic position and opened the gates when the line was clear. In early British Railway days the post was withdrawn and drivers of road vehicles had to telephone the Eggesford signalman for permission to cross. Coal and other supplies for Chenson Crossing were sent from Lapford by porter.

Leaving Chenson Crossing, the line continued along the Taw valley, passed the Eggesford 'down' distant signal, the last surviving LSWR lattice post signal on the line, and ran over the level crossing into Eggesford station, 193¾ miles from Waterloo.

Eggesford

Chronology:

Opened	1st August 1854
Mixed gauge into use	2nd March 1863
First signal box opened	1st October 1873
Broad gauge taken out of use	30th April 1877
Goods yard closed	4th January 1965
First signal box and 'down' loop closed	21st November 1967
Second signal box, 'down' loop and platform opened	28th September 1969
Lifting barriers on level crossing into use	30th November 1969
Second signal box closed	1st December 1987

Eggesford station was an isolated railway community situated in the valley beneath Eggesford House, seat of the Earls of Portsmouth who in Victorian times supported the

EGGESFORD

	1928	1930	1932	1934	1936
Passenger tickets issued	9,040	7,778	6,284	4,815	4,304
Season tickets issued	36	28	13	14	42
Tickets collected	10,176	8,695	7,303	6,240	5,480
Parcels forwarded	1,702	1,770	1,381	1,004	739
Parcels received	4,461	4,692	4,619	5,134	5,076
Horses forwarded	62	49	63	16	23
Horses received	97	64	58	7	24
Milk forwarded (gal) (churns up to 1932)	–	–	–	–	–
Milk received (gal) (churns up to 1932)	–	–	–	–	–
Fish, meat, etc. forwarded (cwt)	131	462	387	470	87
Fish, meat etc. received (cwt)	57	52	35	20	39
General merchandise forwarded (tons)	2,792	2,139	1,459	824	1,053
General merchandise received (tons)	2,491	2,510	2,361	2,292	2,537
Coal forwarded (tons)	–	–	–	11	–
Coal received (tons)	1,195	1,277	1,109	987	925
Other minerals forwarded (tons)	19	130	6	11	138
Other minerals received (tons)	2,244	1,624	1,667	1,284	1,686
Livestock forwarded (trucks)	292	240	179	156	135
Livestock received (trucks)	24	27	17	5	10
Loaded wagons (not livestock) forwarded	890	738	553	561	666
Loaded wagons (not livestock) received	1,174	1,117	956	856	954

North Devon and South Western Railways, as we shall see later. Eggesford was one of those places where the tradition of railway service in a family was strong. In the early 1900s the two signalmen were Michael Southcombe and W. F. Snell, who lived in the two railway cottages overlooking the station. Michael Southcombe had several relations working on the South Western and Mr Snell had seven sons and two son-in-laws who worked on the railway. Half a century later, in the 1950s, their respective

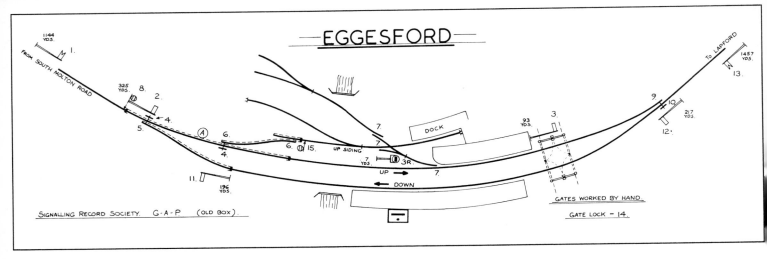

EGGESFORD

SIGNALLING RECORD SOCIETY.   G-A-P   (OLD BOX).

GATES WORKED BY HAND.

GATE LOCK - 14.

sons, W. F. Southcombe and George Snell were the two signalmen at Eggesford, working opposite turns just as their fathers had done before them.

Situated on a long curve between the main road and the river, Eggesford station boasted a passing loop and a medium sized yard on the 'up' side, from which ran the long Fox and Hounds siding. The main North Devon Railway station house, together with several other buildings, was on the 'up' platform, which was later enlarged in the same style. Not quite opposite was the 'down' platform with wooden waiting shelter and the unique 1873 signal box, the station having many standard items of South Western and Southern equipment. The minor road to Wembworthy crossed the line on a gated level crossing at the end of the 'up' platform, and then crossed the River Taw, where a mill leat was channelled away from the river, behind the 'down' platform and then under the tracks and the goods yard. The signal box was perched above the mill leat, with its front supported by the

platform and rear on two cast iron posts, the arrangement working well for 94 years until on 21st November 1967, when the platform started to subside and access to the signal box was possible only through a window! The signal box, 'down' platform and 'down' loop were taken out of use for two years until the entire structure could be rebuilt and a new signal box built adjacent to the level crossing.

The goods yard was well equipped with a crane of 7½-tons capacity, which replaced an earlier 5-ton crane, a goods shed with a 2-ton crane and several stores for various uses. The A. A. Oil Company had a depot in the yard with several high capacity storage tanks which were supplied by rail tankers, and a bitumen depot in the yard was served in the same way. On the long Fox and Hounds siding, which incorporated a loop, were stores, a coal depot, a slaughterhouse and cattle loading pens. Eggesford was apparently the first intermediate station to have a periodic cattle auction market, in pens adjacent to the Fox

Eggesford station in 1900. On the 'up' platform from left to right are H. Snell (porter), M. Southcombe (porter signalman), unknown, Kath Snell (daughter of signalman), W. Snell (signalman), G. Howard (porter), W. Manning (porter) and Mr Braithwaite (Station Master).

Collection W. Southcombe

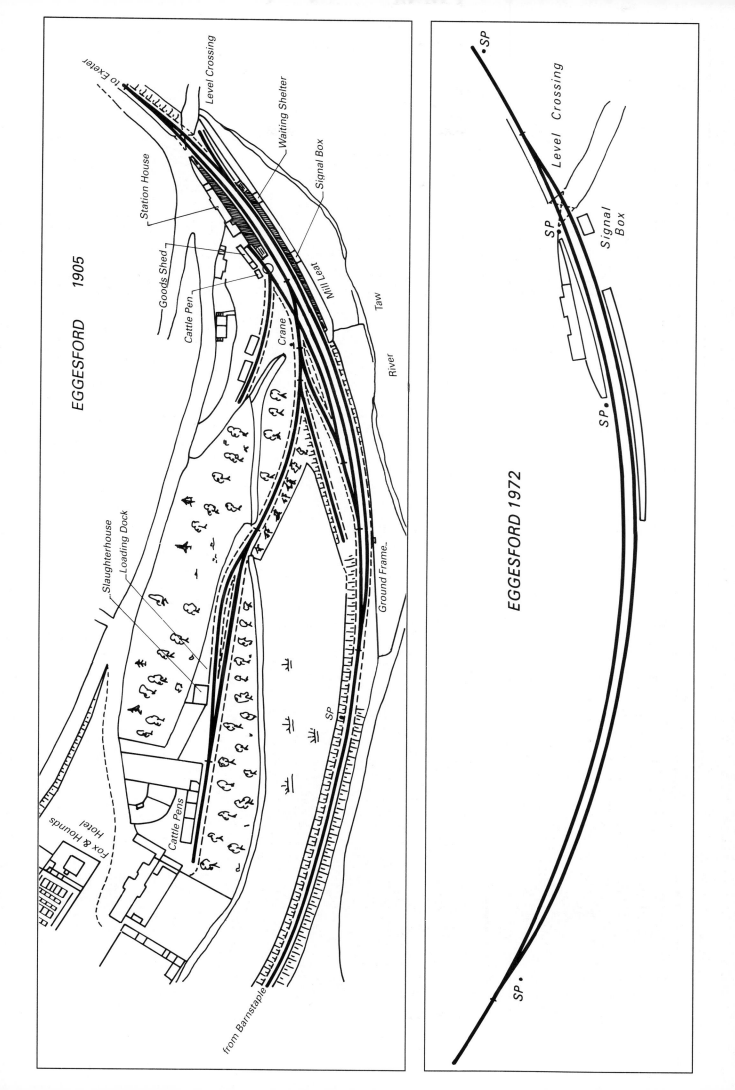

EGGESFORD 1905

to Exeter
Level Crossing
Station House
Waiting Shelter
Signal Box
Goods Shed
Cattle Pen
Crane
Mill Leat
River
Taw
Slaughterhouse
Loading Dock
Ground Frame
SP
Cattle Pens
Fox & Hounds Hotel
from Barnstaple

EGGESFORD 1972

SP
Level Crossing
SP
Signal Box
SP
SP
SP

Eggesford station in 1913. From left to right: M. Southcombe (porter signalman), unknown, unknown, Mr Towning (Station Master), W. Manning (porter), W. Snell (signalman), J. Harding (porter).

Collection W. Southcombe

and Hounds Hotel. Since the 'up' crossing loop could accommodate only a locomotive, brake van and 29 wagons, the Fox and Hounds Siding was sometimes used to shunt long goods trains for crossing purposes, since it could accommodate a train of fifty wagons clear of the running lines and catch points.

Traffic dealt with, according to the Southern Railway statistics in 1928-36, included about 25 tickets a day issued and rather more collected per day, together with a considerable number of parcels and telegrams dealt with. In the yard, three wagons a day were forwarded on average and about four received. The main traffic forwarded was livestock, after the periodic cattle auctions, meat, timber, hay, straw, reeds, horses, eggs and poultry.

The timber included pit props from Eggesford Saw Mills. Traffic received included manure and fertilizers, particularly during the early spring, animal feedstuffs, coal, grain, building materials, oil and bitumen. Goods were delivered to the villages by local carriers including Mr S. Chambers of Winkleigh, Mr Petherick of Chawleigh and Mr J. Richards & Sons of Chulmleigh, who also had a store in the station yard. This was in the days of horse transport, but by the 1950s there were two railway lorries based at Eggesford to operate the collection and delivery service, including that for meat containers. As at Morchard Road, the postman was an overnight visitor, and a combined stable and bunk house was provided in the station yard.

Eggesford station about 1955. From left to right, standing: J. Patt (porter), Mr Sandercock (porter signalman), W. Pollard (lorry driver based at Crediton), J. Western (lorry driver), S. Heal (storeman), unknown, W. Butt (lorry driver). Seated: W. Southcombe (signalman), C. Tett (Station Master), G. Walyers (clerk) and G. Snell (signalman).

Collection W. Southcombe

52

On 20th June 1959 a 'down' train passes Eggesford signal box as the crew prepare to exchange single-line tablets with the waiting signalmen.

R. J. Sellick

The original signalling at Eggesford was quite straightforward with distant, home and starting signals in both directions, although the 'up' starting signal was originally mounted on a tall post with a lower co-acting arm, later replaced with a short rail-built post signal and a repeater at the other end of the platform. At one time the loop points at the north end of the station were worked from a ground frame interlocked with the signal box, later replaced by an electrically worked point, this end of the layout being track circuited.

The level crossing gates were locked from the signal box but worked by hand. The 1969 signal box, the only one between Crediton and Barnstaple until 1987 controlled only the loop points, excluding the fixed distant, and level crossing barriers.

In 1873 there was one signalman, William Sanders, who was relieved by porter John Bird, who worked alternate shifts in the signal box of 4am to 5.30pm or 9.30am to 9.30 pm, with one Sunday in three off, illustrating the long hours worked by railwaymen at that time. The establishment at Eggesford varied over the years, but usually included the station master, two signalmen, one porter signalman, a clerk, one or two porters, permanent way staff and in later years, two lorry drivers. In later Victorian days Mr Bartlett was station master, in 1910 it was Mr F. S. Stretch, then Mr Braithwaite, Mr Towning and Mr Townsend in later South Western days. In Southern days for some time Eggesford was supervised by the Lapford station master, but by 1955 Mr C. Tett was station master here. Mr G. Snell had been porter

Eggesford goods yard from the rear of a long 'up' train on 24th June 1962. The flat wagon under the crane was one of many loaded with meat containers brought here by lorry.

Author

The 16.54 train from Barnstaple to Exeter St Davids waits in the crossing loop at Eggesford for a late running 'down' train on 23rd August 1980. The replacement signal box and lifting barriers on the level crossing can be seen, together with the new 'down' platform, waiting shelter and electric lights.

Author

Eggesford signal box in 1963, built over a mill leat. This 1873 signal box was closed by subsidence in 1967.

Author

signalman in the 1920s and by 1955, the porter signalman was Mr Sandercock. By 1967, there were three signalmen, Messrs W. F. Southcombe, W. Butt, H. Toulson and by 1983, Mr W. F. Southcombe had retired and been replaced by Mr J. Hughes. The station clerk in 1921 was Mr W. Hazelden, and by 1955 it was Mr G. Walters. Porters in 1921 were Messrs E. Maton, L. Down and W. F. Southcombe, in 1955 Mr J. Patt and in 1967, Mr H. Brown. In 1955, the staff also included lorry drivers, Messrs J. Western and W. Butt and storeman Mr S. Heal.

After leaving Eggesford station, the line passed its 'up' distant signal and continued down the Taw valley, crossing the River Taw and other streams and passing under a couple more bridges before passing South Molton Road 'down' distant and running into the station 197¾ miles from Waterloo.

South Molton Road/King's Nympton

Chronology:

Opened	1st August 1854
Mixed gauge into use	2nd March 1863
Signal box opened	1st October 1873
Broad gauge taken out of use	30th April 1877
Renamed King's Nympton	1st March 1951
Public goods yard closed	4th December 1967
Signal box closed	26th July 1970
Remain siding taken out of use	1981

South Molton (or Southmolton) Road station was railhead for the town some eight or nine miles away for almost a generation until the Devon & Somerset Railway opened in 1873, and even after that the South Western sought to gain some traffic by means of a coach service. A particular feature of the station was the very short crossing loop,

King's Nympton station looking south in 1952. The new nameboard has been installed, but the old South Molton Road nameboard is retained at ground level, in case of confusion!

R. J. Sellick

SOUTH MOLTON ROAD

	1928	1930	1932	1934	1936
Passenger tickets issued	6,245	5,462	4,862	4,111	3,645
Season tickets issued	11	11	11	15	38
Tickets collected	6,779	5,892	5,342	4,690	4,209
Parcels forwarded	1,649	1,530	1,293	1,309	949
Parcels received	2,057	2,190	2,303	2,404	2,432
Horses forwarded	34	48	37	28	6
Horses received	21	13	20	9	14
Milk forwarded (gal) (churns up to 1932)	–	1,412	7,456	12,703	12,641
Milk received (gal) (churns up to 1932)	–	–	–	–	–
Fish, meat, etc. forwarded (cwt)	183	203	123	116	197
Fish, meat etc. received (cwt)	108	53	20	11	27
General merchandise forwarded (tons)	2,072	1,123	726	487	655
General merchandise received (tons)	2,273	2,043	1,951	2,210	3,016
Coal forwarded (tons)	26	5	18	16	12
Coal received (tons)	806	941	1,144	974	1,136
Other minerals forwarded (tons)	6	18	–	10	14
Other minerals received (tons)	2,972	3,032	2,594	3,202	2,413
Livestock forwarded (trucks)	361	395	307	156	143
Livestock received (trucks)	38	30	7	3	–
Loaded wagons (not livestock) forwarded	521	337	209	268	271
Loaded wagons (not livestock) received	1,167	1,127	979	1,145	1,165

which could accommodate only a locomotive, van and fifteen goods wagons, which, as we will see, presented considerable difficulties when longer trains had to pass here. There were several sidings, only one of which was convenient for loading and unloading wagons, which first had to be shunted through the goods shed. The main station house, of standard North Devon design with later additions, was on the 'up' platform, with signal box and waiting shelter on the 'down' platform. The platforms were linked with a sleeper-built crossing and the station was well equipped with standard South Western and Southern items. In the yard, was a short spur to a loading dock which was equipped with cattle pens and a 5-ton

King's Nympton goods shed and fertiliser store in 1965.

A. E. West

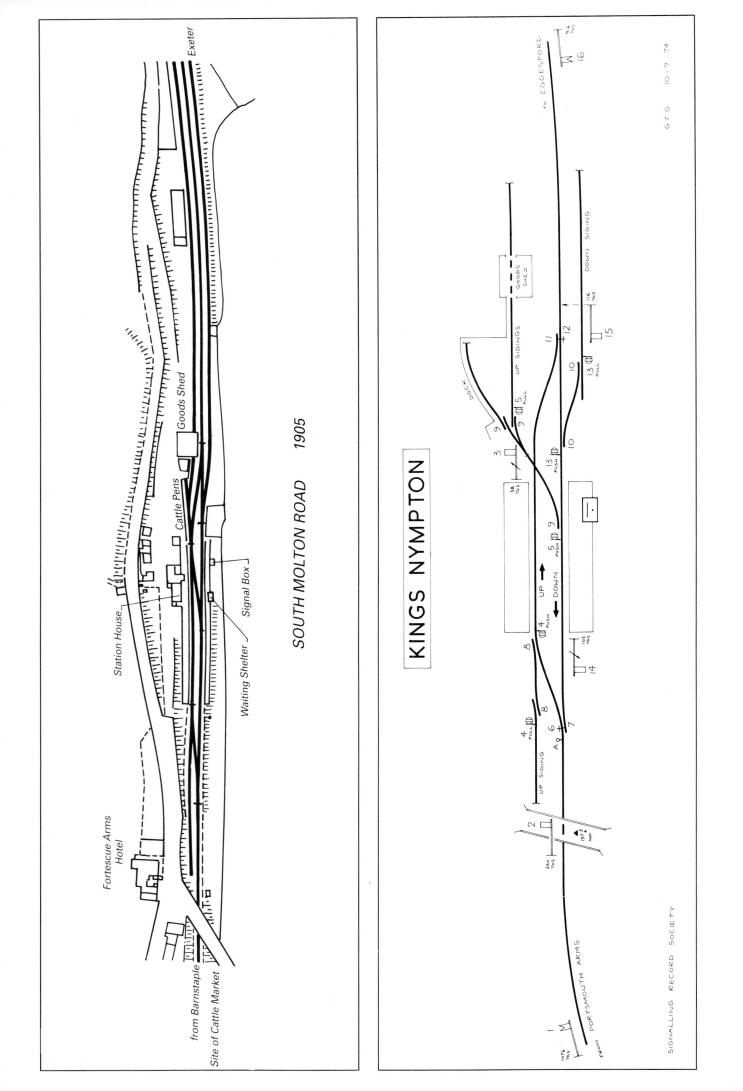

SOUTH MOLTON ROAD   1905

Station House

Fortescue Arms
Hotel

Goods Shed

Cattle Pens

Waiting Shelter

Signal Box

from Barnstaple

Site of Cattle Market

Exeter

KINGS NYMPTON

TO EGGESFORD

GOODS SHED

UP SIDINGS

DOWN SIDING

DOCK

UP SIDING

UP

DOWN

FROM PORTSMOUTH ARMS

SIGNALLING RECORD SOCIETY

GFG 10-9-74

King's Nympton goods siding and warehouse in 1965.

crane. The wooden goods shed had a loading dock, goods office and 2-ton crane, and further along this siding was a depot run by the firm of J. Cole & Co. of Ashreigny.

The station approach to the north ran up to meet the main A377, just outside the Fortescue Arms Hotel, when the road crossed the line on a girder bridge. Immediately beyond the bridge, in a triangle bounded by the road, railway and river, was the livestock auction market which did considerable business on the fourth Wednesday of the month.

The signalling at South Molton Road was quite straightforward, with all points and signals controlled from

the 16-lever frame in the 1873 signal box. We have already considered the difficulties in crossing long passenger trains here, but in South Western days the signalman had three trains on his hands twice a day, at about 2.20pm and again at 3.10pm. The 11.01 am goods from Exeter to Barnstaple Junction was involved on both occasions, in the first case the 1.15pm passenger train from Torrington crossed the 1.02pm passenger train from Exeter, and in the second case, the 2.16pm passenger train from Torrington crossed the 11.10am from Waterloo. The goods arrived at 2.45pm and departed at 3.18pm, having been shunted out of the way of the faster passenger trains,

King's Nympton station building in 1965.

Above: King's Nympton signal box in 1965.   A. E. West

Right: The 'down' starting signal at King's Nympton in 1965.   A. E. West

but no doubt needed to make use of the locomotive water supply then provided at South Molton Road. This facility was taken out of use by the Southern, although the derelict water tower survived into 1960s.

In 1928-36, the Southern Railway traffic figures show that about fifteen to twenty tickets were issued on an average day and slightly more collected. There was also some business in parcels and telegrams, and also some milk churn traffic. Half the loaded wagons forwarded, some thirty to forty per month, were cattle trucks, most of them on market day. There were a further couple of loaded wagons forwarded and about four received per day, the most important traffic being that in fertilizers, animal feedstuffs and coal, much of this being consigned to J. Cole & Sons. After the general closure of the yard, the remaining siding was retained for fertilizer traffic.

The staffing here was similar to that at other stations,

A view of King's Nympton station in 1978, looking south, showing the single track line, together with the siding retained for fertiliser traffic.

P. Swift

being station master, two signalmen, a porter signalman and a porter, together with permanent way staff, and in the later 1960s, three signalmen only. In 1910, the station master was Mr S. Chalkley, and one of the signalmen in later years was Mr R. Baker.

Leaving South Molton Road station the line passed under the A377 road and then over the River Taw on Newnham Bridge, just above the junction pool with the River Mole. It now followed the west bank of the river passing through water meadows until reaching High Doomsford Crossing.

Higher Doomsford Crossing

High Doomsford Crossing was provided for a track running from the main road to the water meadows between the railway and river. Here there was a cottage for the crossing keeper, Mrs Woldridge, who operated the crossing in the same way as others on the line. The post of crossing keeper was withdrawn late in Southern Railway days and a telephone was provided for road users to seek permission to cross from the signalman at South Molton Road, Mrs Wooldridge moving to Chenson Crossing. Coal and other supplies for High Doomsford Crossing were sent from South Molton Road by porter.

The line soon found itself a rare straight stretch of about a mile into Portsmouth Arms station, passing the 'down' distant signal on the way, the station being 200¾ miles from Waterloo.

Portsmouth Arms

Chronology:

Opened	1st August 1854
Mixed gauge into use	2nd March 1863
Signal box opened	1st October 1873
Broad gauge taken out of use	30th April 1877
Goods yard closed	3rd July 1961
Signal box closed	3rd April 1966

As we will see in Chapter 3, the fourth Earl Portsmouth was responsible for the construction of the turnpike road down the Taw Valley, now the A377, and an inn bearing the name Portsmouth Arms was constructed. When the North Devon Railway was built the isolated station was named after the inn. The station could hardly have been more simple, comprising a passing loop with two platforms and a single siding. On the 'down' platform was an attractive but unusual brick-built building, containing the booking office and waiting rooms, and the 1873 signal box. Opposite, on the 'down' platform, was a stone-built

waiting room and a stone-built goods shed, both 'up' and 'down' goods trains calling here to load and unload parcels and other consignments. The crossing loop could accommodate trains of eight coaches or twenty wagons, but the goods siding could take forty wagons from the catch points to the stop blocks. At the station end of the siding was a cattle loading dock and a 5-ton crane. Outside the station was a South Western design of station house, and the platforms were equipped with standard LSWR and Southern items.

PORTSMOUTH ARMS

	1928	1930	1932	1934	1936
Passenger tickets issued	4,997	4,366	3,583	3,603	3,357
Season tickets issued	–	–	–	13	6
Tickets collected	5,873	5,004	4,167	4,332	4,042
Parcels forwarded	853	727	560	750	814
Parcels received	1,115	1,193	1,247	1,323	1,243
Horses forwarded	11	15	7	9	15
Horses received	6	9	2	14	14
Milk forwarded (gal) (churns up to 1932)	–	–	–	2,095	3,434
Milk received (gal) (churns up to 1932)	–	–	–	–	–
Fish, meat, etc. forwarded (cwt)	20	33	8	48	70
Fish, meat etc. received (cwt)	4	–	3	4	–
General merchandise forwarded (tons)	859	524	212	183	243
General merchandise received (tons)	1,132	1,082	1,180	1,008	1,879
Coal forwarded (tons)	–	–	–	10	–
Coal received (tons)	425	493	448	408	362
Other minerals forwarded (tons)	–	–	–	–	103+
Other minerals received (tons)	1,179	1,217	956	859	541
Livestock forwarded (trucks)	245	230	149	170	175
Livestock received (trucks)	45	54	18	12	5
Loaded wagons (not livestock) forwarded	333	161	85	105	140
Loaded wagons (not livestock) received	548	557	472	397	540

(+ Pig manure to Braunton)

The signal box controlled the entire station area from its ten-lever frame, with distant, home and starting signals in each direction, there being some economy in that the home signal levers also operated the facing point locks on the loop points. The signalmen were kept busy with the passing of trains, and sometimes three trains could be seen here at once. For example, in 1936, the 12.35pm freight from Torrington 2.55pm passenger train from Ilfracombe and 11.45am passenger train from Waterloo, were all here

Portsmouth Arms signal box about 1930 with signalman W. Southcombe.
Collection W. Southcombe

PORTSMOUTH ARMS 1905

Waiting Shelter

Goods Shed

SP

Crane

Station House

Cattle Pens

Signal Box

Station Building

Portsmouth Arms
Hotel

SP

SP

from Barnstaple ———— to Exeter

PORTSMOUTH ARMS

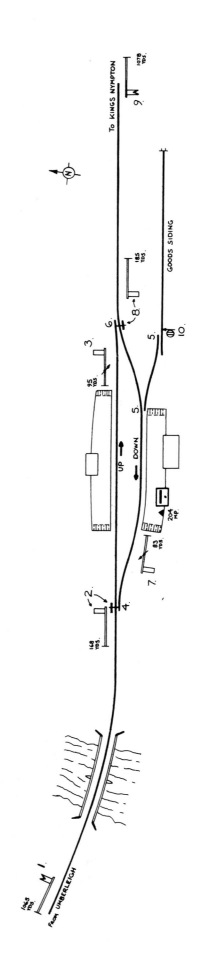

To KINGS NYMPTON

1078
YDS.

9

185
YDS.

8

GOODS SIDING

10

6

5

3

95
YDS.

5

DOWN

UP

204
M.P.

83
YDS.

7

2

4

148
YDS.

1065
YDS.

1

FROM UMBERLEIGH

N

SIGNALLING RECORD SOCIETY.   G·A·P.

Bulleid Pacific No. 34028 *Eddystone* arrives at Portsmouth Arms with a 'down' train on 14th September 1952.　　　*R. J. Sellick*

just after 4pm, presumably, the goods train being shunted into the siding.

The Southern Railway traffic statistics for 1928-36 show the station to be rather busier than its rural situation might indicate, Portsmouth Arms being the railhead for numerous local villages including Burrington, Beaford, Chittlehamholt, Dolton, Roborough and High Bicklington. The station issued a couple of dozen or so tickets a day and collected about the same, there also being regular traffic in parcels, telegrams and milk churns. Although the "Atlantic Coast Express" was booked to pass Portsmouth

Arms without stopping, it was not unusual in the 1930s for the express to be issued with a Stop Order at the station for the benefit of numerous first class passengers travelling to several neighbouring large country houses. On average one or two loaded wagons were forwarded per day and a couple received in the yard, half the loaded wagons forwarded being livestock, mostly after the monthly cattle auction at the station. Meat was another important commodity, in Southern days railway lorries fitted with meat hooks brought the carcasses down from slaughterhouses at High Bickington and Dolton to the

Portsmouth Arms station building in 1965, viewed from the station approach.　　　*A. E. West*

Portsmouth Arms station building from the platform in 1965.
A. E. West

Portsmouth Arms signal box 1965, the year before its closure.
A. E. West

station, where they were loaded into meat vans. Goods traffic received included fertilizers, animal feedstuffs, coal and minerals.

An interesting feature at Portsmouth Arms was the post box at the entrance to the station which was cleared at 8.30pm by the late turn signalman, who padlocked the

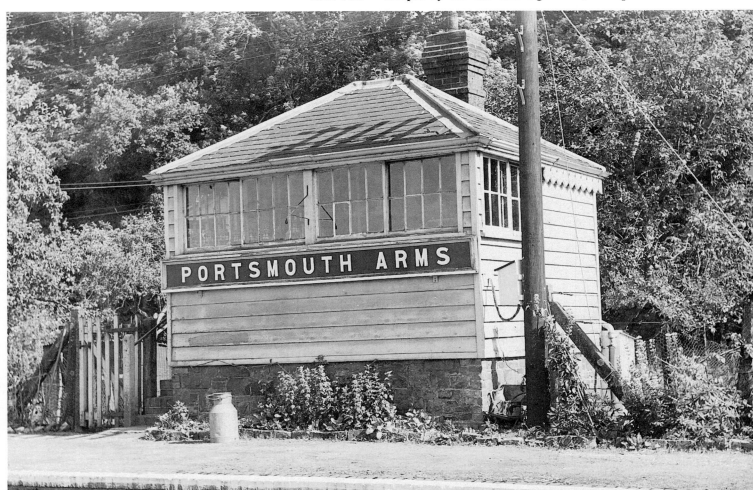

The goods shed at Portsmouth Arms in 1965, unusually sited on the 'up' platform. Goods trains called here to load and unload consignments, there being a similar arrangement at Lapford.

A. E. West

mail bag and forwarded it on the 'up' mail train at about 9pm, the letters being franked and sorted on the mail train. People came from miles around to post their letters at Portsmouth Arms station where the mail was collected much later than most other places.

In 1910, the station master was Mr H. Tate, but for many years Portsmouth Arms was supervised by the Umberleigh station master. The staff, for many years, was two signalmen and a porter signalman who between them attended to all the station duties. In 1936, the men were signalmen W. F. Southcombe and J. Beer and porter signalman R. Baker. One of them usually resided in the railway house at the station.

The line left Portsmouth Arms station and curved away to the north, crossing the River Taw on a viaduct of five spans and then passing under a road bridge at Kingford. It followed the curving river valley in directions varying from north east to west and then north, crossing and re-crossing the River Taw and some streams before arriving at Umberleigh Gates level crossing.

Umberleigh Gates
Chronology:

Signal box opened	18th October 1890
Reduced to ground frame	date unknown
Ground frame closed and crossing converted to automatic operation	19th November 1972

Umberleigh Gates was provided for a minor road which ran along the east side of the valley to cross the line. Initially, according to South Western Instruction No. 115 of 1890, a signal box was established here, operating some

On 23rd August 1980 the 10.58 train from Exeter St Davids to Barnstaple crosses the River Taw on Portsmouth Arms bridge. Typical of many on the line, this was extended for double track in the 1900s, but the second line was never laid.

Author

Umberleigh Gates in 1980 showing the crossing keeper's cottage and associated ground frame building. The crossing has since been converted to automatic operation.

Author

of the signals, but later it was reduced to a ground frame of eight levers, interlocked with Umberleigh signal box. For many years, the crossing keeper was Mrs L. Pratt, the widow of a signalman who had five children and who lived in the adjacent railway house. The gated crossing was then operated in similar fashion to others on the line, until 19th November 1972 when it was converted to automatic operation, approaching trains operating red flashing lights on the ungated crossing. Coal and other supplies for Umberleigh Gates were supplied from Umberleigh station by porter. Leaving Umberleigh Gates, the line quickly ran into Umberleigh station, 204¾ miles from Waterloo.

Umberleigh
Chronology:

Opened	1st August 1854
Mixed gauge into use	2nd March 1863
First signal box opened	1st October 1873
Broad gauge taken out of use	30th April 1877
Line to Pill Bridge doubled, first signal box closed, second signal box opened	19th October 1890
Goods yard closed	4th January 1965
Signal box closed and line singled	21st May 1971

Umberleigh station was one of the most attractive on the line with its two widely spaced tracks curving gently past the platforms, its standard North Devon Railway station house, and under the three-arch bridge and on to Barnstaple, Umberleigh being the end of the single track section from Copplestone. The double track began just south of the station, but further up the line were the points for the very long 'up' siding. There were three sidings, or collections of sidings, on the 'down' side, the first being the main part of the goods yard incorporating a cattle dock and another siding which accommodated a camping coach. The second was a short siding next to the road bridge which served a loading dock and the goods shed, which had its own 2-ton crane, and the third, to the north of the road bridge, which in earlier days boasted a yard crane but in later days was used to store cattle trucks and other wagons. On the other side of the line were two South Western cottages for railway employees, and at the south end of the yard were several stores used by traders. Just

down the road was Umberleigh Bridge with Murch Brothers premises and the Post Office on the station side of the river and the Rising Sun inn on the other.

Umberleigh signal box, situated in the centre of the 'up' platform, was a typical South Western box of the 1890s, quite different to the 1870s vintage boxes seen elsewhere along the line. Built again on a stone base, most of the front and two sides were glazed in small glass panels, and adjacent to it was a waiting shelter built in stone. The 31-lever frame, together with the eight-lever ground frame at Umberleigh Gates, controlled the whole area in more detail than most stations. In the 'down' direction, there were distant, outer home, home, starting and advance starting signals. and in the 'up' direction, distant, home, starting and advance starting signals. There were a considerable number of point locks and ground signals to complete the arrangements.

UMBERLEIGH

	1928	1930	1932	1934	1936
Passenger tickets issued	9,327	9,614	9,619	9,097	8,820
Season tickets issued	10	13	6	26	115+
Tickets collected	10,544	10,591	10,677	10,381	10,026
Parcels forwarded	1,026	946	890	763	725
Parcels received	1,339	1,535	1,658	1,877	1,889
Horses forwarded	20	18	20	6	2
Horses received	10	14	13	8	4
Milk forwarded (gal) (churns up to 1932)	–	37	–	–	–
Milk received (gal) (churns up to 1932)	–	–	–	–	–
Fish, meat, etc. forwarded (cwt)	155	121	74	214	201
Fish, meat etc. received (cwt)	–	–	–	–	6
General merchandise forwarded (tons)	520	507	272	297	218
General merchandise received (tons)	939	908	776	768	816
Coal forwarded (tons)	8	–	–	–	–
Coal received (tons)	989	1,085	1,027	972	823
Other minerals forwarded (tons)	268	–	–	–	12
Other minerals received (tons)	500	663	248	327	454
Livestock forwarded (trucks)	162	167	113*	101	112
Livestock received (trucks)	13	25	3	2	–
Loaded wagons (not livestock) forwarded	148	181	105	134	232
Loaded wagons (not livestock) received	369	557	432	437	569

+ Camping Coach

*Foot and Mouth Disease Order 1932 at Coombe Martin closed market

64

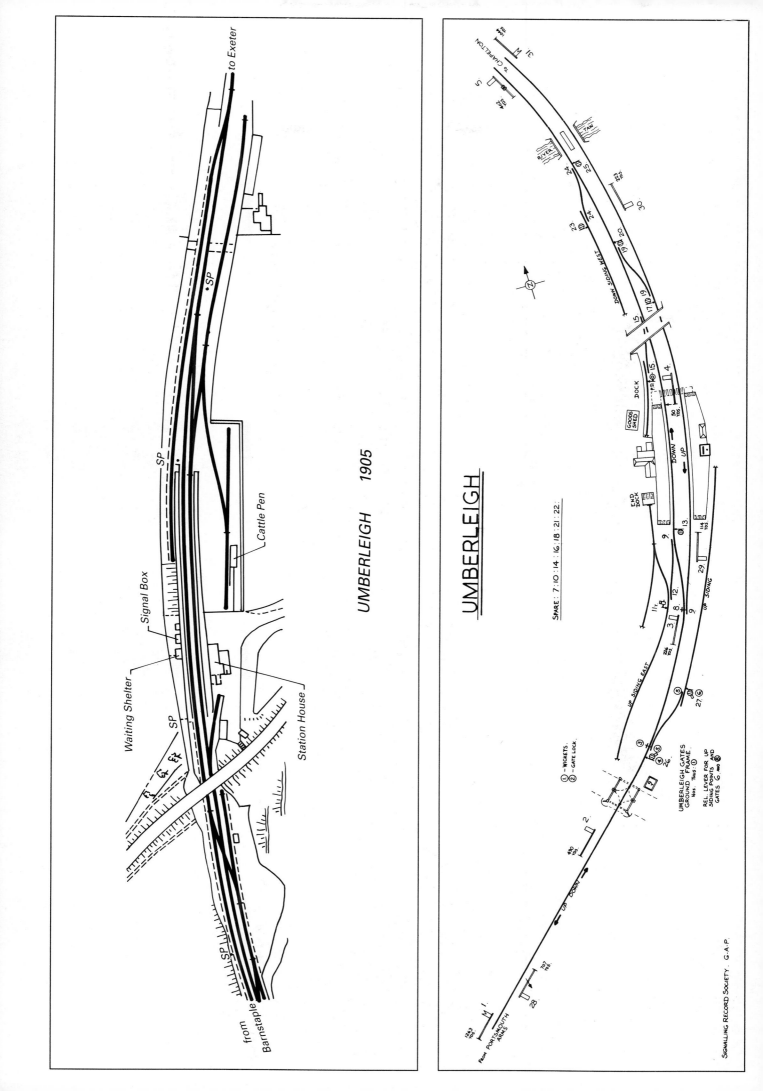

UMBERLEIGH 1905

Signal Box

Waiting Shelter

Station House

Cattle Pen

to Exeter

from Barnstaple

SP

UMBERLEIGH

SPARE : 7 : 10 : 14 : 16 : 18 : 21 : 22 :

To CHAPELTON

RIVER

TANK

DOWN SIDING WEST

GOODS SHED

DOCK

END DOCK

DOWN

UP

UP SIDING

UP SIDING EAST

UP SIDING

① – WICKETS.
② – GATE LOCK.

UMBERLEIGH GATES
GROUND FRAME
Nos. Thus: ①

REL. LEVER FOR UP
SIDING POINTS AND
GATES ⑥ and ⑱

UP DOWN

FROM PORTSMOUTH ARMS

SIGNALLING RECORD SOCIETY. G.A.P.

Umberleigh station looking south from the bridge in 1963. *Author*

The camping coach in the yard was mentioned in the Southern returns for 1936, and after wartime withdrawal was still there in the 1960s, being photographed by the author in 1963. The old South Western coach had been converted into very comfortable accommodation in a beautiful setting in North Devon with a good train service to the seaside resorts. The Southern had a number of camping coaches available in various Devon stations, although the only others in the north of the county were at Wrafton.

During the period 1928-36, traffic statistics show Umberleigh to have more passenger traffic than most on

the line with some thirty tickets a day issued and slightly more collected. The booking office also handled considerable traffic in parcels and telegrams. In the yard, about one loaded wagon a day was forwarded and about two received, with about half the traffic forwarded being loaded cattle trucks. Most of the livestock traffic was loaded after the monthly cattle auction market held adjacent to the station. Other traffic forwarded included manure, reed, apples, timber and meat. Traffic received included agricultural machinery and spare parts for Murch Brothers, coal distributed by local merchants Mr Down and Mr Gardener who had depots in the yard, fertilizers

Umberleigh station looking north in 1963.

Author

Umberleigh signal box in 1965. When the line north was doubled in 1890 this signal box was built to replace an earlier (1873) box.
A. E. West

and animal feedstuffs for Mr Thomas who had a store in the yard, building materials and some livestock.

In 1910, the station master was Mr F. H. Brazier, in 1936 Mr W. Wheeler and then Messrs Chugg, Servden, Woods, Somerfield, Mills and lastly Gregory. The station staff were usually two signalmen and one porter signalman, in 1939 being Messrs W. Snow, E. Lake and W. Passmore respectively. An earlier porter signalman was Mr H. Walters and Mr Pratt had previously been signalman here. There were eight permanent way staff based at Umberleigh under the ganger, Mr King, and the five station houses were occupied by Messrs Snow, Lake, Passmore, King and Willoughby, a platelayer. When the signal box closed in 1971, the three signalmen were Messrs W. Passmore, Bird and Knight. A permanent way gang of about nine men responsible for the northern end of the line is now based here.

Passing under the road bridge, No. 68, the line shortly crossed the River Taw on Black Bridge, a viaduct of iron spans, No. 69, and the ran through the water meadows on the west bank of the river. The double track line was punctuated with the odd culvert and occupational crossing provided for local farmers. Passing the 'down' distant signal, the line then ran round a curve to enter Chapleton station, 207¼ miles from Waterloo.

'Up' home signal at Umberleigh in 1965, looking south through the arches of bridge No. 68 to the station.

A. E. West

The Umberleigh Camping Coach in 1963, a converted LSWR vehicle.

Author

Looking north from Umberleigh road bridge on 4th July 1953 as an N class 2-6-0 on an 'up' train passes a rake of cattle trucks in the siding, which was later lifted.

R. J. Sellick

Class 31 No. 31263 heads the 19.14 train from Barnstaple to Basingstoke on 18th August 1981 as it calls at Umberleigh, showing the limited facilities comprising waiting shelter and electric lights.

Author

Chapleton

Chronology:

Chapleton siding opened	1st August 1854
Temporary platform opened	July 1857
Temporary platform closed	August 1860
Station opened	1st March 1875
Broad gauge taken out of use	30th April 1877
Line doubled and signal box opened	19th October 1890
Goods yard closed	4th January 1965
Signal box closed	26th January 1966
Line singled	21st May 1971

CHAPELTON

	1928	1930	1932	1934	1936
Passenger tickets issued	8,437	7,723	7,021	6,803	5,250
Season tickets issued	4	3	–	1	–
Tickets collected	9,070	8,408	7,350	7.090	5,960
Parcels forwarded	219	330	363	334	262
Parcels received	221	285	376	303	312
Horses forwarded	–	–	–	–	–
Horses received	–	–	–	–	–
Milk forwarded (gal) (churns up to 1932)	55	–	–	4,188	6,590
Milk received (gal) (churns up to 1932)	–	–	–	–	24
Fish, meat, etc. forwarded (cwt)	5	36	9	2	19
Fish, meat etc. received (cwt)	–	–	–	–	–
General merchandise forwarded (tons)	162	755	1,642	1,104	1,694
General merchandise received (tons)	277	1,255	243	794	400
Coal forwarded (tons)	10	–	–	–	–
Coal received (tons)	62	82	87	7	–
Other minerals forwarded (tons)	–	179	–	–	32
Other minerals received (tons)	237	235	90	47	58
Livestock forwarded (trucks)	–	–	–	–	–
Livestock received (trucks)	–	–	–	–	–
Loaded wagons (not livestock) forwarded	67	201	293	301	486
Loaded wagons (not livestock) received	141	335	70	250	118

The quiet station at Chapelton, later Chapleton, was for many years a model of railway efficiency on the North Devon line. Situated on a double-track line the signal box was usually switched out, only being switched into use for an hour or so every midday when the goods train from Exeter to Barnstaple shunted the yard, and on some busy summer Saturdays. One porter signalman, Wilfred Osman, who was there for some 35 years, attended to all station duties including the issuing and collecting of tickets, parcels and telegram traffic, consignment notes for wagon loads of timber forwarded from the yard, and other duties. He did have some assistance from his wife during meal breaks and to shorten his shift the guards of the last two trains of the day were responsible for collecting tickets here.

The layout at Chapleton was quite straightforward, with a crossover and two sidings in the yard on the 'down' side, at least after 1930. Before then there was a second crossover and a long 'up' siding at the Umberleigh end. At the Barnstaple end a gated crossing connected the two platforms for both foot and vehicular traffic, this being operated by a ground frame up to 1928. The South Western designed station house, occupied for many years by Mr and Mrs Osman, was at the Barnstaple end of the 'up' platform and incorporated all the usual booking and waiting facilities. On the 'down' platform was the 1890 signal box and a waiting shelter, with the goods yard behind.

The signalling at Chapleton was rather complicated in earlier years, the signal box having a 23-lever frame, interlocked with a three-lever ground frame for the level crossing. There were distant, home, starting and advance starting signals in each direction, point levers and numerous ground signals, but this was simplified after 1930.

Traffic from the goods yard at Chapleton was very light

Chapelton station in 1950, looking south, with all the signals pulled 'off', the signal box being switched out.   *R. J. Sellick*

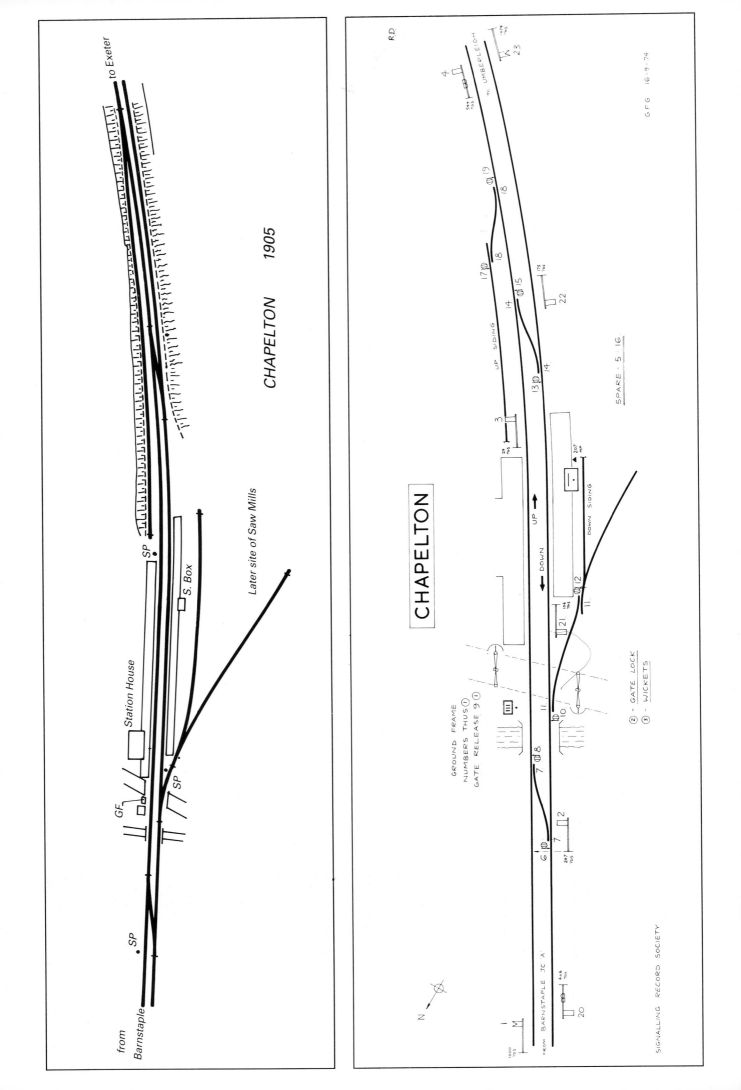

CHAPELTON 1905

to Exeter

from Barnstaple

Station House

S. Box

GF

SP

Later site of Saw Mills

CHAPELTON

FROM BARNSTAPLE JC 'A'

TO UMBERLEIGH

GROUND FRAME
NUMBERS THUS ①
GATE RELEASE 9 ①

② - GATE LOCK
③ - WICKETS

SPARE - 5 · 16

UP

DOWN

UP SIDING

DOWN SIDING

N

R.D.

G.F.G. 16-9-74

SIGNALLING RECORD SOCIETY

Chapelton station looking north 1952.

R. J. Sellick

until March 1930, when the firm Chappell & Walton established their sawmills here. They were joined in 1932 by Mr J. H. W. Parkman, who worked his way up to become manager and director of the company, continuing as manager after the takeover in 1966 by Rawle Gammon & Baker until his retirement in 1981. Mr Parkman has been able to supply considerable information about both the sawmills and the station. Timber was cut from woods in private estates, Forestry Commission land and local farms and brought to the sawmills by road, initially using a Fowler and a Marshall traction engine, and later by lorry. Here it was cut to size, using power saws, initially steam driven and later electric. Although the sawmills did supply most types of timber required it had several specialities.

One was fencing, sawn timber in the form of posts, rails, scantlings, palings and so on, for customers including the Southern Railway and the Astolat Company of Peasmarsh near Guildford. Pit props were supplied to collieries all over the country, together with chocks and other specialised requirements of the mining industry.

Perhaps their most interesting speciality was high quality oak cut to scantlings, solebars, headstocks, middle bearers and various small sizes which were supplied to the Southern, Great Western and LMS wagon workshops and to Wagon Repairs Ltd of Birmingham. When the timber was ready the company workshop was informed and an inspector sent to check each piece of timber and to mark it before forwarding a wagon load to the workshops. Timber

On 19th April 1963, Bulleid Pacific No. 34054 *Lord Beaverbrook* arrives at Chapelton with an 'up' train.

R. J. Sellick

In the 1950s the Chapelton porter signalman Wilfred Osman won the 'Best Kept Station' award for the area. Here he is seen in conversation with Mr J. A. W. Parkman (left), manager of Chapelton Sawmills, the principal railway customer.

Collection J. A. W. Parkman

which was not quite up to standard was still suitable for repairing wagons. The LMS works at Derby and Bromsgrove sent inspectors Thorpe and Browne, the Great Western at Swindon inspectors Hillman and Morris and the Southern at Eastleigh sent Messrs Barton and Taylor. A 10-ton crane in the yard was used for loading some of the timber.

Southern Railway statistics show that although few people lived near Chapelton station about twenty tickets a day were issued and about the same number collected, the booking office also dealing with the odd parcel and telegram. After the establishment of the sawmills about six or seven loaded wagons were forwarded per week almost all loaded with timber. Little other traffic was forwarded, there not being a cattle dock provided, except for hampers of rabbits forwarded by Mr Lester Moore. Traffic received included coal, some for the sawmills, and fertilizers received by local merchant, Mr Snell.

Leaving Chapelton station the double-track line ran over Langham Lake on an iron viaduct, under a couple of

Chapelton goods yard about 1962, with wagons loaded with pit props from Chapelton Sawmills, about the depart on the midday 'down' goods.

Collection J. A. W. Parkman

Chapelton station house in 1965. This South Western structure dates from the opening of the station in 1875.　　　*A. E. West*

overbridges and then continued to Barnstaple for four miles, with an almost dead straight section. The line crossed the River Taw on a viaduct and ran under the main A377 road on a three-arch bridge at Newbridge, past Bishops Tawton on the hillside above, and over Pill Bridge, as rebuilt by the South Western in 1891 and described in Chapter 5, together with the temporary signal box. Meeting the Great Western line coming in from the East, the line ran into Barnstaple Junction station, 211½ miles from Waterloo and the end of our journey.

The large, 10-ton crane in Chapelton goods yard in 1965.　　　*A. E. West*

The rear of Chapelton signal box in 1965.

A. E. West

Throughout the railway age Barnstaple Junction station has been the principal station in North Devon, dealing with all services on the lines to Exeter, Torrington, Ilfracombe and Taunton. On a busy summer Saturday it was possible to take a through express train to Waterloo, Paddington, Manchester, Cardiff or Wolverhampton, many of these running via the Great Western line to Taunton, but the Southern line to North Devon was always the most important. The station has expanded and contracted with the railway traffic, but we shall consider it at its peak after the expansion of 1924.

Situated on a long curve around the side of the hill at Sticklepath there were three running lines, opening out to four through the station, serving No. 1 'up' platform and Nos 2 and 3 'down' platforms. The original North Devon Railway station house, with many additions, was on the 'up' platform and accommodated all the waiting and refreshment rooms, booking, parcels and other offices. On the 'down' platform was similar accommodation including another refreshment room. Connecting the platforms was the 1878 footbridge, extended in 1924, which also gave access to the station form the Sticklepath side of the line. The A and B signal boxes completely controlled the whole station area, the A, former East box, controlling the lines to Chapelton and the Great Western together with the entrance to the goods yard and locomotive depot, the B, formerly West box, controlling the lines to Torrington and Ilfracombe.

Barnstaple/Barnstaple Junction

Chronology:

Opened for standard gauge goods traffic to Fremington	August 1848
Opened for broad gauge services to Exeter	1st August 1854
Passenger services to Bideford opened	2nd November 1855
Mixed gauge into use	2nd March 1863
Ilfracombe branch opened, station renamed Barnstaple Junction, West signal box and 'down' platform opened	20th July 1874
Broad gauge taken out of use	30th April 1877
GWR loop line opened, East signal box opened	1st June 1887
New 'down' loop and island platform, new West signal box opened, old West signal box closed	23rd July 1924
East and West signal boxes renamed A and B	2nd October 1949
Torrington passenger service withdrawn	2nd October 1965
Taunton passenger service withdrawn	3rd October 1966
Victoria Road goods branch closed	30th May 1970
Ilfracombe line closed completely	5th October 1970
Motive power depot closed	1971
Track simplified, B signal box closed, line to Umberleigh singled	21st May 1971
New travel centre opened	10th November 1981
Meeth goods branch closed	31st August 1982
A signal box closed	1st November 1987
New loop opened, 'down' platform closed	August 1990

BARNSTAPLE JUNCTION

	1928	1930	1932	1934	1936
Passenger tickets issued	64,346	52,743	40,507	34,722	32,070
Season tickets issued	11	391	223	238	217
Tickets collected	114,417	103,289	93,028	84,342	76,865
Parcels forwarded	8,597	7,800	8,477	8,466	7,280
Parcels received	29,181	27,377	28,092	29,175	37,661
Horses forwarded	194	80	86	25	42
Horses received	108	99	28	17	30
Milk forwarded (gal) (churns up to 1932)	–	–	–	25,967	595
Milk received (gal) (churns up to 1932)	–	–	–	440	8,639
Fish, meat, etc. forwarded (cwt)	1,016	360	81	355	946
Fish, meat etc. received (cwt)	2,295	1,527	1,385	2,899	5,128
General merchandise forwarded (tons)	8,160	7,979	6,762	5,147	5,810
General merchandise received (tons)	17,860	16,611	13,952	13,284	15,645
Coal forwarded (tons)	1,383	1,442	739	660	63
Coal received (tons)	16,714	17,781	18,931	22,403	23,293
Other minerals forwarded (tons)	1,972	3,420	3,983	3,145	2,848
Other minerals received (tons)	7,703	17,343	13,010	15,207	17,841
Livestock forwarded (trucks)	629	800	422*	451	471
Livestock received (trucks)	513	469	206	92	101
Loaded wagons (not livestock) forwarded	8,658	9,611	8,819	6,892	6,484
Loaded wagons (not livestock) received	11,773	12,804	11,367	9,422	10,466
Wagons transferred (loaded & empty)	27,967	31,205	26,843	30,075	32,263

*Foot and Mouth Disease Order October 1932 Coombe Martin closed Barnstaple Market, also Blackmoor Gate Market

From outside the A signal box the goods yard formed a long curve to terminate near Barnstaple Bridge, although the siding accommodation was at times, inadequate. There was a siding into the wooden goods shed and another served extensive cattle pens. In Victorian days several spurs ran from a wagon turntable to serve various stores, and there was an extensive timber yard and sawmills, operated by the firm of Bartlett Bayliss & Co. At the end of the yard there were three sidings, one of which ran inside a building used first as a manure store and then as a slaughterhouse. Underneath the Sticklepath Road bridge was another wagon turntable with four more spur lines. There were large numbers of loading docks and stores used by the traders who operated from the station yard and by various railway engineers departments. A 7½-ton crane was provided in the yard.

On the Torrington line, under bridge No. 97 which carried the Sticklepath Road, there was a long siding, known as the 'Shipyard Siding' from which ran the private siding of Saw Milling & General Supplies, laid in during the 1914-18 war. It ran on a three-chain radius curve to a wharf on the River Taw and had a long loop siding. There was a concrete works on the wharf and the loop siding served the old Westcotts shipyard shed. During the 1939-45 war, considerable quantities of timber used for aircraft construction were received and forwarded from this siding. However, the main business of the siding was in connection with the Devon Concrete Works, sand and gravel being brought in by sea and cement by rail. The works produced a wide variety of concrete products, particularly large pipes and some of the products were forwarded by rail. Inside the works, concrete items were moved round the extensive storage area by railway flat wagons, and for many years the company had a self-propelled steam crane which was used for lifting the concrete castings and for moving wagons around. The works driver operated and maintained the steam crane.

Barnstaple shed was a two-road affair built in timber with various extensions, including some in stone, which accommodated stores, offices, repair and maintenance shops and a mess room. An early 35ft-diameter turntable outside the shed was replaced by a LSWR standard 50ft-diameter one in late Victorian days, and this could turn all locomotives used on the line, except the Bulleid light Pacifics. Four water columns were provided; one each at the end of the 'up' and 'down' platforms, outside the locomotive shed and next to the turntable. Water was supplied initially from a tank on the hill above the footbridge and later from one mounted on a tower adjacent to the turntable. In earlier years there were coal stacks outside the shed, but these were replaced by a partially mechanized coaling stage.

More than one hundred men were employed at Barnstaple shed for many years, including 44 drivers, 44 firemen, twelve cleaners, four coalmen, two boilersmiths, five fitters, two shed chargeman, two storemen and two clerks, all under the supervision of the running shed foreman. In SR days cleaners were usually taken on for the summer season, then laid off for the winter, and then re-employed the following summer on a permanent basis to work up to passed cleaner, firman, passed fireman and eventually driver, although they often had to move to their sheds as promotions became available. On busy summer Saturdays many of the passed firemen were needed to drive trains, their places being taken in turn by passed cleaners. The boilersmiths and fitters kept the locomotives in good order, having workshops equipped with lathes and milling machines, and much of their work was done through the night. In charge of the depot, was the running shed foreman, a former driver, in 1910 Mr T. Young, Mr R. Nicolson up to 1943, when he was succeeded by Mr Stevens, and the last being Mr F. Cox.

When dieselization came in 1964, several Barnstaple men were sent on a fortnight's course at Plymouth and passed to drive multiple units, North British Type 2 diesels of the D6300 series, and 'Hymek' diesels of the D7000 series. However, duties dwindled with line closures to the extent that by 1968 only ten drivers and four firemen were employed at Barnstaple, which was used as a signing-on point only, and in 1971 the depot finally closed completely, since then all trains have worked back to Exeter at night, usually almost empty.

The Southern Railway traffic statistics show Barnstaple to be a very busy station in all respects. About 150-200 tickets were issued daily, with twice as many collected, together with several hundred season tickets. Every day a hundred parcels were dealt with, and as many telegrams. In 1928-36 Barnstaple Junction was the most important passenger station in North Devon with the sole exception of Barnstaple Town which was more convenient for the town centre, but by 1963 the situation had been reversed. In the yard, some thirty loaded wagons were forwarded per day and about fifty received, the main headings being 7,000 tons of general merchandise, 3,000 tons of minerals,

The view south from Barnstaple Junction in 1965 showing, from right to left; 'down' siding, double-track North Devon line to Exeter, and the ex-GWR loop line curving away to the east to cross the River Taw on the viaduct on the extreme left.

Author

75

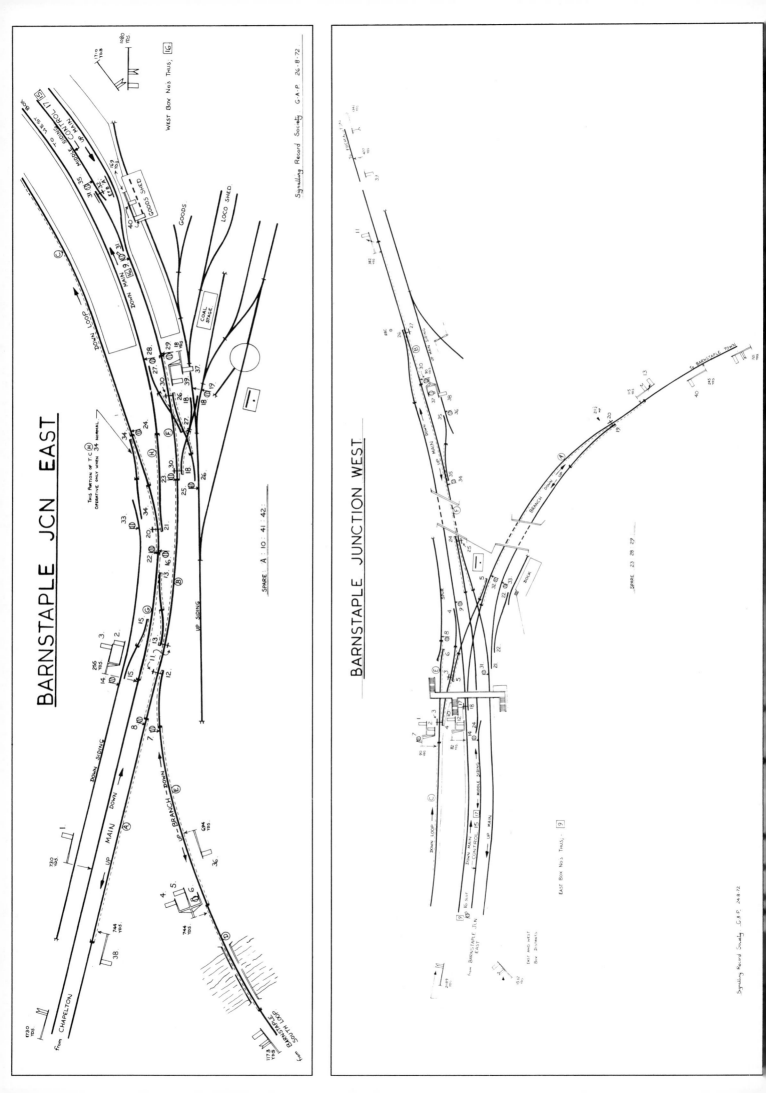

BARNSTAPLE JCN EAST

BARNSTAPLE JUNCTION WEST

WEST BOX Nos THUS, [16]

Signalling Record Society G.A.P. 26-8-72

THIS PORTION of T.C. (H) OPERATIVE ONLY WHEN 34 NORMAL.

SPARE : A : 10 : 41 : 42 :

EAST BOX Nos THUS, [9]

SPARE 23 28 29

Signalling Record Society G.A.P. 24.8.72

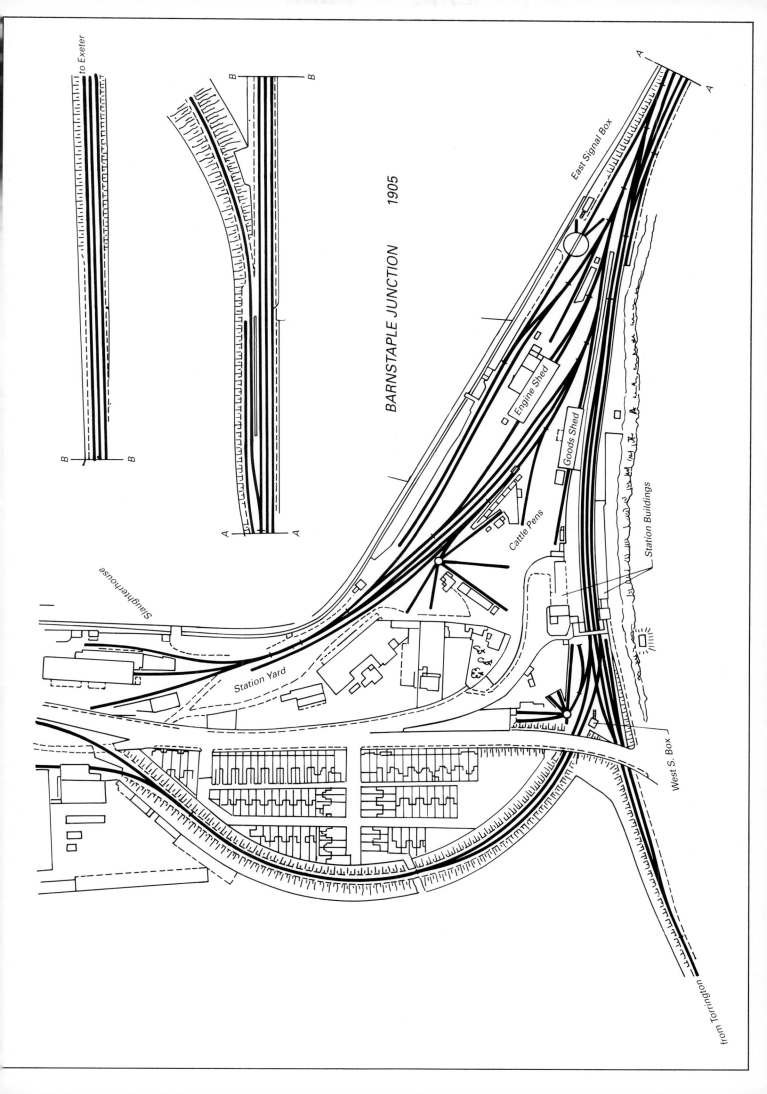

to Exeter

BARNSTAPLE JUNCTION 1905

East Signal Box

Engine Shed

Goods Shed

Cattle Pens

Station Buildings

Slaughterhouse

Station Yard

West S. Box

from Torrington

A A

B B

A A

B B

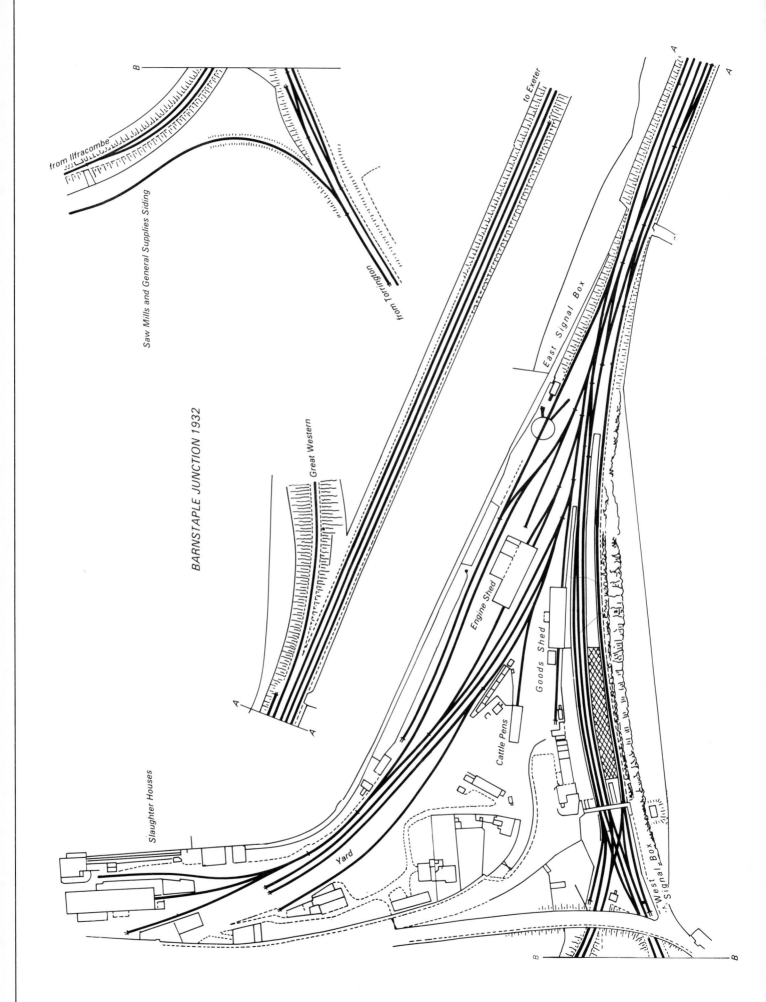

BARNSTAPLE JUNCTION 1932

from Ilfracombe

Saw Mills and General Supplies Siding

from Torrington

to Exeter

East Signal Box

Great Western

Engine Shed

Goods Shed

Cattle Pens

Slaughter Houses

Yard

West Signal Box

78

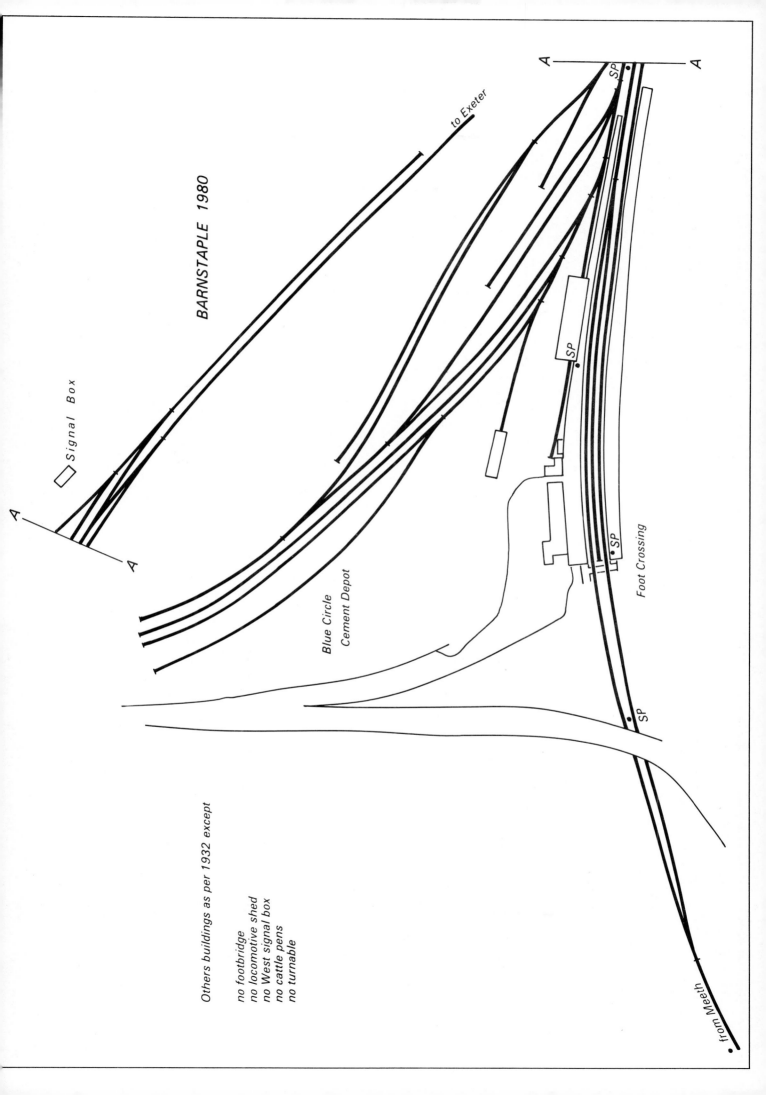

BARNSTAPLE 1980

Signal Box

to Exeter

A
A
A
A

SP
SP
SP
SP

Blue Circle
Cement Depot

Foot Crossing

from Meeth

Others buildings as per 1932 except

no footbridge
no locomotive shed
no West signal box
no cattle pens
no turntable

A fine study of Adams 460 class 4-4-0 No. E0468 at the coaling stage outside Barnstaple shed in the 1920s.

A. Halls courtesy National Railway Museum

A group of South Western staff pose at Barnstaple Junction in 1911. Centre may well be the Station Master, Mr Sommerfield surrounded by booking clerks, platform staff, shunters, guards and a policeman. The group is just a small part of the several hundred employed here by the LSWR.

Harold Mock Collection

Barnstaple Junction shed and goods yard from the 'up' platform on 4th August 1951.

R. J. Sellick

M7 class 0-4-4T No. 30670 shunts the yard at Barnstaple on 20th August 1962.

D. Wigley

800 wagons of livestock forwarded, with 15,000 tons of general merchandise, 20,000 tons of coal for the locomotive depot and coal merchants and 500 wagons of livestock received. These figures included the Rolles Quay branch and the private sidings of Saw Milling & General Supplies, and Shapland & Petter, but even so, Barnstaple Junction accounted for a third of all loaded wagons dealt with at all stations in North Devon.

The rear of Barnstaple shed in 1963 with a selection of Ivatt 2-6-2Ts and an ex-GWR 2-6-0.

Author

Left: The standard LSWR 50ft turntable at Barnstaple Junction in 1963.

Author

Below: Bulleid Pacific No. 34066 *Spitfire* rounds the curve on the Ilfracombe line on 20th August 1962 with an 'up' train arriving at Barnstaple Junction. Behind it is the extensive stockyard of the Devon Concrete Works with the jib of its rail-mounted self-propelled crane visible.

D. Wigley

Barnstaple Junction on 25th July 1964 showing an 08 class diesel shunter in the yard, right.

Author

The west end of Barnstaple station in 1980 illustrating the rationalized track and signalling layout.

Author

A large number of traders had premises in the station yard, and during the railway age there can have been few local businesses that did not use Barnstaple Junction goods yard. One firm of carriers with a depot here was Chaplin & Co., which later became part of Pickfords, and in later years there has been a Blue Circle cement depot supplied by rail.

There have always been many railwaymen employed at Barnstaple Junction station, with several hundred in both South Western and Southern days. In the early 1900s, the station master was Mr Somerfield, assisted by District Inspector Gammon, Station Inspection Pollard and Permanent Way Inspector Pring, who lived in the station house. In the 1930s, Mr Cawsey was station master, and in the 1950s, Mr Kelland assisted by foremen Bill Brock and Reg Ball, and Permanent Way Inspector Jim Chard. In the 1960s, Area Managers were introduced, Mr J. Bellamy followed by Mr E. J. Maclaughlan who was there until 1974 when the post was withdrawn. Passenger station staff included foremen, booking clerks, porters, carriage cleaners, shunters, ticket collectors and rest day relief men for the area. In the goods yard were goods shunters, clerks, checkers, porters and delivery lorry drivers, together with the employees of other firms with premises in the yard.

In Victorian days, shunting horses were employed at the station and there were men looking after them. Here, also were based a district carpenter, gas and water plumber, engineers to maintain signals, telegraphs and telephones, railway policemen and carriage and wagon examiners. Inspector Pring had a large staff of permanent way men working under his direction in the area bounded by Umberleigh, Torrington and Ilfracombe, and also the Lynton & Barnstaple narrow gauge line. Employment at the station has fallen considerably in recent years, first to 74 in 1968, 48 in 1981 and then seven in 1989.

The first revenue-earning visit of an HST to Barnstaple was on Sunday 18th March 1990 and this train from Paddington, was photographed by the train's Senior Conductor. (A clearance test run had been made previously, back in the 1970s).

Andy Robbins

Chapter 2
The Railway Age Begins

The Exeter & Crediton Railway of 1832

At the beginning of the railway age, before the great trunk routes of the Great Western and the Bristol & Exeter had penetrated the West Country, a number of small local lines were mooted. These included the Bideford & Okehampton, Bodmin & Wadebridge, and Exeter & Crediton, all of which were promoted in the early 1830s. In each case the projected railway linked a port with an inland town and was to be used to bring in seaborne goods, such as coal and fertilizers, and to take out agricultural produce, timber and the products of local mills and quarries.

Promotion of the first Exeter & Crediton Railway started at Exeter on 12th and 13th August 1831 when meetings of local landowners were held to discuss the project. The second meeting was called by Thomas Pring, a solicitor from Crediton, to ascertain public support for the project and to ensure that it was completed in the best possible way. The line from Crediton was to terminate at the basin of the Exeter Canal, which accommodated small sea-going vessels, but some advocated that it should be extended to a sea port at Topsham Quay. The promoters took their Bill to parliament in the next session and on 23rd June 1832 gained an Act for a line from the basin of the Exeter Canal to Four Mills, Crediton, with an authorized capital of £35,000. However, after three years no construction had been undertaken and the powers of the 1832 Act lapsed, this railway meeting the same fate as an earlier canal, the Exeter & Crediton Navigation, which gained its Act in 1801.

The Taw Vale Railway & Dock Company

Following a public meeting at Barnstaple Guildhall on 24th November 1836 a railway of similar type was proposed in North Devon. The North Devon Journal of 5th January 1837 carried the prospectus of the Taw Vale Railway to construct a dock at Fremington and a four mile railway linking the dock with Barnstaple, with a capital of £15,000. The objective was the elimination of the need for ships to navigate the difficult waters of the Taw estuary, all the promoters being local men including the Mayor of Barnstaple, and Mr William Thorne. The promoters went to parliament the following year and on 11th June 1838 gained the Taw Vale Railway & Dock Act; capital £15,000 in 300 shares of £50. Passenger traffic was also authorized. However the powers of the Act expired after seven years, with no progress having been made, and so the promoters returned to parliament and on 21st July 1845 gained the Taw Vale Amendment Act which extended powers for another five years and authorized extensions to the quays at Fremington. By now the chairman of the Taw Vale was William Thorne, formerly of Barnstaple but now the resident in London.

The Bristol & Exeter Railway

The Bristol & Exeter Railway gained its Act in 1836 and opened in stages until on 1st May 1844 the whole line from Bristol to Exeter St Davids station was opened. The double track broad gauge line built by Isambard Kingdom Brunel, together with the Great Western, now provided a main line of 194 miles from Paddington to Exeter. Initially the line was leased to the Great Western, but from 1849 the Bristol & Exeter ran its own services, establishing its own locomotive works at Bristol and carriage and wagon works at Bridgwater. Powers for a branch to Tiverton had been obtained in the 1836 Act, but these had lapsed and were renewed in a further Act of July 1845. The Bristol & Exeter remained independent until 1876 when it was amalgamated with the Great Western. The broad gauge main line was extended further to Torquay and Plymouth by the South Devon Railway which gained Acts in 1844 and 1846. After the unsuccessful experiment in atmospheric traction it opened its line in stages, reaching Torre and Laira in 1848.

The Railway Mania

By 1845 the early railway companies were proving to be very profitable for their shareholders, with the Great Western paying 7% and 8% dividends for the two half years of 1844, the South Western 6½% and 8%, and 10% was not unknown elsewhere. A railway mania broke out with promoters falling over each other to present Bills to parliament in the sessions of 1845, 1846 and 1847. By the end of 1847 session in three years parliament had sanctioned 576 Acts authorizing 8,652 miles of railway, and more Bills had fallen. However neither the capital nor the labour markets could cope with so much railway construction and so the mania was followed by a depression when many of the lines authorized were not built and the powers of the Acts expired.

By the autumn of 1844 no less than 220 railway Bills had been deposited for the consideration of parliament in the 1845 session and so the President of the Board of Trade, Mr Gladstone, persuaded parliament to set up a Board of Trade committee to examine the Bills and make recommendations on them. This committee of five was headed by Lord Dalhousie and became known as the 'Five Kings'. On 31st December 1844 the Five Kings reported on the Bills for eight lines in Devon and Cornwall, this being published on 4th March 1845. These included the Cornwall & Devon Central, from Exeter to Falmouth backed by the LSWR, the Exeter & Crediton, and the North Devon from Crediton to Barnstaple. They recommended against the Cornwall & Devon Central on the grounds that the South Devon, authorized in 1844, and the recommended Cornwall Railway would provide the necessary railway accommodation. They also recommended postponement of both the Exeter & Crediton and Crediton to Barnstaple lines so that the merits of the two alternative routes from Exeter to Barnstaple, via Crediton and via Tiverton, might be examined. The advantages of the Tiverton route were that it would save twenty miles on the journey from North Devon to London via Bristol, it would also connect Barnstaple with South Molton and Tiverton, and would require only 34 miles of new railway instead of 54. The committee did not report on Bills submitted by the Taw Vale and by the Bristol & Exeter for its Tiverton branch, presumably because both sought renewal of powers previously authorized.

The Exeter & Crediton Railway

After the opening of the Bristol & Exeter Railway promoters of a line to Crediton now required a shorter line than that authorized in 1832, starting from a junction at Cowley Bridge, north of Exeter. The first meeting recorded in the minute book of the Exeter & Crediton Railway was held on 20th March 1844 at the office of Robert Dymond at Exeter. In the chair was a prominent Crediton resident, J.W.Buller of Downes. Mr Ford and Mr Pring stated the advantages of the proposed line, and a provisional committee was set up. On 19th April 1844 this committee published their prospectus for the Exeter & Crediton Railway, capital £60,000 in 1,200 shares of £50, solicitors Mr Ford of Exeter and Mr Pring of Crediton, and engineer Robert Dymond. The provisional committee had made an agreement with the directors of the Bristol & Exeter for that company to lease the Exeter & Crediton for a rent of £3,000 per annum plus a third of gross receipts should the income exceed £7,000.

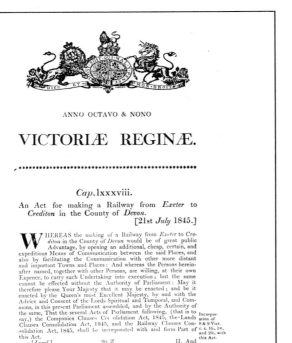

ANNO OCTAVO & NONO

VICTORIÆ REGINÆ.

Cap. lxxxviii.

An Act for making a Railway from *Exeter* to *Crediton* in the County of *Devon*.

[21st *July* 1845.]

WHEREAS the making of a Railway from *Exeter* to *Crediton* in the County of *Devon* would be of great public Advantage, by opening an additional, cheap, certain, and expeditious Means of Communication between the said Places, and also by facilitating the Communication with other more distant and important Towns and Places : And whereas the Persons hereinafter named, together with other Persons, are willing, at their own Expence, to carry such Undertaking into execution ; but the same cannot be effected without the Authority of Parliament : May it therefore please Your Majesty that it may be enacted ; and be it enacted by the Queen's most Excellent Majesty, by and with the Advice and Consent of the Lords Spiritual and Temporal, and Commons, in this present Parliament assembled, and by the Authority of the same, That the several Acts of Parliament following, (that is to say,) the Companies Clauses Consolidation Act, 1845, the Lands Clauses Consolidation Act, 1845, and the Railway Clauses Consolidation Act, 1845, shall be incorporated with and form Part of this Act.

[*Local.*]　　　　20 Z　　　　II. And

Despite the Five Kings recommendation of a postponement the provisional committee decided to press ahead with their Bill on 18th March, and their determination was rewarded when the Exeter & Crediton Railway Act was passed on 21st July 1845, capital £70,000 in 2,800 shares of £25, with powers to borrow another £23,333. The junction at Cowley Bridge was to be made under the superintendence of the Bristol & Exeter engineer, and there was a clause for the protection of the adjacent Exeter Waterworks. Clause 43 authorized a lease of the line to the B&ER or any other railway forming a junction or being united to it, provided that three fifths of the shareholders at a general meeting approved, while Clause 44 authorized similar conditions for the sale of the Company. The gauge was not specified.

Under its Chairman, J.W.Buller, the E&CR board wasted no time, meeting at its offices in High Street, Exeter on 6th August 1845. Tenders were invited and on 15th October the board accepted those of Messrs Waring and Co. of Dawlish for the earthworks and masonry, and from Sir John Guest for iron rails. At the first general meeting of proprietors on 27th February 1846 the directors reported that five sixths of the land had been acquired, all calls on shares had been paid, and that a draft copy of the lease to the Bristol & Exeter was in preparation. Robert Dymond, the engineer, reported:

"...Messrs Waring and Sons, the Contractors, are

proceeding satisfactorily with the works. The heaviest portion of the line, the cutting at Downes Hill, was commenced immediately after the letting of the contract, and the embankments now extend to a considerable distance from each end of that cutting. The diversion of the River Yeo at Downes is completed, and the cuttings at Longbridge and Pynes are in active progress. Drawings for the bridges to carry the various roads over the railway are being prepared, and these works also will soon be commenced..."

At the second general meeting on 28th August 1846 the directors reported that all the land had been acquired at a total cost close to the engineer's estimate. Contracts for laying permanent way, building several timber bridges, and the construction of the station building and outbuildings at Crediton had been let and were progressing well. Dymond reported that there had been some delays but:

"The earthwork and masonry are drawing towards completion. About one half of the line is ballasted, and the permanent way is laid. The station at Crediton, and the viaduct and bridges to connect our line with the Bristol & Exeter are commenced, and I can rely with confidence on the assurance of all the contractors that the utmost exertions shall be made to complete their respective works so as to enable us to open the line in November."

At the next general meeting on 24th February 1847 the directors reported the total expenditure up to 31st December 1846 to be £66,346 3s 3d, the main headings being land and compensation £13,005 4s, and contracts for earthworks and masonry, iron rails, permanent way, timber bridges and Crediton station totalling £44,959 5s. Dymond reported that the whole line, with the exception of the junction at Cowley Bridge, was ready for public traffic,and but for circumstances unconnected with his department, the junction would also have been completed.

He was referring to the outcome of a special general meeting on 11th January 1847 when the Exeter & Crediton shareholders had rejected the recommendation of the directors for the lease of the line to the Bristol & Exeter Railway.

Construction of the Taw Vale started

After gaining its Amendment Act on 21st July 1845 the Taw Vale board also set about its construction. On 17th October the board advertised for sealed tenders to be returned by 10th November, and awarded the No. 1 contract for the construction of a dock at Fremington and the railway to Barnstaple to its former Chairman, William Thorne, Emmanuel Cooper becoming the new Chairman. Although the No. 1 contract was dated 14th February 1846 Thorne was advertising subcontracts for materials and labour on 22nd December 1845, and he cut the first sod himself on 5th January 1846 at Pentole Marsh. Construction continued for more than two years.

The Parliamentary Struggle for North Devon

By the end of 1845 session parliament had authorized construction of the Exeter & Crediton, the Tiverton branch and the Taw Vale. The scene was now set for the 1846 session to consider the route for the main line into North Devon, the two alternative routes running via Tiverton and via Crediton.

The first on the scene was the North Devon Railway which published its prospectus on 30th June 1845. Its line was to run from Tiverton to or near Bampton, Dulverton, South Molton, Barnstaple and Bideford, with a branch to Ilfracombe. The capital was £700,000 and the provisional committee included many residents along the line. By 24th

July the provisional committee had been increased substantially by the inclusion of Earl Fortescue, the Lord Lieutenant of the County, several Lords and numerous directors of the Great Western, Bristol & Exeter and South Devon railways, with Brunel as the engineer. Lines to Taunton and Plymouth were added to give a total of 120 miles of railway; capital £1,750,000. For its Bill to be considered in the 1846 session the engineer was required to deposit with parliament by 30th November 1845 all the plans and sections of the proposed line, but these were not ready in time and were deposited several days later. This was fatal for the North Devon since on 12th May 1846 a parliamentary committee declared that the Standing Orders had not been complied with and that the Bill could not proceed. These events were reported to a subscribers meeting on 20th June by Earl Fortescue, chairman of the provisional committee, when the undertaking was wound up after expenditure of £38,668.

Vale, directors of several lines allied to the London & South Western, and residents along the line. The capital was £700,000 and the engineer, Joseph Locke, the South Western's engineer. After the fall of the North Devon on 12th May 1846, the Bristol & Exeter changed its tactics and courted the promoters of the Taw Vale Extension. After only a fortnight, on 26th May they reached a provisional agreement for the lease of the Taw Vale Extension to the Bristol & Exeter for a rent of four percent of capital for six months, and then approximately five per cent below Bristol & Exeter dividends. Parliament was petitioned in favour of the Taw Vale Extension by meetings at Bideford, Barnstaple and Crediton, and on 7th August 1846, the Act was passed. The Taw Vale Extension Act authorised amendments to the two previous Taw Vale Acts of 1838 and 1845, and the extension to join the Exeter & Crediton Railway. The capital was increased by £533,000 in £20 shares, with arrangements for the

TAW VALE RAILWAY EXTENSION.

AT a most numerous and highly influential Meeting of the inhabitants of the town of *Crediton* and its neighbourhood, called by public advertisement, at the Market-house in that town, on Saturday the 11th day of July instant, to consider the propriety of Petitioning the House of Lords in favor of the Taw Vale Railway Extension;

JOHN SILLIFANT, Esq., in the Chair;

IT WAS RESOLVED UNANIMOUSLY—

1. —On the motion of JOHN QUICKE, Esq., of Newton, seconded by JOHN WILLS, Esq.;—

" That a line of Railway, giving a more ready access to the agriculturists in the valley of the Taw to the market town of Crediton, and opening a communication for the importation of American timber, coal, iron, slate, pottery ware, lime, and other manure, into this district; and for the exportation of timber, cider, and other agricultural and manufactured produce, to Wales and other parts of the kingdom; will be generally and highly beneficial to all classes in this town and neighbourhood."

2. —On the motion of WILLIAM WREFORD, Esq., of Claonaborough, seconded by EDWARD DAVY, Esq., of Crediton :—

" That the proposed Extension of the Taw Vale Railway, from Barnstaple to Crediton, will be highly beneficial to the district through which it passes, and will be essentially advantageous to the county of Devon generally, inasmuch as, in connexion with other lines of railway already formed or about to be constructed, it will connect the Bristol and English Channels, and thus avoid the dangerous passage round the Land's-end; and will open to this important county a ready access to all parts of the kingdom; and by means of the works now in progress at Fremington, and by the Exeter and Crediton Railway, facilitating the shipment of cider—an article of considerable growth in this district—to Ireland and Wales, and the embarkation and landing of passengers to and from that country will be greatly promoted."

3. —On the motion of JOHN BROWNE, Esq., of Sandford, seconded by JOHN MOORE, Esq., of Kelland Barton ;—

" That a Petition to the House of Lords in favour of the Taw Vale Railway Extension be adopted and signed by this meeting."

(Signed) JOHN SILLIFANT, *Chairman.*

On the motion of the Rev. CHARLES GREGORY, of Sandford, seconded simultaneously by Mr. MADGE, of Copplestone, and several other gentlemen, the thanks of the meeting were voted to the Chairman by acclamation.

Crediton, 12th July, 1846.

North Devon Journal Thursday 23rd July 1846

Second on the scene for the 1846 session was the Taw Vale Railway Extension & Dock Company which published its prospectus on 18th September 1845 for a line from Barnstaple to Exeter with branches to Bideford, Ilfracombe and South Molton. In many respects it was a similar proposal to the North Devon from Crediton to Barnstaple of the previous year, but the provisional committee now included directors of the original Taw

ANNO DECIMO TERTIO

VICTORIÆ REGINÆ.

●●

Cap. xxiv.

An Act to enable the *Exeter and Crediton* Railway Company to enlarge their *Cowley Bridge* Station, and to raise a further Amount of Capital
[10th *June* 1850.]

WHEREAS an Act was passed in the Ninth Year of the Reign of Her present Majesty Queen *Victoria*, intituled *An Act for making a Railway from Exeter to Crediton in the County of Devon*, whereby a Company for carrying such Undertaking into effect was incorporated by the Name of " The *Exeter and Crediton* Railway Company," and the said Company were thereby authorized, amongst other things, to raise a Capital of Seventy thousand Pounds, and to borrow on Mortgage or Bond any Sum not exceeding in the whole the Sum of Twenty-three thousand three hundred and thirty-three Pounds : And whereas, under the Powers conferred on the said Company by the said recited Act and the Acts incorporated therein, the said Company have constructed a Railway from the City of *Exeter* aforesaid to *Crediton* aforesaid, but the same has not yet been opened for public Traffic ; and the said Company have raised, and have laid out and expended in and about the said Railway and the Works connected therewith, the whole of the said

[*Local.*]   4 *F*   Capital

8 & 9 Vict. c. 88.

original £15,000 Taw Vale capital to be reconstituted in £20 shares. Parliament was also considering the Gauge Act in the 1846 session, it being passed after the Taw Vale on 18th August, so a clause in the Taw Vale Extension Act stated that "the gauge shall be such as the Board of Trade shall in its discretion approve".

The Bristol & Exeter twice rejected

At this stage the Bristol & Exeter had made provisional agreements to lease both the Exeter & Crediton and the Taw Vale. On 5th September 1846 two Taw Vale directors reached a new provisional agreement for the lease, but the Taw Vale board considered it on the 9th and decided to recommend its rejection to a special proprietors meetings on the 26th. At this meeting, Emmanuel Cooper and his board reported the terms of the provisional agreement of the 5th, stating that the terms were far less favourable to Taw Vale shareholders than those agreed on 26th May. There were accusation of bad faith on both sides, but the resolution rejecting the lease to the Bristol & Exeter was carried unanimously. The Taw Vale board now turned to its distant ally, the South Western, which had ambitions to extend into Devon and Cornwall but by 1846 its nearest line was that from Bishopstoke (Eastleigh) to Salisbury, then under construction. The Taw Vale board negotiated with the LSWR and on 24th December 1846, reached a provisional agreement for the lease of the Taw Vale for a rent of five per cent on capital. The Taw Vale proprietors approved the lease at a special meeting on 18th January 1847, when three South Western directors joined the Taw Vale board. However, this lease had not been provided for in either Taw Vale Act so required parliamentary authority for its implementation. At Barnstaple, the North Devon Journal waxed eloquent over the benefits of the South Western lease of the Taw Vale.

TAW VALE RAILWAY AND DOCK COMPANY.

NOTICE is Hereby Given,—That a SPECIAL GENERAL MEETING of the Proprietors of the Taw Vale Railway and Dock Company will be held at the London Tavern, Bishopsgate-street, London, on MONDAY, the 18th day of JANUARY, 1847, at 1 o'clock p.m. precisely, for the purpose of confirming or rejecting the agreement, bearing date the 24th of DECEMBER instant, entered into between this Company and the London and South-Western Railway Company, for leasing the Taw Vale Railway and Dock to the London and South-Western Railway Company.
EMANUEL COOPER, Chairman.
Office, 76, King William-street, London, Dec. 30, 1846.

Meanwhile, the board of Exeter & Crediton had negotiated the lease of their line to the Bristol & Exeter in accordance with their provisional agreement of 1844. In November 1846, they gave notice to the B&ER that their double-track broad gauge line would be ready for opening on 22nd December and requested them to work their line on the same terms as they were worked by the Great Western. A special Exeter & Crediton proprietors meeting to confirm the lease was held on 11th January. Mr J. W. Buller and his board knew that many shares had recently changed hands, indeed, some of the directors had made handsome profits by selling some of their shares at twice their nominal value, so several new shareholders attended, including William Thorne and Emmanuel Cooper of the Taw Vale. When Mr J. W. Buller put the lease to the meeting it was passed by a show of hands by thirteen to eleven, but rejected by a poll of shares by 1,542 to 561. At Barnstaple, the North Devon Journal congratulated Thorne

and Taw Vale camp on their coup, but it was denounced in the Exeter press.

At the next Exeter & Crediton proprietors special general meeting on 17th February, Cooper proposed that the line be leased to the Taw Vale at a rent of five per cent on capital, the same terms as the South Western lease of the Taw Vale, the lease to be guaranteed by the LSWR. This lease was in accordance with Clause 43 of the Exeter & Crediton Act since the Taw Vale, when constructed, would join the E&CR. Thorne spoke warmly in favour of the lease which was approved by 1,681 votes to 700. At the proprietors general meeting of 24th February, Cooper gave an assurance that the line would open for traffic given the assent of the directors, although he did not give any details. Three Taw Vale directors, Cooper, Thorne and Woolmer, were elected to the board. However, of the ten directors there was still a majority, led by the Chairman, Buller, who were connected with or sympathetic to the Bristol & Exeter. Indeed, on 11th March, Buller himself was elected Chairman of the Bristol & Exeter, but the situation where the board did not reflect the interest of the shareholders could not last for long. A two year contract with Mr George Hennett to work the line was agreed by the board without discussion, despite the protests of the minority directors, and Buller signed the contract on 7th April, thus precipitating a final showdown.

EXETER AND CREDITON RAILWAY.
FOURTH CALL OF £5 PER SHARE.

NOTICE is hereby Given,—That in pursuance of a resolution of the Board of Directors, the Proprietors of Shares in this Company are required to pay a Call of £5 per Share to either of the undermentioned Bankers, on or before Tuesday the Ninth day of February next.
Messrs. Glyn, Halifax, Mills, and Co. .... London.
The West of England and South Wales District Bank .... } Bristol.
The West of England and South Wales District Bank .... } Exeter.
A circular will be sent to each Proprietor previously to the date of payment of the above Call, which must be deposited with the Bankers.
Interest at the rate of 5 per cent. per annum will be charged on all Calls in Arrear.
By order of the Board of Directors,
THOS. HARTNOLL, Secretary.
Exeter, January 13th, 1847.

The Taw Vale party called an extraordinary general meeting on 12th April 1847, to consider resolutions approving the lease to the Taw Vale, reducing the board from ten to six by removing Messrs Buller, Brown, Bastard and Fripp, who were all directors of the Bristol & Exeter, and restraining the board from opening on the broad gauge. Thorne spoke at length and to acclamation, but Buller declared his resolution to be illegal. After further discussion Thorne himself put the resolution to remove Buller and the other Bristol & Exeter directors. This was carried unanimously on a show of hands, Thorne's opponents not voting, having accepted Buller's ruling. The Bristol & Exeter party were now in disarray when Mr Wilkinson pointed out that Buller was no longer Chairman and proposed Thorne, being seconded by Cooper. Buller refused to leave the chair, but "closed" the meeting, leaving escorted by the Bristol & Exeter directors who took the minute book with them after a scuffle. Thorne then took the chair and the other resolutions were passed. Legal proceedings followed in the which the court ruled against Buller and the other Bristol & Exeter directors, and Thorne was properly elected Chairman at the next proprietors meeting on 26th August. The takeover was complete but many questions were being asked.

The Railway Commissioners Investigate
Early in 1847 the directors of both the Bristol & Exeter

The Exeter and Crediton Railway Company
Number 2042   Certificate of £25 Share.

This is to Certify that James Billings Badham of Bristol Gentleman is the Proprietor of the Share, Number 2042 of The
EXETER AND CREDITON RAILWAY COMPANY, subject to the Regulations of the said Company. Given under their Common Seal the 28th Day of August, in the year of our Lord, One Thousand Eight Hundred and Forty five.

REGISTERED N° 43

Secretary.

and the Exeter & Crediton railways had complained to the Railway Commissioners about the circumstances of the rejection of the lease on 11th January. The complaints alleged that most of the shareholders involved had been on the Company's register for less than a week, and that they were only the nominal holders of shares. These nominal shareholders were connected with the Taw Vale and South Western and the shareholdings had been carefully subdivided to conceal their ownership.

The Railway Commissioners reported to parliament on 14th April 1847. "The South Western company have laid a statement before the commissioners, in which they explain, that having agreed to subscribe towards and to take a lease on the Taw Vale lines, and having applied to parliament for powers to ratify this agreement, it has become desirable to be possessed of the Exeter & Crediton Railway, as forming an important link in their intended line of railway communication, and they admit that they have advanced £30,000 to the Taw Vale company and that the Taw Vale company, with the aid of this money, have purchased 1,700 shares in the Exeter & Crediton line. They also state that previously they had, in anticipation of the sanction of parliament, paid a deposit and a call amounting together to £4 a share, upon 6,850 shares of £20 each in the existing capital of the Taw Vale company, and also a deposit of 10 per cent on one fourth part of the proposed capital. Both these transactions appear to the commissioners to involve illegitimate application of the capital of the South Western company, but the proceeding seems to be more particularly objectionable in the case in which the funds have been misapplied for the purpose of controlling the directors and shareholders of an independent company".

In turn, the Taw Vale then complained to the Railway Commissioners who reported again on 29th April. The Bristol & Exeter admitted that they had also purchased 800 Exeter & Crediton shares with funds provided by one individual. In self defence the B&ER had also acted illegally, too late to control the lease but had almost succeeded in denying the lease to the South Western. Three fifths of the shares were needed to control the lease. The South Western needed 1,680; it got 1,700.

Taw Vale Branches Authorised
Having gained its Act in the 1846 session for the main line from Barnstaple to Crediton, the Taw Vale immediately set about gaining authority for two branches, to Bideford and South Molton, in the 1847 session. On 9th November 1846 it gave notice of the Bill, which also authorised deviations in the main line. By June 1847, after negotiations with landowners, the Bill was unopposed and the Act passed on 22nd July 1847. The authorised Taw Vale capital was increased by another £180,000 to a total of £713,000 for enlarging the dock at Fremington, extending from Fremington to Bideford and building a branch from near Umberleigh to South Molton.

Construction of the Taw Vale
At the Taw Vale proprietors general meeting on 21st February 1847, the engineer, Lock, reported that "The original line from Fremington Pill to Barnstaple is now nearly completed, and the permanent way will be laid very shortly. These works, constructed upon tidal lands, over the Penhill marsh and beach at Fremington have been subject while partially finished to a considerable wash of the river, but their stability has not been affected to any degree. Since obtaining the Act for extending the railway to Crediton the line has been re-surveyed, and the first

contract from Barnstaple to Umberleigh Bridge, a distance of nearly seven miles, let to Mr Thorne the contractor for the original line to Fremington Pill and they will be commenced immediately on possession of the land being obtained. The next contracts up to Crediton, which are now in a forward state of preparation, may be advertised for letting during the next month...."

On 11th March 1847, the Rev. James Arthur, Chairman of the Barnstaple Turnpike Trustees, turned the first sod on the Taw Vale Extension at a ceremony at Newbridge. On 23rd March Thorne invited tenders for labour and materials for this the No. 2 contract, it being stated that work would commence on 5th April. The No. 2 contract between Thorne and the Taw Vale was for a double-track railway of six miles and fifty chains, and was dated 1st July 1847. However by June several hundred men had worked to clear a site of several acres for Barnstaple station, to the east of the Sticklepath turnpike gate, excavating an old cannon ball in the process. On 1st August Thorne himself laid the foundation stone of the Sticklepath Road bridge at Barnstaple, and at that time it was hoped to open the line from Bideford to Umberleigh by the spring of 1848. On the debit side, two men working on the line had been admitted to the North Devon Infirmary after accidents. In October a jury awarded damages of £300 in favour of an Umberleigh Barton farmer as compensation to be paid by the Taw Vale.

Sadly, in November 1847, the Taw Vale succumbed to the pressures of the money markets and Thorne was forced to lay off most of his men. Taw Vale accounts for the six months up to 3rd June 1847 were healthy with receipts of £98,223 3s 4d, exceeding expenditure of £81,482 2s 7d, but up to 31st December, receipts of £119,189 7s 3d were set against expenditure of £117,559 18s 10d and debts of more than £10,000. At the proprietors general meeting of 12th February 1848 the engineer, now Mr W. R. Neale, stated that the Barnstaple to Fremington line was almost complete and would shortly be available for coal and other goods traffic, whilst considerable progress had been made on the Umberleigh line. But much of the meeting was spent discussing the decision of the Railway Commissioners as to the gauge of the Taw Vale Extension.

The Gauge Question
As we have seen in its 1846 Act the gauge of the Taw Vale Extension was to be decided by the Board of Trade. On 27th August 1847 the Taw Vale petitioned the Railway Commissioners to order that it be built on the 'narrow' gauge (4ft 8½in). However, on 3rd December 1847 the board of the Exeter & Crediton ordered its existing unused broad gauge tracks to be narrowed and this brought a complaint from the Bristol & Exeter to the Railway Commissioners, who were powerless to act in this matter. The Railway Commissioners sent Capt. Simmons, an Inspecting Officer of Railways, to inspect the Taw Vale and to assist them, he also looked at the Exeter & Crediton. Capt. Simmons reported that "The junction with the Bristol & Exeter was to have been made at a point near Cowley Bridge, and about one and three quarters of a mile from the city of Exeter, where the Bristol & Exeter Railway is carried on an embankment close to the left bank of the river, and the original intention of the Exeter & Crediton Railway is evident from the construction of a timber viaduct, curved to suit the junction and standing partly on the embankment of the Bristol & Exeter Railway. The stations have been entirely completed, and the line ready for inspection previous to it being used by

the public as a broad gauge railway for many months, but its opening was prevented by legal proceedings, and the company have lately commenced to narrow the gauge to 4ft 8½in, and to construct a temporary station at Cowley Bridge, with an approach to it from the turnpike road; this station and approach have become necessary since the determination to alter the gauge as by doing so the company can no longer avail themselves of the Exeter station of the Bristol & Exeter Railway, which is adapted to only one, the broad gauge."

On 8th February 1848, the Railway Commissioners issued their order that the Taw Vale Extension be constructed to the broad gauge, on the grounds of general local convenience, and the need to avoid a break of gauge. Reference was also made to their previous report on the illegitimate takeover of the Exeter & Crediton. The order applied to the Taw Vale lines authorised in 1846 and 1847, but did not apply to the 'narrow' gauge Barnstaple to Fremington line, nor to the Exeter & Crediton.

Public opinion in North Devon was very much in favour of the Taw Vale; in April and May there were public meetings in favour of the 'narrow' gauge at Barnstaple, Bideford and Chawleigh, and the North Devon Journal waxed eloquent in favour of the Taw Vale and the 'narrow' gauge. The Taw Vale itself took a Bill to parliament to authorise the South Western lease and to empower its construction on standard gauge, thus reversing the Railway Commissioners order. However, in committee it was declared that the case for the Bill had not been made out and it fell on 28th June 1848.

First Openings in North Devon

The Bristol & Exeter opened its Tiverton branch on 12th June 1848, and at the opening celebrations, Mr Saunders, Secretary of the Great Western, and Mr Badham, Secretary of the Bristol & Exeter, both spoke of their hopes of extending the line from Tiverton into North Devon. The North Devon Journal commented that "if the Bristol & Exeter company can have its way, the Taw Vale line will never be made". Then with complete absence of ceremony, the original Taw Vale 'narrow' gauge line from Barnstaple to Fremington was opened in August 1848. Goods traffic only was worked by William Thorne using horse-drawn wagons, charging ¾d per ton mile.

Post-Mania Depression

At the Exeter & Crediton proprietors general meeting on 12th February 1848, Thorne and his board reported that they had had the gauge altered to the national gauge, and on 15th the company gave notice to the Railway Commissioners of their intention to open the line, but nothing came of this. By now the company meetings were being held at the London Tavern, Bishopsgate Street, London, which the Taw Vale also used, and accounts up to 31st December 1847 showed an expenditure of £93,797 2s 4d which slightly exceeded authorised capital and borrowing. The cost of the contract for construction had now risen to £66,154 18s 6d. To remedy this situation the board promoted another Bill which passed parliament on 10th June 1850. The Exeter & Crediton Amendment Act empowered the company to purchase more land for the enlargement of Cowley Bridge station and to raise another £20,000 of capital in £25 shares, allocated in proportion to existing shareholders. The unfortunate citizens of Crediton could only look on as their railway gathered rust, having been ready for opening since January 1847.

There was no progress either on the Taw Vale as the engineer, Mr W. R. Neale, reported to proprietors on 31st

ANNO NONO & DECIMO

VICTORIÆ REGINÆ.

****

Cap. ccclv.

An Act for amending the Acts relating to the *Taw Vale* Railway and Dock, and for making an Extension therefrom to the *Exeter and Crediton* Railway in the County of *Devon*.

[7th *August* 1846.]

WHEREAS an Act was passed in the First Year of the Reign of Her present Majesty Queen *Victoria*, intituled *An Act for making a Railway from* Penhill *in the Parish of* Fremington *in the County of* Devon *to the Town of* Barnstaple, *and for constructing a Dock in the said Parish of* Fremington, to be called "The *Taw Vale* Railway and Dock:" And whereas another Act was passed in the last Session of Parliament, intituled *An Act to amend the Act relating to the* Taw Vale *Railway and Dock*: And whereas the several Works by the said firstly-recited Act authorized are in the course of Construction: And whereas the making of a Railway from the said *Taw Vale* Railway in the Parish of *Tawstock* in the County of *Devon* to the Town of *Crediton* in the said County, there to form a Junction with the *Exeter and Crediton* Railway now in course of Construction to the City of *Exeter*, would be of great public Advantage: And whereas the Company incorporated by the said firstly-recited Act, together with others, are willing to carry the said

[*Local.*]   71 R   Undertaking

August 1848. "The second contract, extending from Barnstaple towards Umberleigh Bridge, a distance of about 6½ miles, with the exception of the bridge over the Taw at Barnstaple, is now nearly completed, and a considerable proportion of this and the whole of the line from Barnstaple to Fremington ballasted, and a single line of permanent way laid. No further steps have been taken in progress of the other contracts towards Exeter on the main line, or of the branch from Fremington to Bideford, and those portions of the second contract to which operations have been confined are accommodation works for public and private use which would entail additional expense by delays, until the wet season".

In answer to a shareholder's question the Chairman, Emmanuel Cooper, stated that the South Western had 6,850 shares on which £6 was paid, and they had paid calls in advance to the amount of £6,300, making a total of £47,400 invested in the Taw Vale. The South Western Chairman, William Chaplin, had put the Taw Vale investments at £98,920 4s 7d, but this also included Exeter & Crediton investments. Even so, the South Western had financed a large proportion of the Taw Vale income of £133,591 4s 4d.

When the Taw Vale next tried to raise funds for construction by a call on shares only £16,000 out of £44,000 due was received, it was reported to proprietors on 2nd January 1849. Due to failure of the 1848 Taw Vale Bill, the lease to the South Western was terminated in September 1848. John Sharland, the new chairman, reported to shareholders on 28th August 1849, the continued suspension of construction due to lack of funds.

By the end of the decade there was little to show for all the exertions and expenditure of the 1840s in promoting and building railways to North Devon. Starting from Cowley Bridge, there was almost six miles of a double-track line to Crediton, which had been ready since January 1847, but had not seen a revenue-earning train. From Crediton to Umberleigh construction had not yet started, from Umberleigh to Barnstaple, there has been some construction and some track laid; only the three miles of line from Barnstaple to Fremington was open, albeit only for horse-drawn goods traffic. To this end, the Exeter & Crediton and the Taw Vale companies had spent almost a quarter of a million pounds, much of this coming from the LSWR. Promoters of other lines had lost all, such as the £40,000 spent on the unsuccessful North Devon Railway of 1846. Only Tiverton was connected to the national railway network, while Crediton, Barnstaple and Bideford had to wait.

The South Western had promoted companies which together gained Acts for a central line to Exeter Queen Street, but a vital Exeter and Cowley Bridge Junction Bill had been rejected on 28th June 1848. The post-mania depression reduced the South Western half year dividend from a peak of 8½% in 1845 and 1846 to a mere 3% in the first half of 1850, so the Company was in no position to build its expensive main line to Exeter. There was now no hope that the Exeter & Crediton and Taw Vale railways could be linked to their principal ally and shareholder in the near future. The outlook for the railway to North Devon in 1850 looked very bleak.

Chapter 3
The Broad Gauge Era

Re-appraisal

In the aftermath of the mania several issues became clear to those involved with the railways projected for North Devon. Firstly any lines opened for public traffic would have to be built to the broad gauge. Secondly there would have to be harmonious relationships with the Bristol & Exeter, which might be required to work either line. Thirdly, in the prevailing financial climate only essential construction was feasible and this must be completed at minimal expense. These considerations were particularly delicate for the largest investor, the London & South Western, which owned 40% of Taw Vale shares and 60% of the Exeter & Crediton. The South Western board took the long term view that they would eventually reach Exeter and link up with the North Devon lines, so they held on to their shares but allowed the two companies to negotiate the best deal they could for the interim period. A delicate aspect of this arrangement was that the South Western was still liable for calls on its Taw Vale shares when construction re-commenced.

Opening of the Exeter & Crediton Railway

At the Exeter & Crediton proprietors general meeting on 28th February 1851 the chairman was now William Chaplin MP, the South Western chairman, and the board reported that they had provisionally agreed a lease of the line to the Bristol & Exeter. The rent paid was to be one third of gross receipts, and the lease would run until seven years after the date of opening of the Taw Vale from Crediton to Fremington. The Bristol & Exeter would supply all necessary servants and plant, and run the traffic of the line. The Exeter & Crediton would restore one line of rails to broad gauge and pay for the junction at Cowley Bridge, and was also liable for all the repairs including flood damage to Pynes Bridge and New Bridge. The Bristol & Exeter were to nominate one director and a second director was to be appointed. The proprietors approved the lease, the works were put in hand, and the line was ready a couple of months later. At last, on 8th May 1851, Capt. Mynne, on behalf of the Railway Department of the Board of Trade, made his inspection of the line and reported:

"I have this day inspected the Exeter and Crediton Railway which commences from a junction with the Bristol and Exeter Railway about one mile from the city of Exeter, and extends to the town of Crediton, its length being 5 miles 55 chains.

The line starts from the Bristol and Exeter Railway as a double line on the broad gauge, and then at a few chains from the junction it falls into a single broad gauge line, the second line being a narrow gauge line, the explanation offered me for this apparently singular arrangement was that the line was originally laid as a double broad gauge line, it was afterwards altered to a double narrow gauge line in which state it has remained for some years, at length arrangements having been entered into for working in connection with the Bristol and Exeter Railway, it became necessary to have it laid on the same gauge as that line, viz the broad gauge; and until it has been ascertained whether the amount of traffic would warrant the expense of an alteration to the double line, only one line has for the present been altered to the broad gauge. I found that the single line, which is constructed to work continuously

with the Bristol and Exeter Railway in good order, the works properly constructed and of sufficient strength and I am of the opinion that the line may be opened with safety for the conveyance of passengers. The Exeter and Crediton company are provided with no stock rolling or other but have entered into arrangements with the Bristol and Exeter Railway for working the line and providing all the stock.

As I inspected the line as a single one of the same gauge as the Bristol and Exeter Railway, and recommend its opening as such, it is necessary that proper precautions should be adopted for preventing two engines proceeding on the line in opposite directions at the same time, and to this end I would suggest that the traffic should be worked both ways between Exeter and Crediton by one engine."

The ceremonial opening took place on Monday 12th May 1851 when at one o'clock a five coach train left Exeter St Davids station for Crediton carrying the

IMPORTANT NOTICE.
OPENING OF THE EXETER AND CREDITON RAILWAY.

One hour saved in time between Exeter, Bideford, or Barnstaple, being only thirty miles of Coaching, and
A REDUCTION OF FARES.

The Public are respectfully informed that the Great Western Railway have appointed for (on and after the 2nd of June) Trains to leave Exeter and Crediton in connexion with the Bideford and Barnstaple Coaches.

FOR THE "HERO" ROYAL MAIL FOR TORRINGTON AND BIDEFORD

The Express Train leaves Exeter for Crediton at 2·40 p.m., after its arrival from Paddington, which it leaves at 9·50 a.m., Bath 12·10 a.m., Bristol 12·45 a.m., reaching Crediton at 3·0 p.m., Torrington at 6·10 p.m., and Bideford at 7·0 p.m.
The "HERO" will return from Bideford daily at 7·30 a.m., Torrington 8·20 a.m., reaching the Crediton station for the 12·0 Express Train to Exeter at 12·30, Bristol, 2·35, Bath 2·55, London 5·15; also Teignmouth 3·20, Torquay 3·50, Plymouth 4·55. Also for Mails to Dorchester, Weymouth, Southampton, Sidmouth and Budleigh.

FOR THE "QUEEN" AND "RUBY" COACHES FOR BARNSTAPLE AND ILFRACOMBE

The Train will leave Exeter for Crediton daily at 12·55, which train leaves Plymouth at 10·20, Totnes 11·12, Torquay 11·17, Newton 11·45, Teignmouth 11·57, Dawlish 12·7; also from the train leaving Chippenham 8·45, Bath 9·15, Bristol 10·0. Also after the arrival of the Weymouth, Dorchester, and Southampton Mails, the Mails from Sidmouth, Exmouth, Budleigh Salterton, &c., and reach Barnstaple at 4·30, and Ilfracombe at 7·0.
The "QUEEN" and "RUBY" will leave Pridham and Lake's Office, the Fortescue Arms, and the Golden Lion, Barnstaple, every morning at 9·0 a.m., reaching Crediton station for the 1·20 train for Exeter, the South of Devon, and London; also for the mail for Dorchester, Weymouth, and Southampton; also for Sidmouth, Exmouth, Budleigh Salterton, &c.

FOR THE LONDON AND BIDEFORD ROYAL MAIL

The Train will leave Exeter for Crediton at 4·20 a.m., after its arrival from Paddington, which it leaves at 8·55 p.m., Bath 12·50, Bristol 1·25, Taunton 3·15, reaching Crediton at 4·10 a.m., and Bideford at 9·30 a.m.; half-an-hour allowed for Breakfast at the Ship Hotel, Crediton.
The Mail will return from Bideford daily at 3·40, arriving at the Crediton station for the 8·25 Mail Train for Exeter and London.

	IN.	OUT.
Fares from Crediton to Barnstaple,	10s.	6s.
„ Crediton to Southmolton,	6s.	3s.
„ Crediton to Winkleigh,	6s.	3s.
„ Crediton to Bedford,	8s.	4s.
„ Crediton to Torrington,	10s.	5s.
„ Crediton to Bideford,	12s.	6s.

PENFOUND AND SON, PRIDHAM AND LAKE,
Proprietors.

This advertisement was placed in *Woolmers Exeter and Plymouth Gazette* of 7th June 1851 and details the coach services run to North Devon in connection with the newly-opened Exeter & Crediton Railway. Pridham and Lake were the principal operators of coach services in North Devon.

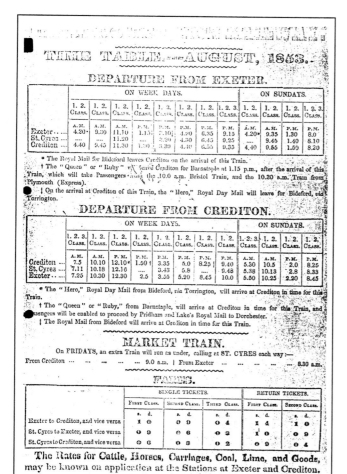

Robert Ward was one of the earliest traders at Crediton station and his family firm continue to trade there to this day. This advertisement appeared in *Woolmers Exeter and Plymouth Gazette* of 24th May 1851.

directors of the Bristol & Exeter Railway, led by its chairman James Buller, and other guests. A second train of nine coaches followed half an hour later to accommodate several hundred more passengers. At Crediton the train was met by a procession of the inhabitants, led by the band of the Royal East Devon Yeomanry of which James Buller was Colonel, and they all walked back into the town through streets decorated with flowers, trees and triumphal arches to the Market House for a banquet. Some 230 people sat down to the banquet including most of the directors of the Bristol & Exeter and also Messrs Hartnoll, Dymond and Pring, the secretary, engineer and solicitor of the Exeter & Crediton. There were a score of speeches and toasts, with the toast to the Chairman and Board of Directors of the Bristol & Exeter Railway being received with prolonged and enthusiastic cheering, as was James Buller's reply. For Thomas Pring the opening was the culmination of twenty years work. Notable absentees were the chairman and many of the directors of the Exeter & Crediton company, but as we have seen in Chapter 2 there was good reason for William Chaplin and his South Western associates to be absent - but for them this opening would have occurred more than four years previously. The passenger service started immediately with seven trains each way daily and one intermediate station at St Cyres, Cowley Bridge station never being opened, and to all intents and purposes the line appeared to be just another branch of the Bristol & Exeter Railway.

Thorne v Taw Vale Railway & Dock Co.
From August 1848 William Thorne had worked the line from Barnstaple to Fremington for goods traffic using horses. At Fremington he had leased land from the Taw Vale, constructed two limekilns and warehouses and a tramway linking them to the Taw Vale tracks, and imported coal and limestone from Wales to manufacture lime which was sold to farmers for fertilizer. His coal and lime were brought to Barnstaple by rail for sale and storage at his warehouse, and he had built up a considerable business. His lease expired on 18th May 1850, and he sold his business to Messrs Richards, but on the 22nd the Taw Vale board decided to stop this traffic because of the damage to the track by horses. A court case followed when Thorne sought an injunction against the Taw Vale's action, but he was eventually unsuccessful.

Construction having ceased Thorne sold off his contractors equipment at two auctions, the second being on 6th February 1851 at Barnstaple station. William Thorne now faded out of the North Devon railway story having played a very prominent role from the start in 1836. He had been chairman of both the Taw Vale and the Exeter & Crediton, contractor and lessee of the first line and had masterminded the takeover of the second, all in the space of four years.

Financial Re-construction of the Taw Vale
At the Taw Vale proprietors general meeting of 28th August 1849 a committee of shareholders had been set up to investigate and report on the future of the line. They met interested parties at Barnstaple, Bideford, Eggesford and Crediton and reported back to the next general meeting on 28th February 1850. Mr Wilkinson presented the report which reviewed the company's progress. Of the 22,040 shares issued 4,649 had been forfeited, leaving 17,400 of which the South Western held 6,850. They had persuaded many landowners along the line to accept shares in payment for their land, and suggested that the calls on South Western owned shares could be paid in kind

from that company's large stock of surplus rails. They recommended that the line be completed as a single broad gauge line, that tenders for construction be obtained, that £50,000 of shares be taken up locally, and that the company go back to parliament for an Act for deviations and a reduced capital of £435,000. At the board's request a decision was postponed to an extraordinary meeting on 29th May when they reported considerable progress on the recommendations, and at the general meeting of 28th August the board themselves made a substantially similar recommendation.

On 4th July the board had advertised for two tenders, one for the construction of the Umberleigh to Crediton line as a single broad gauge line, and the other for a seven year lease of the line when open. On 9th November they gave notice of a Bill as recommended by the committee of shareholders, which also changed the name to the North Devon Railway & Dock Company. The Act passed parliament on 24th July 1851, reducing capital to £426,000 by a complex arrangement protecting both the Bristol & Exeter and South Western shareholdings, some £20 shares being replaced by £16 shares and £8 half shares. The Act provided for deviations at Presbury, Eggesford and Nymet Rowland and alterations in levels at Chulmleigh, Chawleigh, Nymet Rowland and Down St Mary. Clause 49 authorized a seven year lease to Thomas Brassey, given a three fifths majority of shareholders, and Clause 51 allowed North Devon trains to run over the Exeter & Crediton and Bristol & Exeter lines by agreement. Thus at the third attempt a North Devon Railway gained its Act, previous attempts in 1845 for a line from Crediton, and 1846 from Tiverton having failed.

Back on 3rd January 1851 the chairman, John Sharland, had announced that Thomas Brassey the prestigious international railway contractor had been provisionally engaged on both contracts for construction and leasing, and invited the local subscription of £50,000 in shares. This sale turned out to be very had work for the board, a committee of directors visiting every town and large village in the area during February, but by July only £30,000 worth had been taken up. It was not until Christmas Day 1851 that the £50,000 target was reached, and the board then sanctioned the re-starting of the construction of the line, which had ceased four years previously.

Construction of the North Devon Railway
On 2nd February 1852 the ceremony of cutting the first turf was held at Copplestone, the third such event on the line following similar ceremonies on the Taw Vale in 1846 and the Taw Vale Extension in 1847. The ceremony took place in Great Meadow, about a quarter of a mile from Copplestone Cross, on the site of the heaviest earthworks on the line, the deep cutting through the village at the summit of the line. A large party including the chairman, John Sharland, engineer, W. R. Neale, and contractor, William Brassey, assembled at the Copplestone Inn at 12 noon and walked to the field where, in front of an audience of more than 500 people and two bands, the ceremony was performed by the Hon. Newton Fellowes. After the ceremony there was a dinner provided by Mrs Tucker at the Copplestone Inn followed by a number of speeches. The Hon. Newton Fellowes, later Fourth Earl of Portsmouth, lived at Eggesford House and was a leading local supporter of and shareholder in the railway. Back in the 1830s he had financed the turnpike road built along the Taw valley, the route also followed by the railway.

Thomas Brassey's main No.3 contract was for the entire

works between Crediton and Umberleigh, but he also undertook the No.4 contract for completing the works between Umberleigh and Fremington and converting from 'narrow' gauge to broad for £23,000. Brassey himself recommended a deviation at Eggesford which saved £4,530, and here a level crossing was substituted for a road bridge which had been planned. In May 1852 the first consignment of 600 tons of iron rails and chairs was shipped by the South Western to Teignmouth and Fremington to be brought by rail to each end of the works. Later on there was some dispute with the South Western about the quality of the bridge rails supplied. By June 1852 Brassey reported that 700 men and 100 horses were at work on the line, and by February 1853 this had risen to 1,075 men, 195 horses and one locomotive, although there had been delays to the works due to floods. By August progress had been maintained; work was in hand on the largest bridge on the line, over the River Taw at Barnstaple, although a temporary wooden bridge was in use by the contractor. At the North Devon proprietors general meeting on 27th February 1854 the engineer, W. R. Neale, reported from his Crediton Office.

"Since my last report the prevalence of the wet weather, and occurrence of several heavy floods, have together much impeded the progress of the works. The floods alone, the highest known in this district for many years, occasioned considerable injury to the unfinished parts of the line, but the contractor is executing the necessary repairs as well as additional works where requisite. At Copplestone summit the contractor has encountered serious difficulty from the slips which have taken place, these are now got out, and the permanent way is laid through the cutting. At Weir Marsh as very extensive slip has occurred, this has also been, to a considerable extent, removed and there appears no reason to apprehend further delays at these points. Notwithstanding these obstructions, the works generally are in a forward condition. The bulk of the earthwork and masonry with the exception of the bridge over the Taw at Barnstaple, which is in hand, is completed. A great portion of the permanent way is laid down, and the electric telegraph is nearly fixed through the entire length. The station works are well advanced. From these causes, the anticipation formed that in the absence of any unforseen contingency, the line might be ready for traffic during this month, will not be realized, and the opening must be deferred".

The chairman, now the eminent railway architect William Tite, added that of almost 80 bridges only four had failed in the foods. He also reported that Brassey had come to an arrangement with the Bristol & Exeter Railway for them to supply locomotives, carriages and wagons when the line opened, although the line would be leased to Brassey.

Final calls on shares were made by the North Devon on 15th March 1854 and on 22nd May a large party of officials and gentlemen inspected the works. On 26th May Brassey's men commenced widening the road to the broad gauge from Umberleigh Bridge to Fremington Pill at the rate of half a mile per day, so it would appear that the original Taw Vale 'narrow' gauge tracks had been utilized during construction. On 28th June progress was such that a Bristol & Exeter engine ran from Crediton to Barnstaple in 58 minutes. Sadly a number of accidents and other misfortunes attended the construction of the line. A cow had strayed on to the line through an unsecured gate and had been killed by a locomotive. Two men had been blasting rocks on the slope between Barnstaple station and Sticklepath Farm when there was an unexpected explosion which severely injured both of them. Between Crediton and Uford a man was killed when he slipped under a horse-drawn train of four wagons loaded with earth, the coroner returning a verdict of accidental death.

The Opening of the North Devon Railway

Capt. Tyler on behalf of the Railway Department of the Board of Trade, made his report on 30th June 1854 after his inspection the previous day.

"I have inspected the North Devon Railway from Crediton to Fremington Pill, in compliance with the instructions contained in your letter of 20th instant.

This line is 34 miles and 66 chains in length, it was commenced some 8 years since but its completion had been hitherto postponed, principally in consequence of the disputed question as to the width of the gauge.

The North Devon Railway has now been constructed with a gauge of 7 feet between the rails, but with double I rails and transverse sleepers, the former weighing from 68 to 80 lbs per lineal yard, and the latter being placed at intervals of 3ft 2in excepting for 7 miles between Fremington Pill and Langham, where they are laid at distances of 4 feet from each other. I understand that it is not the intention of the company to employ any but moderate speeds on this line: but I would recommend that particular attention should be paid in respect of the working of that part of the line on which the sleepers are 4 feet apart. The sleepers are of normal timber, and of large size.

The works over the line are generally light and are in satisfactory condition. The bridges and viaducts are 89 in number varying in span from 8ft to 83ft 6ins. The principal bridge is constructed to carry the railway over the River Taw at Barnstaple. It consists of 3 openings the span of each measuring 51 feet on the square and 83ft 6ins on the skew, and the permanent way is supported on timber baulks resting on cast iron arched girders. There are three girders to each opening and the centre girder carries half the weight of the passing load, but although it is not stronger than the others I estimate the compression per square inch to which is would be subjected by the heaviest load added to its own weight, at about 9 tons. In testing this bridge with a weight of 150 tons I obtained deflections on the centres of the girders varying from 0.24 to 0.36 inches, and a rise at the haunches of 0.06 inches when the opposite half of the girders were weighed, also a rise of 0.18 of an inch at the centre under the same circumstances. I may remark however that although they carry more weight I obtained less deflection from the centre of the central girders than from the others apparently in consequence of the increasing lateral stiffness which the construction of the bridge gives them. The foundations of this bridge are composed of cast iron cylinders filled with concrete, both at the piers and the abutments. The cylinders have been sunk to various depths, and weighted, when empty with 150 tons each, and I have every reason to believe that in this respect, as well as in all others, the bridge is sufficiently strong.

There are 5 bridges composed of cast iron straight girders on masonry abutments and piers, some of them with 3 and some with 4 openings. The spans of these vary from 17 to 30 feet. They all appear to be of ample dimensions, the distributed breaking weights, as I calculate them, being in every case upwards of 9 times the passing load added to the weight of the girder. The deflections also were very small, not exceeding ¼in in the longer girders under the heaviest moving weights that could be put upon them. I therefore believe these bridges to be amply strong enough, and I am of the same opinion in regard to all the other bridges on the line, which are constructed generally with timber tops on masonry abutments, but in some places on piles.

In the above statement I have not alluded to any of the works between Barnstaple and Fremington Pill. I found that it was not intended to open this portion of the line for public traffic until the completion of the railway between Fremington and Bideford, which is now in progress and that consequently no station arrangements had been prepared at Fremington and I have therefore obtained from the Secretary the enclosed letter, withdrawing the notice of opening already forwarded, in so far as it relates to that portion.

The North Devon Railway being a single line and having the electric telegraph laid down throughout it appears to be only necessary in order to provide against the possibility of collision, to take care that no two trains shall under any circumstances be permitted to be on any portion of line between any two working telegraph stations at the same time, and I beg to enclose a certificate from the Secretary stating that this mode of working will be adopted.

The signals at the stations are at present placed one at each end of the station sidings and I have recommended that instead of erecting two signals so near to each other, a plan which would render it necessary to have also additional signals at a greater distance to be used as auxiliary signals, there should be placed at each station a main signal showing signals in each direction as well as an auxiliary signal in each direction, at 500 or 600 yards distant, according to circumstances, to be worked by means of wires by the signalman at the station signal. I would beg to recommend that similar arrangements be adopted in reference to a siding which is to be used for goods at a point where there is not any station for passengers, and that chockblocks be added to the sidings at Barnstaple station.

Until these requirements shall have been completed I am obliged to report that the opening of the North Devon Railway between Crediton and Barnstaple would by reason of the incompleteness of the works be attended with danger to the public using the same."

The ceremonial opening of the North Devon Railway took place on 12th July 1854, when a special train conveying a civic party from Exeter and Pinneys band arrived at Barnstaple station at 11.30am, but only the first half of the train. The remaining coaches had inadvertently been left behind at Umberleigh and the engine had to return there for them, the reception received there by the driver not being recorded! A long civic procession wended its way through the decorated streets to the station, led by a troop of the North Devon Mounted Rifles and including representatives of civic, commercial and social interests of Barnstaple and surrounding towns. There were many banners devoted to the railway, the lace trade, shipping, commerce, shareholders and masons. On the station platform the Town Clerk, Mr Bencraft, presented an Address to the directors of the North Devon Railway to which the chairman, William Tite, responded. The procession, together with the chairman and directors, now returned back over the long bridge to the New Corn Market where a banquet for 760 people was held. There were the usual large number of toasts and speeches reviewing the history and progress of the North Devon Railway and the men connected with it.

When the additional signals required by Capt. Tyler had

OPENING OF THE NORTH DEVON RAILWAY - ARRIVAL OF THE TRAIN AT BARNSTAPLE

THE IRON RAILWAY BRIDGE, OVER THE RIVER TAW, NEAR BARNSTAPLE

been installed public train services began on the North Devon Railway on 1st August 1854 with a service of four weekday and two Sunday passenger trains. The rolling stock was provided by the Bristol & Exeter Railway until 28th July 1855 when Brassey provided his own locomotives and rolling stock. There were stations at Yeoford, Copplestone, Morchard Road, Lapford, Eggesford, South Molton Road, Portsmouth Arms and Umberleigh, with the siding referred to by Capt. Tyler at Chapeltown. Here a temporary platform was built, first appearing in public timetables in July 1857, but closing in August 1860.

During 1852 the North Devon's Land and Works Committee had dealt with considerable correspondence from Earl Fortescue and others concerning the siting of stations, particularly in respect of Chulmleigh. The four largest communities between Crediton and Barnstaple in 1851 were Chulmleigh, Morchard Bishop and Winkleigh each with the best part of 2,000 inhabitants and South Molton with more than 4,000. Morchard Road station was some three miles from Morchard Bishop and about eight miles from Winkleigh along the old coaching road, with

HIGH STREET, BARNSTAPLE

TRIUMPHAL ARCH, BARNSTAPLE-BRIDGE

South Molton Road station some eight miles from the town. Sometimes a 'Road' station later became a Junction station when a branch was opened to the town, examples being Chard Road and Tiverton Road. Eventually South Molton got its own station on the Devon & Somerset line, but Morchard Bishop never did. The line passes within about a mile of Chulmleigh, at Lee Cross, and there was considerable dissatisfaction at the failure of the company to provide its largest intermediate community with a convenient station. Instead the townspeople had to go three miles to Eggesford station which was very convenient for Earl Portsmouth (formerly the Hon. Newton Fellows) at Eggesford House, but few others. Portsmouth Arms station was convenient for the Portsmouth Arms Hotel built on the turnpike road of the 1830s, but was otherwise remote, but several other stations such as Yeoford, Lapford and Umberleigh were quite convenient for their villages.

When the North Devon Railway was re-structured in 1851 the powers to build branches to South Molton and Bideford were not renewed, and expired. The former was never built, but an independent Bideford Extension Railway was promoted in 1852, gained its Act in 1853 and opened for public services on 2nd November 1855. Although independent the Bideford Extension had much in common with the North Devon including six directors, the engineer W. R. Neale, contractor and leasee Thomas Brassey. By now Brassey was operating the North Devon with his own rolling stock, running trains from Bideford to Crediton, from where a Bristol & Exeter locomotive took the train on to Exeter. It was only at this stage that the original Taw Vale line from Fremington to Barnstaple gained a passenger service, before November 1855 only a goods service having been operated.

Early Years on the Broad Gauge

As we have seen, the very wet winter of 1853 delayed the construction of the North Devon, but the floods also damaged bridges on the Exeter & Crediton to the extent

97

Opening of the North Devon Railway

These advertisements appeared in *Woolmers Exeter and Plymouth Gazette* of 5th August 1854 immediately after the opening of the North Devon Railway. The train service comprised four trains daily each way, with two on Sundays, with minimal provision for third class passengers. A side effect of the opening was the reduction in work available for the coach proprietors, and the trade advertisements illustrate the influence of the new railway on businesses.

that train services had to be suspended for a period. Many of the wooden bridges had deteriorated since their construction in 1846 and subsequent lack of maintenance, and had to be propped up. Further propping had to be carried out on the Exeter & Crediton in 1856. Thomas Brassey was a railway contractor of international importance, so he appointed a manager, Robert Ogilvie, to manage the North Devon and Bideford Extension lines from his office at Barnstaple station. There were some difficulties to start with. Initially, the North Devon mail was still carried to Exeter by cart, and there were poor relations with the Bristol & Exeter which leased the Exeter & Crediton. The difficulty with the General Post Office was resolved and the mails carried by train, apparently from 28th May 1855.

A court case earlier that year, May v Brassey and Ogilvie, illustrated the bad relations between the lessees of the two lines. The plaintiff, a Barnstaple grocer, brought an action to recover £3 13s 7d which he alleged he had been overcharged for the carriage of goods on the North Devon Railway. It came out that if a ton of goods were sent from Exeter to a tradesman in Crediton, he would have to pay 2s 6d (12½p) carriage, but that if that same ton of goods were sent to Barnstaple the North Devon would be charged 5s (25p) by the Exeter & Crediton. For the passenger fare of 1s (5p) the North Devon was charged 1s 6d (7½p). Since trains from North Devon to Exeter usually spent between five and ten minutes at Crediton where the locomotives were changed, it was a common practice for passengers to re-book here in order to avoid extra expense. Robert Ogilvie eventually overcame these and other problems and built up a good reputation in North Devon to such an extent that on 6th January 1857 a public dinner was held at the Kings Arms Hotel, Barnstaple, attended by 70 people. It was stated that Robert Ogilvie had discharged his duties with fidelity to the lessees and liberality to those placed under him and he was presented

Two advertisements which appeared in the *Western Times* in May 1860. Cheap fares were advertised on the North Devon line to stimulate traffic, and an interesting coach service operated by Blatchford & Co. operated between Holsworthy and Copplestone station.

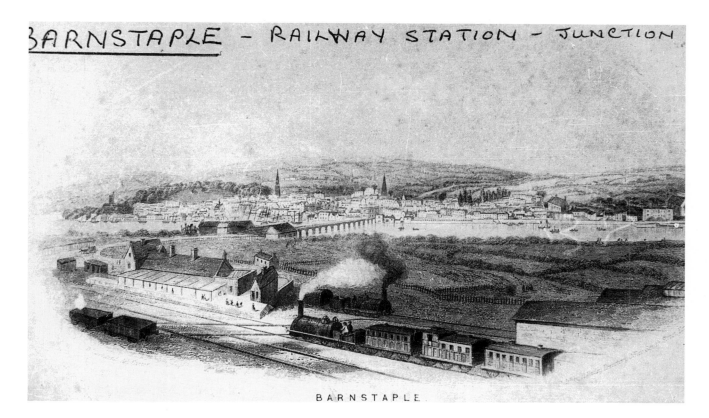

BARNSTAPLE - RAILWAY STATION - JUNCTION

BARNSTAPLE.

Barnstaple station from an early engraving circa 1860.

Collection John Nicholas

with two pieces of plate. Two years later he had been joined by Mr Patey as traffic manager and by their efforts traffic was increasing steadily.

The North Devon lines saw their share of misfortunes and accidents, major and minor. On 13th December 1854, the Mail Train was delayed for an hour at Morchard Road station when a truck collided with a crane and was derailed. On 31st January 1855 the morning 'down' train was delayed for an hour at St Cyres when a railwayman forgot to change the points, the train running into a siding,

Barnstaple station in broad gauge days from Sticklepath Hill, showing how much of the goods yard was constructed by building up the level of the salt marshes. On the left is a wooden carriage shed, the short vehicles reaching it via a turntable. At the end of the yard adjacent to Barnstaple Bridge is the warehouse built by William Thorne in 1848 for his lime traffic. In front of this is a timber yard, later extended considerably by Messrs Bartlett, Bayliss & Co.

Collection B. D. Hughes

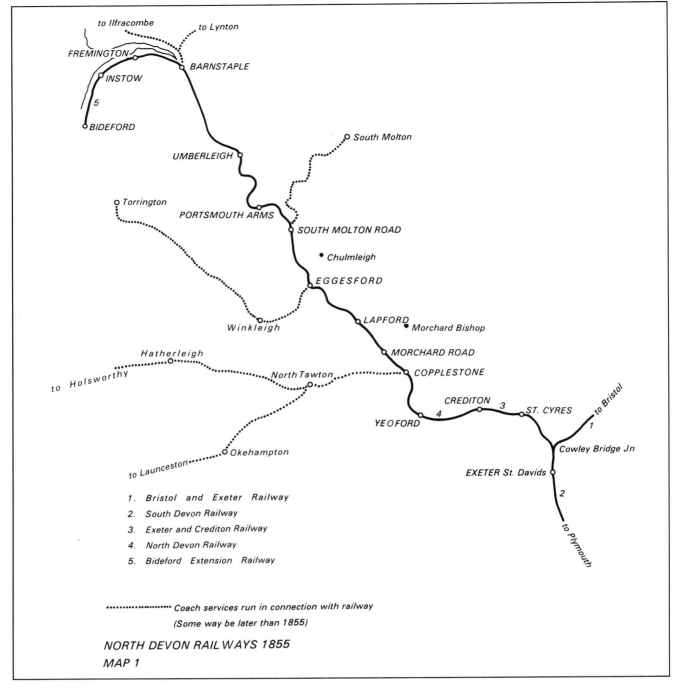

1. Bristol and Exeter Railway
2. South Devon Railway
3. Exeter and Crediton Railway
4. North Devon Railway
5. Bideford Extension Railway

•••••••••••• *Coach services run in connection with railway*

(Some way be later than 1855)

NORTH DEVON RAILWAYS 1855

MAP 1

where it collided with some wagons. On 11th January 1857 the 'down' Mail Train ran into a luggage van at Tawton, destroying the van which had been blown along the line from Barnstaple by very strong winds the previous night. It was humorously suggested in the North Devon Journal that this was an example of the atmospheric principle, which had recently been so disastrous for the South Devon Railway.

Apparently, none of these minor mishaps, which involved no injury to passengers and caused little damage, were of interest to the Board of Trade and its inspecting officers, but in three years, there were three accidents on the North Devon lines investigated by Lt Col., later Col. Yolland, who was to become a regular visitor and whose professional reports give a reliable picture of the lines and their operation. The first of these accidents occurred on 4th January 1859 when the 6.15pm passenger train from Exeter to Bideford, consisting of the 2-2-2 tender engine *Taw* and two carriages, came to grief on the Bideford Extension line at Yelland. A tyre on one of the locomotive driving wheels broke, causing the locomotive, tender and first carriage to be derailed. The fireman was slightly hurt,

but the passengers escaped without injury.

Next, on 24th August 1859, the 9.45am excursion train from Exeter to Barnstaple, for the North Devon races, was derailed at Cowley Bridge Junction. Several passengers and train crew suffered minor injuries while the superintendent of Exeter station, Mr Mears, who was travelling on the footplate, suffered a broken leg. The locomotive ran down a bank and turned over on its side, followed by the three front coaches, two of which were smashed. Fortunately, these were empty and the remaining nine coaches stayed on the rails. Col. Yolland held an enquiry and reported to the Board of Trade on 16th September in lengthy terms, here abridged.

The original curved wooden viaduct of 1846 carrying the double broad gauge tracks and built on a curve of radius 26 chains had deteriorated to such an extent that it had been replaced by an iron girder bridge. The new single track iron grider bridge, brought into use in November 1858, was built to the same 26 chain radius, but the curve at the junction had been reduced to just over 14 chains radius and all Exeter & Crediton line trains now had to negotiate facing points. Only Bristol & Exeter locomotives

Broad gauge at Barnstaple station with 2-2-2 locomotive *Tite* on a two-coach 'up' train at the only platform. A shunting horse deals with a wagon laden with timber. Note the electric telegraph wires in the foreground, gas lamp on the left and in the right background the outline of the engine shed and repair shops.

Collection P. J. T. Reed

worked trains from Exeter to Crediton where North Devon locomotives were put on to work to Bideford. This excursion train consisted of some North Devon and some Bristol & Exeter coaches. Apparently, on this occasion, the locomotive had mounted the guard rail opposite the crossing. The locomotive was a 4-2-2 with 7ft 6in driving wheels and a rigid wheelbase of 18ft 4in built by Slaughter & Co., a standard Bristol & Exeter express passenger tender engine, but not the usual type used on the Crediton line. The regular locomotive was a double or single bogie framed engine, but this was under repair.

Col. Yolland blamed the accident on a combination of the very sharp curve and the employment of an engine with a very long wheelbase. Indeed, three similar derailments had happened with that class of locomotive in less than a month since this accident. He was also of the opinion that the Exeter & Crediton should be compelled to restore the line to its original state with at least a 26 chain radius throughout, on both the viaduct and the junction. However, on 16th December the Board of Trade declined to compel the company to restore the line to its original curvature, and so began a long running campaign to improve the junction in several more of Col. Yolland's reports.

Col. Yolland's third accident report concerned a collision between the 6.30am 'up' train from Bideford and 7.45am 'down' train from Exeter at Copplestone on 16th July 1861, his report being made on 30th September. Thirteen passengers and the second guard of the 'down' train were injured. At the time there were four stations on the North Devon, with passing places or loop sidings, and two were also provided with water tanks for the locomotives, these being Copplestone and South Molton Road. However at each station only one platform was provided and when trains were to cross each other the first one to arrive was turned into the loop siding which was provided with the platform. The second train was then run along the main line and shunted back to the other end of the platform when the first train had left. The station was protected by 'up' and 'down' main signals at the end of the loop siding, about 200 yards apart, and by distant signals another 500 yards away, all the signals being of the cross bar and disc variety.

The first train to arrive was the 6.30am from Bideford, consisting of engine and tender and four carriages with one guard, which was turned into the loop siding and came to a halt with the locomotive opposite the water crane. By a lapse in concentration, the signalman William Shobbrick, turned the 'up' train in to the loop platform where the collision took place. The 'up' train was travelling at about seven miles per hour and comparitively little damage was done to the rolling stock. Subsequently, the signalman was imprisoned for a month by the local magistrates, after admitting that he had caused the accident by his carelessness. However Col. Yolland was critical of the lack of mechanical safeguards which would have prevented the accident and recommended that 'up' and 'down' platforms should be provided at all passing places on single lines.

North Devon Railway 2-4-0 locomotive *Creedy* on the Barnstaple turntable in August 1863, together with the extensive staff of the locomotive depot and repair shops who maintained not only the North Devon but also the locomotives belonging to Thomas Brassey.

J. B. N. Ashford courtesy B. D. Hughes

North Devon Railway & Dock Company Meetings

After 1854, the North Devon proprietors usually met for general meetings twice a year, in February and August, and from time to time, some interesting facts were reported. For the first three weeks of operation in August 1854 the receipts were as follows:

	Passengers	Goods	Total
1st - 6th (6 days)	£307 13s 8d	£20 11s 1d	£328 4s 9d
7th - 13th (1 week)	£348 17s 2d	£69 12s 8d	£418 9s 10d
14th - 20th (1 week)	£366 3s 1d	£60	£426 3s 1d

At this time the main goods traffic was coal and lime from Fremington, which required more siding and other accommodation, together with some livestock and timber. On 28th February 1855, the chairman, William Tite, reported that the cost of construction of the line would exceed the estimate by £29,000 due to Admiralty requirements, additions to the stations and sidings, cost of land and the additional signals required by Capt. Tyler. For some years the earnings of the line were insufficient to clear Brassey and Ogilvie from loss after paying their rent of £12,000 per year. However earnings in the second half of 1858 improved considerably, and this continued in 1859 when the Bath and West Show was held at Barnstaple and generated more traffic.

The rent received from Brassey and Ogilvie yielded a return of less than 3% on the capital invested in the North Devon, and the company itself had to pay expenses before dividends could be paid. For the half year (of five months revenue) ending 31st December 1854, the company made a surplus of £2,319 10s 3d and declared its first dividend of 3s 1½d (15½p) on £20 shares and 2s 6d (12½p) on £16 and £8 guaranteed shares. Company earnings rose slowly, but the second half of 1859 had reached £14,665 and dividends on ordinary stock were 17s 6d (87½p) percent.

At the meeting on 22nd February 1860 the directors reported that the South Western was now approaching Exeter and that arrangements would be made for laying down the standard gauge over the Exeter & Crediton, North Devon and Bideford Extension lines. A special meeting was held on 24th April 1860 to consider the South Western's Bill promoted to authorise these changes and a resolution approving the Bill was carried.

Chapter 4
The Mixed Gauge Era

The Approach of the South Western
During the 1850s the London & South Western Railway board, led by William Chaplin, successfully promoted, both directly and indirectly, several lines which together formed their central route from Basingstoke through Salisbury and Yeovil to Exeter. The South Western opened its own line to Salisbury (Milford) on 1st May 1857, the Salisbury & Yeovil Railway (worked by the South Western) opened in stages, reaching Yeovil on 1st June 1860, while its own Exeter & Yeovil line opened on 18th July 1860. Among those present at the opening ceremony were the Hon. Ralph Dutton, William Tite MP and George Braginton, chairmen of the Exeter & Crediton, North Devon and Bideford Extension companies, and Thomas Brassey, the lessee of the last two. Public services began on the following day, with Exeter Queen Street the terminus of the main line from Waterloo, but efforts were already in hand to extend the South Western line westwards.

The Missing Link
As construction of the Exeter & Yeovil line progressed, the LSWR board considered how best to link its Exeter Queen Street station with the North Devon lines in which it was a large shareholder. Relations with the broad gauge companies were now better, so the 1848 proposal for an independent line to Cowley Bridge was dropped in favour of negotiations with the Bristol & Exeter. There was a comprehensive agreement reached on 14th March 1860 between the two companies, which was authorized by parliament when on 3rd July 1860 it passed the London & South Western Railway (Exeter & North Devon) Act. The South Western would build a connecting line down the hill from Exeter Queen Street station to St Davids. From here to Cowley Bridge the Bristol & Exeter would lay mixed gauge track. The South Western was empowered to take over the leases of the Exeter & Crediton, North Devon and Bideford Extension lines and mix the gauge. The South Western would enjoy running powers over the B&ER as far as Cowley Bridge, and the latter had running powers over the Exeter & Crediton, limited to freight services after the LSWR took over its lease. The South Western was to retain the broad gauge tracks as far as Bideford, and another agreement protected the interests of the South Devon Railway. The South Western let the contract for the line between Queen Street and St Davids to James Taylor, its contractor for the Exeter & Yeovil, for £19,550.

Meanwhile, the proprietors of the Exeter & Crediton, North Devon and Bideford Extension companies started to prepare for the arrival of the South Western. A special general meeting of the Exeter & Crediton proprietors was held at Waterloo Bridge station on 21st November 1861, when they agreed a lease to the South Western for seven years from 1st January 1862 at a rent of 55% of gross receipts, the South Western being responsible for all repairs and maintenance. The South Western was not to give less accommodation to the public than the Bristol & Exeter had given. The lease was proposed by Charles Castleman, seconded by James Buller and agreed unanimously under the Chairmanship of Ralph Dutton, all of whom were directors of the LSWR or B&ER. In fact, the South Western took over the lease on 1st February 1862 and commenced their 'narrow' gauge service on 3rd.

It is curious to note that according to the Exeter & Crediton Act 1874, this lease was dated 25th February 1864.

At the North Devon proprietors general meeting on 27th February 1861 the lease of the line to Thomas Brassey was extended by one more year, until 31st July 1862, at the same rent of £12,000 per annum. The Bideford Extension proprietors extended their lease to the same date. The South Western then took over both leases as from 1st August 1862 and worked the entire service between Bideford and Exeter St Davids with Brassey's rolling stock until the gauge was mixed the following year.

Mixed Gauge to Crediton
Col. Yolland inspected and passed the LSWR line from Queen Street to its junction with the Bristol & Exeter on 27th January 1862. It was double track standard gauge line built mainly on a 1 in 37 gradient, passing through St Davids Tunnel. However, he understood that the South Western proposed to commence its 'narrow' gauge service to Crediton on 3rd February without the sanction of the Board of Trade, the tracks of the Bristol & Exeter and the Exeter & Crediton having been passed only for broad gauge traffic. He had no doubt that there were some details of the new arrangements which he would be unable to approve.

Clearly, there was a difference of opinion between the two railway companies on the one hand and Col. Yolland on the other, as to the need for a further inspection when broad gauge tracks were converted to mixed gauge. This did not stop the South Western from taking over the lease of the Exeter & Crediton on 1st February and running 'narrow' gauge trains through to Crediton from the 3rd. However, the Board of Trade decided that further inspection was necessary and in minutes of 14th and 25th February instructed Col. Yolland to inspect the Bristol & Exeter and Exeter & Crediton lines involved. On 19th February, he inspected the 'narrow' gauge tracks laid down on the Bristol & Exeter and reported on the following day. He required some minor changes but was able to pass the lines concerned, although he specifically excluded the junction at Cowley Bridge from this sanction.

Col. Yolland's third report was made on 10th March 1862.

"I have inspected the additional rail laid down by the London & South Western Railway Company between the Cowley Bridge Junction and Crediton station on the Exeter & Crediton Railway, a length of about 5¾ miles.

The additional rail is laid on longitudinal sleepers similar to the original line - many of the under bridges and flood openings have fallen into a state of decay since the line was originally opened as a broad gauge line, and been replaced by more permanent structures of iron and wood - others have been repaired with wood and some still remain that will require to be carefully watched so that they may be renewed before they become dangerous - I have received a drawing of the bridge over the Exe near Cowley Bridge Junction which shows that the wrought iron girders are sufficiently strong by calculation and when tested with a rolling load of two locomotives, the deflections observed are very moderate. I have not received drawings of two other bridges reconstructed with wrought iron girders but expect to receive them from the Company's resident engineer - but from the deflections observed and the look of these structures, I have no doubt as to their sufficiency for a single line of railway as now laid.

The supports placed on a wooden over bridge are a trifle less then 3 feet from the edge of one of the broad gauge rails - while on the other side the space is more than 3ft 9in - the line should therefore be shifted, or an accident similar to that in which Captain Mathias was killed some years ago since on the South Devon Railway may take place on the Exeter & Crediton Railway.

I think their Lordships decision of 16th December 1859 not to call upon the Exeter & Crediton Railway Company to restore their line at the Cowley Bridge Junction to the state (a complete double junction with a curve of 30 or 26 chains radius) in which it was sanctioned to be opened by the Commissioners of Railways was an ill-advised and injudicious one - I do not deal with the legal, but only with the engineering question as there can be no doubt whatsoever that a curve of 30 chains radius is more safe than one of 15 chains radius, and it was proved to be so by the accident which occurred as soon as the alteration had been effected.

Their Lordships should, in my opinion, always stand between the public and the railway company - and not shelter a railway company from its illegal acts. If an application for a similar reduction in the radius of a curve at a junction were made to the Board of Trade now it must undoubtedly be refused, unless very good grounds are shown for granting it. In this case there were no such grounds and no such application was made and the bridge was actually so constructed that only an additional outer girder would have been required to complete the double bridge, so as to form the double junction which had received the sanction of the Inspecting Officer and of the Commissioners of Railways.

Eggesford station in mixed gauge days, between 1863 and 1873 when the signal box was built, with an 'up' South Western standard gauge goods train hauled by a Beyer, Peacock double-framed 0-6-0 goods engine, possibly on a coal train from Fremington.

LGRP

I have now therefore, to report that the narrow gauge line of rails between Cowley Bridge Junction and Crediton station on the Exeter & Crediton Railway is complete as regards the position and state of the broad gauge line after it was altered in 1859, but incomplete as regards the works originally sanctioned by the Parliamentary Plans under which the line was made and opened".

For the next year the situation on the Exeter & Crediton line was somewhat complex with three companies operating trains on it. The South Western operated 'narrow' gauge passenger and goods trains from Exeter Queen Street to Crediton. The Bristol & Exeter operated broad gauge goods trains between Exeter St Davids and Crediton, and from 1st February until 31st July 1862, Brassey and Ogilvie operated their North Devon Railway passenger service between Bideford and Exeter St Davids. From 1st August 1862, until 1st March 1863, these broad gauge services were maintained by the South Western using rolling stock inherited from Brassey. There were, during this period, advertised through coaches from Bideford to Bristol and Paddington. On 17th May 1862, whilst hauling the 4.20pm passenger train from Exeter Queen Street to Crediton the South Western 2-4-0 well tank No. 144 *Howe* left the road at Cowley Bridge Junction, but this did not lead to another inspection by Col. Yolland.

longitudinal sleepers according to the ordinary Great Western system of permanent way. The additional rail now laid down by the London & South Western Railway Company is a double headed rail weighing 80 lbs per lineal yard, fixed in joint and intermediate chairs on the North Devon Railway with bridge rails weighing about 60 lbs per yard on the longitudinal system adopted by the Bideford Extension Railway. The joint chairs weigh about 36 lbs, the intermediates 24 lbs and they are secured to the transverse sleepers by iron spikes. On some parts where the line is on a sharp curve the joints of the new rails, laid on the transverse sleepers are secured by bracket chairs but this has not been adopted throughout, a large number of damaged sleepers have already been taken out and been replaced by new and sound ones, but it is proper to state that if the whole line is carefully overhauled an additional number of new sleepers will be found to be necessary. Again the ballast on some portions of the line is now very indifferent, it never was good, but it has greatly deteriorated and should, with as little delay as possible be removed.

There are a very large number of under bridges and viaducts on the lines, mostly of stone abutments and timber tops, in some instances the wooden trussed beams have been replaced by iron girders, and in the course of a few years it will probably be found necessary to replace a large number of these timber tops by others of the same description or in iron.

The London & South Western Railway Company should, in my opinion, with as little delay as possible drive spikes through the whole of the treenails that secure the old rails to the sleepers. No person can say when the treenails may give way. The joints on the old rails require to be carefully looked at as many of them are very bad and the joint chairs require to be fish sealed.

Mixed Gauge to Bideford

During this period the South Western had taken over the leases of the North Devon and Bideford Extension lines and mixed the gauge of both. Col. Yolland made his inspection and reported on 26th February 1863.

"I have inspected the additional rail laid down by the London & South Western Railway Company within the broad gauge rails of the North Devon & Bideford Extension Railways so as to render these lines available for the narrow gauge traffic.

The North Devon Railway was inspected and opened for traffic in August 1854, the Bideford Extension Railway in November 1855. Neither of these lines of railway have been kept up in first class order, so that when they passed into the hands of the London & South Western Railway Company in the course of last year, that company proceed to lay down the additional rail required to accommodate narrow gauge traffic, extensive reparations were found necessary.

The North Devon Railway as far as Fremington Pill was originally laid with a double sided rail fixed in cast iron chairs fastened down to transverse sleepers by means of wooden treenails - and the Bideford Extension Railway from Fremington to Bideford, with bridge rails laid on

It would also be desirable in some way or other to fish the joints of the old and new rails - in the first instance over the viaducts and under bridges. In a great many instances the baulks carrying the rails over viaducts and small bridges require to be properly wedged up. In many respects it would be desirable and safe to work the traffic on the narrow rather than on the broad gauge. I understand it is intended to work the passenger traffic on the narrow gauge and some if not all of the goods traffic on the broad gauge. While, therefore, it is necessary to keep up the broad gauge it is right that the mixed gauge should be rendered complete.

1. Thus at all the stations and at some sidings the complete mixed gauge is not carried out in most instances the broad gauge is in existence but the narrow gauge has not been completed - in a few cases the narrow gauge siding has been added where no broad gauge siding exists. This should be attended to at once before the narrow gauge trains begin to run.

2. The mode of transforming the narrow gauge from the north to the south side by means of moveable facing points at the greater proportion if not at the whole of the stations is objectionable and should be changed. A mistake by the signalman in opening the points to the wrong train would be followed by its being thrown off the rails - instead of

merely continuing along the wrong line.

3. The Platform at the Portsmouth Arms station is too narrow.

I have therefore to report that their Lordships sanction for the opening of the narrow gauge lying between Crediton and Bideford cannot by reason of the incompleteness of the works (as referred to Nos 1, 2 and 3) be sanctioned without danger to the public using the same."

The South Western quickly attended to these matters and on 2nd March 1863 the 'narrow' gauge service was extended from Crediton to Bideford. Some trains, or through coaches, now ran between Waterloo and Bideford although there was usually one daily broad gauge mixed passenger and goods train run between Crediton and Bideford. The Bristol & Exeter continued to work two or three broad gauge goods trains between Exeter and Crediton.

An LSWR notice for Wednesday 12th August 1863 shows special trains ran to Bideford Regatta. A standard gauge special left Exeter Queen Street at 10.05am (five minutes after the 10am ordinary) and broad gauge specials from Barnstaple at 2.20pm and 4pm with return workings at 8pm, 9pm and 10.05pm respectively.

Amalgamations

For two of the local companies the end of their independent existence was now in sight. After lengthy and at times difficult negotiations, the South Western Act of 25th July 1864 was passed with the support of the North Devon and Bideford Extension companies. This provided for their amalgamation with the LSWR with the following exchanges of stock:

For £100 of	
North Devon Ordinary, not exceeding £245,415	£49 LSWR Ordinary
North Devon A, not exceeding £25,152	£19 12s LSWR Ordinary
North Devon B, not exceeding £25,152	£98 LSWR Ordinary
Bideford Extension £55,000	£100 LSWR 4% preference

The amalgamations both took place on 1st January 1865, the remaining North Devon shares having been owned by the South Western since 1847.

Due to the years when the unfinished line had earned nothing the North Devon Railway had proved to be a poor investment for its shareholders, paying only a 1¾% dividend for most of its existence when 4% was quite normal elsewhere. Advocates of the broad gauge could point to the Great Western as a fine example of a high speed well maintained line, but the North Devon was the very opposite of this. When opened in 1854 it was a slow line with trains taking some two hours for the 39 miles from Barnstaple to Exeter, and over the next decade the permanent way had deteriorated alarmingly. Most of the locomotives and rolling stock, together with iron rails and chairs, had been acquired second hand and the South Western was now faced with considerable expenditure to bring the line up to modern standards. Yet for the South Western the North Devon had great strategic value as it had kept the Bristol & Exeter out of the area, and now it was feeding considerable through traffic on to their main line to Exeter. Having secured the North Devon, the South Western could now expand its network west of Exeter using the Exeter & Crediton and North Devon lines.

In contrast to these amalgamations it suited the South

EXETER AND CREDITON LINE.

NORTH DEVON RAILWAY SERVICE TIME TABLE.
All Trains are Narrow Gauge, except the Goods Trains marked "Broad," viz.: No. 4 Down and No. 8 Up.

NORTH DEVON RAILWAY SERVICE TIME TABLE.
All Trains are Narrow Gauge, except the Goods Trains marked "Broad," viz.: No. 8 Up and No. 4 Down.

Western and Bristol & Exeter to allow the Exeter & Crediton Railway to retain its nominal independence. Although it held the whip hand with 60% of the shares the LSWR needed to maintain harmonious relations with the B&ER, particularly in respect of its running powers through Exeter St Davids. There had been disagreements between the two but these were resolved by arbitration which established the right of the South Western to employ its own booking clerks at St Davids, a practice which continued during the Southern Railway period. Another advantage of the arrangements for the South Western was that when further expenditure on the Exeter & Crediton in respect of new bridges, doubling of track, signalling and so on was required the Bristol & Exeter was liable for 40% of the cost.

South Western Extension to Plymouth

As was seen in Chapter 2 with the Cornwall & Devon Central proposal of 1845 the South Western's strategic plans had always included a line to the north of Dartmoor to Truro, Falmouth and Plymouth, the largest city in the South West beyond Bristol, with its great naval base. With South Western and North Devon support the standard gauge Okehampton Railway gained its Act on 17th July 1862 for a line from a junction with the North Devon at Colebrook to Okehampton. An agreement of 21st May 1863 gave the South Western a lease and option to purchase, and an Act of 13th July 1863 authorised an extension from Okehampton to join the Launceston and South Devon line at Lidford. A third Act of 23rd June 1864 authorised deviations, replaced the junction at Colebrook with a second line to Yeoford station, and re-named the company the Devon & Cornwall Railway. At last, on 31st March 1864, the first sod was cut by Countess Portsmouth, wife of the Fifth Earl Portsmouth of Eggesford House, the company chairman. Three men employed by the contractors Messrs Sharpe and Son were killed in accidents over the next year before the line to North Tawton was ready.

On 26th October 1865 Col. Yolland made his inspection of the portion of the Devon & Cornwall Railway between its junction with the North Devon and North Tawton railways. The line was single with passing places at the stations at Bow and North Tawton with land purchased and bridges constructed for a double line. The sharpest curve was of 20 chains radius at the divergence with the North Devon line at Colebrook. A turntable was provided at North Tawton but not at Yeoford, and trains were to be controlled by train staff between these two places. There was a siding at Colebrook serving a ballast pit. This had been disconnected but it was intended to re-connect it when semaphore signals had been installed, the location being at or near what later became Coleford Junction. Col. Yolland passed the line and the ceremonial opening took place on 28th October, with public services beginning on 1st November 1865 with six weekday trains between Exeter Queen Street and North Tawton. Yeoford station now became Yeoford Junction and it began to grow in importance as the Devon & Cornwall and other lines were extended.

Construction of the Devon & Cornwall over the granite of Dartmoor was slow; the line was opened to Okehampton Road on 8th January 1867, to Okehampton on 3rd October 1871 and Lidford on 12th October 1874. Finally, on 17th May 1876 South Western trains first ran to Plymouth and Devonport, running over the mixed gauge tracks of the South Devon Railway's Launceston branch. The opening of the 'narrow' gauge to Devonport

was celebrated in great style at Plymouth, where the breaking of the broad gauge monopoly was most welcome.

Four More Accidents

Over a period of five years there were four more accidents involving North Devon line trains and the inspecting officer's reports give a detailed picture of the line and its operation at this time. On 19th October 1865, the 7.43pm Bristol & Exeter 'up' goods from Crediton, consisting of locomotive, 33 wagons and a brake van left more than an hour late at 8.49pm and slowed at Cowley Bridge Junction, finding the distant signal at danger. The 9.10pm South Western 'up' passenger train from Crediton, consisting of tank engine, four carriages and two brake vans ran into the back of the slowly moving goods train just outside Cowley Bridge Junction. Three passengers were slightly injured and the guard of the goods train seriously injured while the material damage was extensive. The engine of the passenger train had its buffer beam and buffers broken, and the guards van next to it was damaged. On the goods train, the brake van, a meat van and a truck were thrown off the rails and seriously damaged. Col. Yolland reported on 4th November and criticised the St Cyres station master for allowing the faster passenger train to leave at about 9.20pm without warning the driver that the slower goods train had left at 9.13pm. The siding at St Cyres was not long enough to shunt the goods train out of the way of the passenger train. He recommended the introduction of the electric telegraph, and pointed out that if the passenger train had continuous brakes it would have probably stopped before hitting the goods train.

Col. Yolland was given another opportunity to visit Cowley Bridge Junction, when on 17th February 1866, the 4.50pm passenger train from Bideford to Exeter was partially derailed, without injury to anyone. Col. Yolland made his detailed report on 13th April. The locomotive was a Beattie 2-4-0 of the 'Falcon' class, No. 79 *Harpy*, only two months out of Nine Elms works. The train consisted of engine and tender, one third class, one first class, two second class carriages and a brake van, and having come off the single track Exeter & Crediton line was passing over the crossover to the 'down' track of the Bristol & Exeter line when the engine and first class carriage left the track and came to rest in the ballast underneath the road bridge.

On examination it was found that a guard rail 16ft in length had been forced off by the passage of a number of previous trains. The curvature at this crossover was only 12½ chains and in the absence of the guard rail the train was inevitably derailed. No blame could be attributed to the platelayers, the quality of the iron plate holding the guard rail having been defective. However, Col. Yolland went on to repeat the recommendations of his 1859 and 1862 accident reports, namely that the whole layout on a curve of 14 chains was unsatisfactory and that the Exeter & Crediton should re-build the line to the 26 or 30 chain radius double junction originally inspected and approved in 1851. He also suggested that the Board of Trade withdraw permission for cheap excursion trains on the line since they removed or restricted liability towards passengers.

On 23rd September 1869 there was a collision at Fremington between the 3.15pm broad gauge mixed train from Bideford to Crediton and the 1.25pm standard gauge passenger train from Exeter to Bideford. The broad gauge train consisted of engine and tender, brake van, two loaded wagons, a composite carriage and a second class carriage with brake compartment, whilst the standard gauge train consisted of a Beattie 2-4-0 well tank No. 196, two second class, two first class and two third class carriages, and two brake vans. Col. Hutchinson in his report blamed a pointsman and the driver of the 'down' train, but pointed out that the single platform at Fremington was inadequate, echoing Col. Yolland's recommendation following the Copplestone collision in 1861.

On 30th June 1870 an accident occurred on the incline from St Davids to Queen Street station when ten passengers were injured, Col. Yolland making his report on 15th July. The 7.40pm passenger train from Bideford to Exeter had been strengthened with seven additional carriages and a brake van at Barnstaple to accommodate extra passengers returning from a flower show at Barnstaple, making the train up to seventeen vehicles including two brake vans. At St Davids a second locomotive was put on to assist the train up the 1 in 37 incline, but the train came to a standstill after 350 yards. The train was then divided into two between the ninth and tenth carriages with the brakes on the wheels of the second half of the train scotched with stones. However, when the locomotives attempted to re-start the first half of the train they set back about six feet, pushing the last eight carriages down the incline where, after 130 yards, they crashed in catch sidings. Col. Yolland was very critical of this mode of operation and also called for continuous brakes.

The Exeter & Crediton Lease Renewed

At the Exeter & Crediton proprietors meeting held at Waterloo station on 27th August 1868, Capt. Mangles in the chair, it was now a more prosperous scene. The half yearly accounts showed an income from the South Western passenger and goods traffic of £2,432 11s 1d and from Bristol & Exeter goods traffic of £111 4s 8d, both after deduction of 55% for working expenses. This enabled the company to pay a dividend of 4%. At this stage the capital account amounted to £112,950 consisting of original share capital of £70,000, £20,000 in 5% preference shares and £22,950 in debentures and temporary loans. The lease to the South Western expired on 31st January 1869 and was renewed for a further seven years on the same terms of income less 55% for working expenses this second lease being dated 21st January 1869.

Resignalling the North Devon Railway

The London & South Western Railway, having already spent a considerable sum on acquiring the North Devon, mixing the gauge and other improvements, now turned its attention to the signalling. Much of the signalling was still provided by the cross bar and disc signals described by Capt. Tyler in 1854 and Col. Yolland in his 1861 Copplestone accident report. Much of this was swept away

London and South Western Railway Time Table.
FOR THE MONTH OF AUGUST, 1874.

DOWN TRAINS.—WEEK DAYS.   **SUNDAYS.**

STATIONS. By South Western Railway.	1 & 2 class p.m.	1 2 3 B class 1 2 3	1 2 3 Exp class a.m.	A 1 & 2 class a.m.	Fast Ex. 1 2 cl class p.m.	Mail 1 & 2 class	1 2 3 1 & 2 class	1 2 3 1 & 2 class a.m.	1 & 2 class
London, Waterloo Station, dep	...	...	6 45	10 45	11 50	2 10	4 5	9 45	5 0
Do., Kensington "			6 10	10 15	11 17		2 52	10 15	
Basingstoke "			8 23	12 2	1 19	3 20	5 33	12 25	7 15
Salisbury "			9 59	1 8	2 45	4 17	6 48	1 55	9 10
Southampton "			8 30	11 40	1 0		4 50	9 30	7 45
Portsmouth "			7 55	10 50	12 30		4 20	8 40	
Yeovil "		7 15	11 10	2 5	4 0	5 8	7 50	3 15	
Exeter arr		9 26	1 20	3 43	6 10	6 25	9 55	5 27	

By Bristol & Exeter Railway.	1 & 2 class a.m.	1 2 3 class a.m.	Exp class p.m.	1 & 2 class p.m.	1 & 2 class a.m.
Exeter arr					

STATIONS. By Crediton & North Devon.	1 & 2 class a.m.	1 2 3 class a.m.	1 & 2 class a.m.	1 2 3 class Ord. p.m.	1 & 2 class p.m.	1 2 3		1 2 3	1 2 3	1 & 2 a.m.	1 2 3 p.m.	1 & 2 p.m.	1 2 3 p.m.
Exeter, Queen-street dep	3 20	7 0	10 0	1 25	3 55	6 35	6 35	10 10	3 20	9 50	1 50	6 40	
Exeter, St. David's "	3 30	7 6	10 7	1 40	4 8	6 45	6 45	10 25	3 30	9 57	1 57	6 55	
St. Cyres "	3 42	7 17	10 17	1 51	4 21	6 56	6 56	10 35	3 42	10 8	2 8	7 5	
Crediton arr	3 49	7 24	10 25	1 58	4 28	7 2	7 2	10 41	3 49	10 15	2 15	7 11	
Crediton dep	3 50	7 26	10 28	2 1	4 29	7 3	7 3		3 50			7 12	
Yeoford Junction "	4 2	9 8	10 45	12 8	2 15	4 45	7 18	7 18				7 20	
Bow arr		9 18	10 56	12 34	2 26	4 58	7 29	7 29					
North Tawton "		9 24	11 4	12 56	2 34	5 4	7 37	7 37					
Okehampton "		9 40	11 20	1 20	2 51	5 20	7 53	7 53					
Copplestone dep	4 14	7 43	10 48		2 19		7 21	7 21	4 14				
Morchard Road "		7 49	10 55		2 26	4 50	7 26	7 26					
Lapford "	4 28	7 57	11 3		2 35	4 56	7 34	7 34	4 28				
Eggesford "	4 38	8 7	11 14		2 45	5 2	7 43	7 43	4 38		7 45		
Southmolton Road "	4 51	8 18	11 23		2 55	5 10	7 52	7 52	4 51		7 52		
Portsmouth Arms "		8 26	11 34		3 5	5 17	8 0	8 0		1 2 3	7 58	1 2 3	
Umberleigh "	5 8	8 37	11 44	1 2 3	3 14	5 27	8 10	8 10	5 8		8 8		
Barnstaple arr	5 20	8 50	12 0		3 24	5 41			5 24		p.m.	p.m.	
Barnstaple dep	5 30	9 30	8 52	12 5	3 29	5 44	8 24	8 24	5 30	2 40	8 30		
Fremington "	5 42	9 36	8 57	12 12	3 44	5 50	8 37	8 37	5 42	2 47	8 37		
Instow "	5 51	9 45	9 7	12 20	3 44	5 57	8 44	8 44	5 51	2 57	8 52		
Bideford "	6 3	9 50			3 51	6 3	8 51	8 51	6 3	3 5	9 4		
Torrington arr	6 18	10 8	9 30	12 42	4 6	6 17	9 5	9 5	6 18	3 20	9 5		

On Fridays only.

L This Train will stop at Lapford on Fridays to set down Passengers by application to the Guard. B The 10.40 a.m. Train from Exeter to North Devon will convey 3rd class Passengers with Through Tickets from Yeovil, &c. C This Train will stop at Portsmouth Arms to set down Passengers from Exeter.

UP TRAINS.—WEEK DAYS.   **SUNDAYS.**

STATIONS. By Bideford & North Devon.	1 & 2 class a.m.	1 2 3 class a.m.	1 2 3 & 2 class a.m.	1 2 3 class a.m.	1 & 2 class p.m.	C 1 2 3 class p.m.	1 & 2 1 & 2 class p.m.	Mail	1 2 3 class a.m.	1 2 3 & 2 class a.m.	1 2 3 class p.m.	1 2 3 class p.m.
Torrington dep		7 5		8 45	10 35	2 20		4 20	7 45	7 10	1 45	7 45
Bideford dep		7 20		9 0	10 47	2 34		4 33	8 0	7 25	2 0	8 0
Instow "		7 26		9 7	10 53	2 40		4 39	8 6	7 31	2 6	8 6
Fremington "		7 34		9 16	11 1	2 48		4 46	8 13	7 39	2 18	8 13
Barnstaple arr				9 24							2 25	
Barnstaple dep		7 47	8 20		11 12	3 0		4 56	8 25	7 55		8 25
Umberleigh "		8 0	8 42		11 20	3 15		5 10	8 38	8 9		8 38
Portsmouth Arms "		8 10	9 0		11 35	3 24		5 18	8 46	8 20		8 46
Southmolton Road "		8 19	9 20		11 42	3 31		5 26	8 54	8 30		8 54
Eggesford "		8 29	9 37		11 49	3 39		5 35	9 3	8 42		9 3
Lapford "		8 38	9 55			3 47		5 44	9 12	8 55		
Morchard Road "		8 46	10 16		12 1	3 54		5 52	9 19	9 4		
Copplestone "		8 52	10 22			4 0		5 59	9 24	9 14		
Okehampton "	8 0	8 20	10 0		11 30	3 20		5 30				
North Tawton "	8 16	8 36	10 16		11 45	3 37		5 46				
Bow "	8 22	8 44	10 24		11 51	3 45		5 54				
Yeoford Junction dep	8 33	9 2	10 55		12 11	4 6		6 7	9 31	9 22		9 31
Crediton arr / dep	8 44	6 20	9 12	11 25	12 20	4 16	6 17	9 40	9 37	1 15	2 30	9 40
St. Cyres "	8 52	6 36	9 21	11 35	12 27	4 22	6 23	9 48	9 46	1 21	2 36	
Exeter (St. David's) arr	9 2	6 37	9 33	11 48	12 37	4 33	6 34	9 58	9 55	1 32	2 48	
Exeter (Queen-street) arr	9 10	6 42	9 45	11 55	12 44	4 45	6 40	10 4	10 0	1 37	2 53	10 4

Goods and Passenger Train every Week Day.

Exeter—Departure by South Western Trains (Queen-st.)	1 & 2 class a.m.	1 2 3 class a.m.	1 2 3 class a.m.	Exp 1 & 2 p.m.	1 & 2 class p.m.	1 2 3 class p.m.	1 2 3 p.m.	1 2 3 class a.m.	1 2 3 class p.m.
Yeovil dep		7 0	10 10	1 40	5 5	7 0		8 15	2 15
Salisbury arr		8 40	11 55	2 5	6 15	8 30		6 50	3 50
Basingstoke "		10 27	1 41	3 39	7 57			8 30	5 30
London arr	11 14	2 27	4 46	6 10	10 53	12 37		8 58	
Southampton "	12 0	3 36	5 29	10 37				8 31	
Portsmouth "	2 19	4 10	6 15	10 30				9 3	
Exeter—Departure by Bristol and Exeter Trains ...	a.m.	a.m.		Exp	p.m.	p.m.	p.m.		p.m.

LSWR Timetables

This timetable for August 1874 appeared in the *North Devon Journal*

when, on 1st October 1873, the South Western opened new signal boxes at every station from Copplestone to Umberleigh inclusive, with new semaphore signals and block signalling using Preeces Three Wire system. Full details were published in LSWR Instruction No. 133 of 1873. However, some cross bar and disc signals remained and were replaced by semaphore signals which were brought into use on 20th March 1879 according to details given in LSWR Instruction No. 75 of 1879. As we shall see the South Western had other intentions to the east of Copplestone in the early 1870s.

Railway Expansion in North Devon

Within North Devon no new railways were opened

INSTRUCTION
No. 133, 1873.

SOUTH WESTERN RAILWAY.

NORTH DEVON LINE.

INSTRUCTIONS TO SUPERINTENDENTS, STATION AGENTS, INSPECTORS, ENGINEMEN, GUARDS, SIGNALMEN, POINTSMEN, AND ALL CONCERNED.

EXTENSION OF THE ELECTRIC SYSTEM OF BLOCK SIGNALLING FROM COPPLESTONE TO UMBERLEIGH.

On Wednesday, 1st October, 1873, commencing at 12.0 noon, the Electric System of Block Signalling will come into use between Copplestone and Umberleigh, and it will be continued without intermission (while Trains are running) in future, according to the Regulations. See Instructions as to working No. 132.

The Electric Apparatus provided will be **Preece's Three-Wire System** as it is adapted to Single Lines, blocking forwards as well as backwards. The following is a List of the New Signal Stations. This completes the Electric Block System from Exeter (Queen Street) to Umberleigh and to Okehampton.

LIST OF SIGNALLING STATIONS.

Copplestone.
Morchard Road.
Lapford.
Eggesford.
South Molton Road.
Portsmouth Arms.
Umberleigh.

All the above Stations and Signal Boxes are supplied with Out-door Home and Distant Signals complete, as well as with Electric Semaphores and Bells; and the whole will be worked according to the Regulations for Signalling Trains on Single Lines, as provided in Instruction 132, 1873, a copy of which is framed and hung up in each Signal Box for the guidance of the Signalmen on duty, and a copy is also kept by each Station Agent to be retained by him for his guidance.

	SECTIONS AND DISTANCES.	Miles.	Chains	Average Time of Running, see Note below.*
1	Copplestone to Morchard Road	1	60	4 min.
2	Morchard Road to Lapford	3	...	7 ,,
3	Lapford to Eggesford	3	20	8 ,,
4	Eggesford to South Molton Road	3	40	8 ,,
5	South Molton Road to Portsmouth Arms	3	...	7 ,,
6	Portsmouth Arms to Umberleigh	4	40	10 ,,

* The average time of running between the Sections is computed as that of an Ordinary Passenger Train, excluding stoppages.

NOTICE TO ENGINEMEN AND GUARDS AS TO NEW OUT-DOOR SIGNALS.

The following Additions and alterations have been made to the existing Out-door Signals, &c., at the undermentioned Stations. Enginemen are requested to keep a good look out in approaching the Stations on Wednesday morning during the time the workmen are employed in connecting up the New Signals, and removing the Old Ones. The New Signals are to be obeyed on and after 12.0 noon on Wednesday.

COPPLESTONE STATION.

The only addition to the Signals at this Station is a new Semaphore starting Signal for Down Trains, which is erected on the Down side of the Line, 55 yards from the end of the Down Platform.

MORCHARD ROAD STATION.

A new Signal Box has been erected at the Western end of the Up Platform, in which all the Signal Levers and Electric Instruments have been concentrated. The following new Semaphore Signals have been erected:—

A **Down distant** Signal on the Down side of the Line, close to and to replace the present Cross Bar and Disc Signal, which will be removed. This Signal has an electric Repeater attached to it.

An **Up distant** Signal on the Up side of the Line, 800 yards from the Station and 240 yards beyond the old Cross Bar and Disc Signal, which it will replace.

A **Down stop** Signal on Up side of the Line, 30 yards east of the old Cross Bar and Disc Signal, which it will replace.

An **Up stop** Signal on the Up side of the Line at the end of the Loop points, to replace the old Cross Bar and Disc Signal.

Up and Down Starting Signals, 50 yards from the ends of the respective Platforms.

LAPFORD STATION.

A new Signal Box has been erected on the Down side of the Line at the Western end of the Loop, in which all the Signal levers and Electric instruments have been concentrated.

The following new **Semaphore Signals** have been erected:—

An **Up Starting** Signal on the Down side of the Line, at the East end of the new Down Platform, 50 yards from (East of) the Loop points.

A **Down Starting** Signal on the Down side of the Line, close to the new Signal Box. The Up and Down Distant Signals and Stop Signals will not be altered, but an Electric Repeater has been fitted to the Down Distant Signal.

EGGESFORD STATION.

A new Signal Box has been erected on the Down Platform, in which all the Signal levers and Electric instruments have been concentrated.

The following new **Semaphore Signals** have been erected:—

An **Up Starting** Signal on the Up side of the Line, 20 yards from the end of the Up Platform.

A **Down Starting** Signal, on the Down side of the Line, 140 yards from the end of the Down Platform.

There will be no change made in the Stop or Distant Signals, either Down or Up, but the Up Distant Signal has an Electric Repeater fitted to it.

SOUTH MOLTON ROAD STATION.

A new Signal Box has been erected at the Up (East) end of the Down Platform, in which all the Signal levers and Electric instruments have been concentrated.

The following new **Semaphore Signals** have been erected:—

A **Down Starting** Signal on the Down side of the Line, 10 yards from the end of the Down Platform.

The Down Distant Signal has not been changed, but Electric Repeaters have been fitted to both the Up and Down Distant Signals.

An **Up Distant** Signal on the Up side of the Line, 850 yards from the Station, and 300 yards beyond (west of) the old Cross Bar and Disc Up Distant Signal, which it will replace.

An **Up Stop** Signal on the Up side of the Line just at the west side of the Over-bridge, and it will replace the old Disc and Cross Bar Signal.

An **Up Starting** Signal on the corner of the Goods Shed.

PORTSMOUTH ARMS STATION.

A new Signal Box has been erected about the centre of Down Platform in which all the Signal levers and Electric instruments have been concentrated.

The following new **Semaphore Signals** have been erected.

A **Down Distant** Signal on the Up side of the Line, close to the old Cross Bar and Disc Down Distant Signal, which it will replace.

A **Down Starting** Signal on Down side, 50 yards from the end of Down Platform.

An **Up Starting** Signal on Up side, 15 yards from the end of Up Platform.

UMBERLEIGH STATION.

A New Signal Box has been erected at the East end of Up Platform, in which all the Signal levers and Electric instruments have been concentrated.

The following new **Semaphore Signals** have been erected:—

A **Down Stop** Signal on the Up side of Line at Loop points, close to the old Cross Bar and Disc Signal, which it will replace.

A **Down Starting** Signal between the Main Line and Loop, 5 yards West of the Over-bridge.

An **Up Distant** Signal on Up side of the Line, 800 yards from the Station and 400 yards West of the old Cross Bar and Disc Up Distant Signal, which it will replace.

An **Up Starting** Signal on Up side of Line, 40 yards from the end of Up Platform.

The **Warning Signal** for Up Trains will be given from Umberleigh to Portsmouth Arms as soon as a Train is in sight.

IMPORTANT NOTICE.

When any Trains have to be crossed out of their regular course, by order from the authority in charge of the working of the Single Line, a copy of the Crossing Order must always be given to the Signalman on duty, who will file it for reference.

WATERLOO STATION,
September 29th, 1873.

BY ORDER.

between 1855 and the early 1870s when three lines were opened in as many years. First in 1872 came the South Western's Torrington Extension. Powers for this had been gained in an Act of 19th June 1865 but due to railway politics construction did not start until 1870. The line opened in two stages with the Bideford Junction to Bideford New line opening on 10th June 1872, the original terminus becoming a goods station, and on 18th July the Bideford New to Torrington section opened, both sections being standard gauge single track lines.

Second, in 1873, was the Devon & Somerset Railway. This railway gained its Act on 29th July 1864 for a single track broad gauge line from Taunton to Barnstaple, opening throughout on 1st November 1873. An independent company until 1901 it was leased first by the Bristol & Exeter and then the Great Western, it being converted to the standard gauge in May 1881. When the Tiverton & North Devon Railway opened on 1st August 1884, the two lines completed the line of the ill-fated North Devon Railway promoted in 1846. Initially, there was no connection with the South Western at Barnstaple, but in 1887 a loop line was opened to Barnstaple Junction to enable Great Western trains to run through to Ilfracombe.

This brings us to our third line, the Barnstaple & Ilfracombe Railway which gained its Act on 4th July 1870, after an earlier abortive scheme. The line was constructed by James Taylor, who contracted for several South Western lines, and was opened on 20th July 1874. The line was worked by the South Western and amalgamated with it in 1875. The Ilfracombe line started from a junction with the North Devon line at the station, which now became Barnstaple Junction.

Lt Col. Hutchinson made an inspection of the Barnstaple and Ilfracombe and reported on 15th July in lengthy terms. It was constructed as a light railway with a single track and passing places. At Barnstaple station (old) he required that points No. 10 should precede Nos 8 and 9. He returned on 30th September to re-inspect and recommended "Judging from the amount of interchange traffic that takes placed at Barnstaple (old) station and from the fact that passengers arriving by 'down' trains are allowed to cross the rails on their way to the town, it seems to me very desirable that a footbridge or subway should be constructed at the station."

Although not explicitly mentioned by Lt Col. Hutchinson it appears that the 'down' platform and the first West signal box at Barnstaple Junction were opened at his time. His recommendation for a footbridge was acted upon, the bridge carrying a stone inscribed "L&SWRy 1878". It may be noted here that on 1st March 1875 the South Western opened a new station at Chapleton, replacing an earlier wooden platform used in the 1850s.

Doubling the Track to Yeoford

As the South Western network was gradually extended onward to Torrington, Ilfracombe, and in particular Plymouth, traffic passing over the single track of the Exeter & Crediton was increasing to the extent that the line had to be doubled to accommodate it. A Bill was prepared and on 30th June 1874 parliament passed "An Act for the widening of the Exeter & Crediton Railway and for laying down an additional line of rails upon that railway, and the connecting of them with the Bristol &

SOUTH WESTERN RAILWAY. SPECIAL NOTICE. No. 1877.

STATION MASTERS are required personally to distribute this Notice to their Staff; and every person supplied with a copy is held responsible to read it carefully through, to note the general information it contains, and to act up to and obey the instructions particularly applicable to himself. No excuse of want of knowledge of these Special Arrangements can be admitted for any failure or neglect of duty.

TO THE OFFICERS AND SERVANTS OF THE SOUTH WESTERN RAILWAY, AND OTHER COMPANIES CONCERNED.

NORTH DEVON LINE.

Today on Monday, 12th _____ 1877, and following week days up to and including —

An extra Goods Train will run as follows:—

FROM EXETER TO FREMINGTON AND BACK.

STATIONS.	ARR.	DEP.	Crossing Instructions, &c.
	P.M.	P.M.	
Exeter (Queen St.)...	..	2 0	
„ (St. David's)..	2 5	2 7	
Cowley Junction, B.&E.	2,10		
„ „ S.W.	2 11		
St. Cyres ...	..	2 18	
Crediton ...	2 25	2 33	
Yeoford Junction ...	2 43	2 55	
Copplestone ..		3 5	
Morchard Road ...		3 10	
Lapford ...		3 20	
Eggesford ..	3 30	3 40	After No. 10 Up has arrived.
Southmolton Road ..	3 50	4 0	After No. 12 Up has arrived.
Portsmouth Arms ...		4 10	
Umberleigh ..	4 20	4 40	After No. 16 Up has arrived.
Chapelton ...		4 50	
Barnstaple ..	5 0	5 20	After No. 14 Up has arrived.
Fremington ...	5 30		

All wagons, loaded and empty, that can be got ready, are to be sent by this Train.

STATIONS.	ARR.	DEP.	Crossing Instructions, &c.
	P.M.	P.M.	
Fremington ...	..	5 45	After No. 15 Down has arrived.
Barnstaple ..	5 55	6 10	
Chapelton ..		6 20	
Umberleigh ..	6 30	6 35	
Portsmouth Arms ..	6 47	6 52	
South Molton Road ..	7 7	7 12	
Eggesford ..	7 22	7 45	After No. 17 Down has arrived.
Lapford ...	7 57	8 2	
Morchard Road ..	8 12	8 17	
Copplestone ..	8 25	8 35	To do shunting at Yeoford, but
Yeoford Junction ..	8 45	9 45	follow No. 19 up.
Crediton ..	9 55	10 0	
St. Cyres ..		10 18	
Cowley Junction, S. W.		10 25	
„ „ B. & E.		10 26	
Exeter (St. David's)..	10 30	10 35	
„ (Queen St.)..	10 40	...	

‡ This Train to take coal from Fremington, and any other Goods from any Station that can be got ready for it.

EXETER STATION. 17 J-77 12 3. 187

BY ORDER.

SOUTH WESTERN RAILWAY. SPECIAL NOTICE, No. , 187

NORTH DEVON LINE.

To the Officers and Servants of the South Western Railway, and other Companies concerned.

Instructions to Station Masters, Inspectors, Enginemen, Guards, Signalmen, Porters, Platelayers, Gatemen, and all concerned, as to

A SPECIAL TRAIN WITH PASSENGERS,

From YEOFORD to TORRINGTON.

On SATURDAY, _____ 187

STATIONS.	ARR.	PASS.	DEP.	Crossing Instructions, &c.
	P.M.		P.M.	
Yeoford Junction	..		2 40	
Copplestone	..		2 45	
Morchard Road ...	..		2 49	
Lapford	..		2 57	
Eggesford			3 3	No. 11 Down Goods to shunt at Eggesford for this Special.
South Molton Road ...			3 11	No. 10 Up Ordinary and this Special are to cross at Portsmouth Arms.
Portsmouth Arms ...	3 19		3 24	
Umberleigh	3 33		3 34	No. 12 Up Goods and this Special are to cross at Umberleigh.
Chapelton	3		3 38	
Barnstaple	3 45		3 49	
Fremington	..		3 54	
Instow	..		4 1	
Bideford Junction ...	..		4 5	
„ Station ...	..		4 8	No. 13 Up Ordinary is not to leave Torrington until this Special has arrived.
Torrington	4 20			

A Special Tail Board is to be attached to the 1.30 p.m. Down Train from Exeter.

You are requested to take such steps as will leave the line clear. Telegraphists must remain on duty while this Train is running.

BY ORDER.

EXETER.

_____ 187

South Western engineers replacing a bridge on the mixed gauge Exeter and Crediton line, illustrating the track described in Col. Hutchinson's 1875 report. The steam crane, carrying the plate "L&SWR Loco DEPᵀ EXETER No 2" is from Appleby Brothers, Leicester, and the locomotive Adams 0-6-0 goods No. 509 of 1885. The location appears to be a bridge over the river Yeo to the east of Crediton, with a signal in the background. 1886-1892 period.

Adrian Vaughan Collection

Exeter Railway, and for other purposes". The Act provided for an increase of £40,000 in capital with the Bristol & Exeter taking its share. Other clauses protected the interests of the Bristol & Exeter in various ways. The powers for doubling expired twelve months after the passing of the Act so progress had to be rapid. Although originally authorised and built as a double track line the Exeter & Crediton had been inspected and opened as a single track line so the earthworks were ready, but a number of bridges required rebuilding, and in particular the 1858 single track Cowley Bridge viaduct had to be converted to double track. At last, Col. Yolland's reports were having their effect here.

Doubling the Exeter & Crediton was just part of the South Western scheme to double its Plymouth line throughout as far as Lidford. It was carried out in stages, the first three involving the Exeter & Crediton line. First Col. Yolland reported on 11th November 1874.

"I have inspected the new Loop line rather more than 330 yards in length which the London & South Western Railway have constructed near the Junction of the Exeter & Crediton Branch with the Bristol & Exeter Railway at Cowley Bridge.

The company are engaged in doubling the line to Crediton and I am informed that they contemplate making a complete double line as far as Crediton, but the bridge over the River Exe close to the Cowley Bridge Junction is at the present time only for a single line but arrangements are being made for laying down a second line across the River Exe.

The object of this Loop line is to save the delay in working the single line between Exeter and Crediton. A signal box has now been established in the centre of the Loop line supplied with the requisite instruments for working the absolute block in both directions towards

Crediton on one side and to the Bristol & Exeter signal box close to Cowley Bridge Junction on the other side.

A staff must be supplied for the portion of single line between this new signal box and the Bristol & Exeter signal box.

The permanent way on this loop line is substantial but I have not been supplied with details of the works and it will be desirable that the whole length between the Bristol & Exeter Railway and Crediton should be included in the details when this second line is reported ready for inspection.

The points and signals are properly interlocked with each other, and I therefore recommend that the sanction of the Board of Trade be given for the use of this loop line as a temporary measure and until the second line is complete and fit for traffic".

Next, Lt Col. Hutchinson made an inspection and reported on 23rd February 1875.

"I have inspected the additional line of rails which has been laid down from the Cowley Loop to St Cyres station on the Exeter & Crediton branch of the London & South Western Railway. The additional line is about 2½ miles in length and the works inspected comprise the renewal of 6 timber bridges and the remodelling of the arrangments at St Cyres station.

The new permanent way consists of double headed wrought iron rails weighing 80 lbs per yard, secured on cast iron chairs weighing 35 lbs each. The rails are 24ft long and are fished at the joints. The sleepers measure 10ft (the gauge being mixed) by 10in by 5in, there being some beech and larch and the chairs being fastened to them by two spikes and hollow treenails, the ballast is gravel and broken stone and is stated to have a depth of 12in below the under surface of the sleepers.

One of the new underbridges has spans of 38½ ft each and consists of wrought iron main and cross girders with the central pier formed of wrought iron cylinders and the abutments of masonry. In the other five under bridges which have each a span of about 20ft wrought iron main and cross girders have been laid on stone abutments.

The bridges appear to possess sufficient theoretical and practical strength and the deflections were moderate. The overbridges were originally constructed for a double line and appear in sound condition. I made note of the following requirements a) The line should be slewed over the first overbridge so as to equal the space between the rails and abutments. b) In the renewal of a long length of post and rail fencing the fence posts should be placed on the inner instead of the outer side of the fence. c) At Cowley Loop the up home signal should be moved nearer the cabin. d) At St Cyres station the normal position of the points at the west of the station leading to the down line should be reversed, and the additional line now laid continuing from St Cyres to Crediton provided with extra points. e) The down siding points should be interlocked with the up home signal and the shunt siding slewed away from the main line. The down starting signal should be moved back to the fouling point of the siding. Nos 3 and 5 levers should be interlocked.

The engineer has promised to have these matters at once attended to and upon condition that this is done and that I have an opportunity of re-inspecting it at some convenient opportunity, I can recommend the Board of Trade to sanction the use of this additional line of rails."

When it came to the inspection of the widened viaduct and new double junction at Cowley Bridge the Board of Trade again sent Lt Col. Hutchinson, rather than allowing Col. Yolland to record a satisfactory conclusion to a long campaign. He reported on 2nd June 1875.

"I have inspected the additional line of rails between Cowley Bridge Junction and a point a short distance from it (whence to St Cyres station the additional line has been previously inspected) and from St Cyres to Crediton on the North Devon branch of the London & South Western Railway.

The permanent way employed is similar to that described in previous reports and the gauge is mixed. The additional line has involved the reconstruction or alteration of 4 under bridges and viaducts and of one over bridge - of these the most important is a viaduct of 6 openings (from 54ft to 63ft span) over the River Exe in which wrought iron continuing girders resting on cast iron columns have been employed: there is also another iron bridge of one span of 80ft, and the over-bridge had a span of 60ft: wrought iron girders resting on masonry having in both cases been employed. These bridges and viaducts appear to have been substantially constructed and to be standing well: they possess sufficient theoretical strength and in the case of those of 1 mile 5 chains, 5 miles 22 chains and 6 miles 36 chains the girders gave moderate deflections under a load of heavy engines. I was not however, able to test the deflections of those at 5miles 47 chains and 6 miles 62 chains as the old half of the bridges were under repair and the engineer could not run over both lines of rails I must therefore take a future opportunity of testing these girders.

A new junction has been laid in at Cowley Bridge where the North Devon line joins the Bristol & Exeter Railway and there are 2 new cabins at Crediton station in which the points and signals are all interlocked. I made note of the following requirements. 1) Cowley Bridge Junction. The down branch distant signal No. 3 to be an arm below the up home signal at Cowley Junction SW cabin, which up home signal should slot the down distant signal arms. No. 4 down branch home signal should be moved to the Crediton end of the bridge. The normal position of the facing point should be open for the North Devon line. Some alterations are required in the surrounding of the lever plate. 2) Crediton West Cabin. No. 2 lever is unnecessary. Siding signals are required for No. 11 facing points and down trains. 3) Crediton East Cabin. Nos 5 and 12 levers should interlock. No. 10 starting signal should precede Nos 7, 11 and 14. The down home signal should be moved nearer in. Two signals are required for Nos 5 and 7 points. No. 13 lever is unnecessary. 4) More ballast is required at places. 5) Transoms and ties are required to protect the gauge on those bridges where they have not been put in.

Upon condition that these requirements are complied with, that their completion is notified to the Board of Trade with a view to reinspection and that I have a further opportunity of testing the 3 bridges above alluded to I can recommend the opening of this additional line being sanctioned."

So the entire length of the Exeter & Crediton had been doubled with a month to spare, and the doubling was continued on the line to Plymouth, which included the North Devon line as far as their divergence at Colebrook. So on 29th May 1876 Col. Yolland reported that:

"I have re-inspected the 2nd line of rails which has been laid down by the London & South Western Railway Company between Crediton station and Yeoford Junction a length of somewhere about 4 miles.

The line is laid with steel rails weighing about 80 lbs per linear yard fixed in cast iron chairs that each weigh about 35 lbs in accordance with that now usually adopted by this railway company. The line is laid with the mixed gauge. There are a large number of bridges under the line, mostly of small span and constructed of stone abutments and wrought iron girders which are sufficiently strong theoretically and exhibited moderate deflections under a rolling load, all of which are standing well. New signal boxes have been provided both at Crediton station and Yeoford Junction; at the former the signal box has 19 levers in it of which 3 are spare ones - and at Yeoford Junction there are 18 levers of which 4 are spare ones, in the signal box. The large gates at the level crossing at Crediton station are now worked, and the wicket gates controlled, from the signal box and the up platform is to be lengthened and improved. The station buildings on the new down platform at Yeoford Junction are not quite complete but will be finished in a few days: and when this second line is opened for traffic a crossover road with facing points at Crediton is to be taken out. At several of the under bridges the company have yet to fix handrails at the sides and to lay down flooring between the handrails and the rails, but this work is steadily being proceeded with. An up home signal lever No. 6, for the main down line is to be removed at Yeoford Junction.

In some respects the work at Yeoford Junction is of a temporary nature, as the company intend to make a junction between the North Devon and the Devon and Cornwall lines about a mile further to the north, and thence to double the Devon & Cornwall line on to Bow station. I am also informed that the mixed gauge is to be taken up north of Crediton station as soon as the company's Bill, now before parliament, has received the Royal Assent.

SOUTH WESTERN RAILWAY.

Instruction, No. 135, 1877.

EXETER, CREDITON & NORTH DEVON LINE.

BROAD GAUGE GOODS TRAINS.

After the expiration of the present month of April, no Broad Gauge Trains will run on the North Devon Line below Crediton. All Goods for Broad Gauge Lines will thereafter be transferred either at Exeter or Crediton.

Any Goods intended to be handed to the Great Western Company at Crediton must be forwarded to that Station for transfer.

A Road Box Wagon, labelled "Crediton Transfer," must be attached to the 1.40 p.m. Up Goods Train for important Transfer Goods only. All rough Goods for transfer must be sent either by the 6.30 a.m. from Torrington or the 5.40 p.m. from Bideford.

ARCH^{D.} SCOTT,

General Manager.

Waterloo Bridge Station,
20th April, 1877.

SOUTH WESTERN RAILWAY.

INSTRUCTION No. 167, 1877.

NORTH DEVON AND LIDFORD LINES.

Instructions to Superintendents, Station Masters, Inspectors, Enginemen, Guards, Signalmen, Pointsmen, and all concerned,

INCLUDING THE SERVANTS OF OTHER COMPANIES

AS TO

THE OPENING OF THE NEW DOWN LINE BETWEEN YEOFORD AND BOW STATIONS AND OF THE NEW JUNCTION AT COLEFORD.

STATION MASTERS are required personally to distribute this Notice to their Staff; and every person supplied with a copy is held responsible to read it carefully through, to note the general information it contains, and to act up to and to obey the instructions particularly applicable to himself. No excuse of want of knowledge of these Special Arrangements can be admitted for any failure or neglect of duty.

On and after 1.0 p.m. on Wednesday, 16th May, the New Down Line between Yeoford and Bow will be open for traffic, thus forming a complete double line from Exeter to Bow. See revised pages of Service Book, Nos. 58 and 59.

At the same time the Train Staff and Ticket working between Yeoford and Bow will be abolished, and the Block system in operation between the same Stations will be in accordance with the Instructions for the working of Double Lines instead of Single Lines, as heretofore.

The section of Line between Yeoford and Copplestone will be worked under the Train Staff regulations for which separate Instructions will be issued.

All Down Trains going on to the Lidford Line, will, of course, run on the new Down Line from Yeoford to Bow.

All Down North Devon Trains will also run on the new *Down Line* from Yeoford Station to Coleford Junction, and thence on the Single Line towards Barnstaple as at present, but no North Devon Train, either Down or Up, must leave Yeoford or Copplestone Station without the Train Staff or Ticket, see special instructions.

2

SPECIAL INSTRUCTIONS

ELECTRIC SIGNALLING.

The Line between Yeoford Station and Coleford Junction will form one Double Line Section.

The Line between Coleford Junction and Bow Station, one Double Line Section, and

The Line between Coleford Junction and Copplestone Station, one Single Line Section.

In signalling Down Trains from Yeoford to Coleford Junction, those going over the Main or Lidford Line, will be distinguished from North Devon Trains by means of the Bell Signals.

The usual Signals will be given for Lidford Line Trains.

For North Devon Trains the Signals will be as follows:—

> Warning Signal. Four Beats given twice ● ● ● ● — ● ● ● ●
> Departure Signal, Four Beats   ● ● ● ●

The regulations applying to Trains when approaching Junctions as laid down in rule No. 284, page 126 of new Book of Instructions must be complied with, as also the Notice at foot of page 2 of this Instruction.

WHISTLE SIGNALS, COLEFORD JUNCTION.

The Whistle Signals for this Junction will be as follows:—

Down and Up Trains between Yeoford and Bow	**One Whistle.**
Down and Up Trains between Yeoford and Copplestone	**Two Whistles.**

ENGINE HEAD SIGNALS.

Down and Up Lidford Line Trains will carry by day two White Discs, one at the foot of the funnel and the other on the centre of the buffer beam, and by night, two Green Lights in the same position.

Down and Up North Devon Trains will carry by day two White Discs, one on each side, and by night, two lights in the same position, one Red and the other White, the white light being on the near side.

BY ORDER.

Waterloo Bridge Station,
12th May, 1877.

3

NEW AND ALTERED SIGNALS AT YEOFORD STATION.

The five-armed signal post on the Down Side of the Line, 140 yards west of the Signal Box will be removed.

A new Starting Signal for Down Trains has been provided by placing a Semaphore arm on the existing Up Stop Signal.

The existing Up Distant and Up Stop Signals, each of which have hitherto had two arms, one applying to Up Trains from Lidford, and the other to Up Trains from North Devon, will hereafter each have only one arm, which will apply to *all* Up Trains both from Lidford and North Devon.

All other Signals at Yeoford Station remain unaltered.

COLEFORD JUNCTION.

A new junction has been constructed about three-quarters of a mile West of Yeoford Station, and has been completed with a new Signal Box containing a Locking Frame and Electric Block Instruments, and this Junction is signalled in the following manner:—

A new Down Distant Signal has been erected on the Down Side of the Line, 800 yards east of the Junction points.

A new Down Bracket Stop Signal, with two arms has been erected on the Down Side of the Line, close to the Junction points, the left arm will control Down Trains going towards Bow, and the right arm will control Down Trains going towards Copplestone.

A new Up Distant Signal has been erected on the Up Side of the North Devon Line, 800 yards west of the Signal Box.

A new Up Stop Signal has been erected on the Down Side of the North Devon Line, near the Loop Points—the two lastnamed Signals will control Up North Devon Trains.

A new Up Distant Signal has been erected on the Down Side of the Lidford Line, 800 yards west of the Stop Signal.

A new Up Stop Signal has been erected on the Up Side of the Line 280 yards west of the Signal Box—the two last-named Signals will control Up Trains from the Lidford Line.

IMPORTANT NOTICE TO ENGINEMEN AND GUARDS.

As Trains may be expected to approach Coleford Junction from the direction of Bow and Copplestone at the same time, Drivers of all Up Trains are warned to stop at the Distant Signal on either Line when it is at danger, and after stopping, proceed slowly to the Stop Signal.

BOW STATION.

All out-door Signals at this Station remain unaltered.

I beg now to recommend that the sanction of the Board of Trade may be given for the opening of the second line of rails between Crediton station and Yeoford Junction for public traffic."

The End of the Broad Gauge from Crediton to Bideford

The Bill referred to by Col. Yolland was the London & South Western Railway (Exeter & Crediton and North Devon) which became an Act on receiving the Royal Assent on 13th July 1876. An important clause in the Act removed the obligation of the 1860 London & South Western Railway (Exeter & North Devon) Act for the retention of the broad gauge tracks from Crediton to Bideford. For many years there had only been one train daily on the broad gauge between these places and the South Western's surviving broad gauge rolling stock was now well past its prime. The broad gauge service between Crediton and Bideford was withdrawn after 30th April 1877, which enabled the South Western to save the £2,300 needed for mixed gauge tracks at Coleford Junction. Indeed the South Western might have used such powers a year earlier when doubling from Crediton to Yeoford on the mixed gauge. From 1877 goods in transit between the South Western's North Devon and Plymouth lines and the broad gauge system were transhipped at Crediton or Exeter.

Further Doubling to Plymouth

With the complication of mixed gauge track eliminated the doubling of the Plymouth line now continued and Col. Rich reported on 16th May 1877.

"I have inspected the doubling of the London & South Western Railway between Yeoford and Bow stations.

The whole length of line is about five miles. Three quarters of a mile of this consists of the old single lines from Yeoford to Okehampton and from Yeoford to Barnstaple. These two single lines are now to be used as a double line between Yeoford and Coleford Junction. Coleford Junction is formed as an ordinary double junction and a new second line of rails has been laid from Coleford Junction to Bow (a distance of 4¼ miles).

The permanent way consists of an 80 lbs steel rail which is fished and fixed with wooden keys in chairs that weigh about 35 lbs each. The chairs are fixed to transverse sleepers with two spikes driven inside wooden treenails. The sleepers are laid at an average distance of 3ft apart, those next to the joints being about 2ft 2in apart. The sleepers are 9ft long by 10ins by 5ins and there are nine of them to each 24feet length of rail. The gauge of the line is 4ft 8½in. The works consist of five masonry under bridges, three under bridges that have iron girders, and three masonry over bridges. These works were all constructed when the single line was originally formed to Okehampton. The line is well ballasted and well fenced.

At Yeoford signal cabin No. 18 lever required to be locked with No. 20 and in the cutting at the 186 mile post a severe slip has taken place which will require to be watched.

The engineer has promised to attend to these and I submit that the Board of Trade may sanction the opening of the second line of rails between Yeoford and Bow.

The South Western continued doubling its line to Plymouth, stage by stage, until on 22nd December 1879 the Meldon Junction to Lidford double track was opened, giving double track all the way from Exeter to Lidford. South Western trains were often delayed on the single track South Devon line from Lidford to Plymouth until 2nd June 1890 the new Plymouth, Devonport & South Western Junction Railway opened from Lidford giving the LSWR its own independent double track main line to Plymouth. West of Exeter the Plymouth line was now the main line, with that to North Devon a secondary line.

The South Western Purchase of the Exeter & Crediton

Returning to the London & South Western Railway (Exeter & Crediton and North Devon) Act 1876 there were also powers for the South Western to purchase the

---

SOUTH WESTERN RAILWAY.

INSTRUCTION No. 75, 1879.

NORTH DEVON LINE.

Instructions to Superintendents, Station Masters, Inspectors, Enginemen, Guards, Pointsmen and all concerned.

NEW AND ALTERED SIGNALS

At the undermentioned Stations on the North Devon Line, to be brought into use at 12.0 noon, on THURSDAY, 20th MARCH, 1879.

NEW SIGNALS HAVE BEEN ERECTED AS FOLLOWS:—

COPPLESTONE.

An Up Semaphore Stop Signal on the Up Side of the Line about 10 yards from the Loop Facing Points.

A Down Semaphore Stop Signal on the Down side of the Line about 10 yards from the Loop Facing Points.

SOUTH MOLTON ROAD.

A Down Semaphore Stop Signal on the Down Side of the Line about 10 yards from the Loop Facing Points.

A Down Distant Semaphore Signal on the Up Side of the Line about 800 yards from the Loop Facing Points.

PORTSMOUTH ARMS.

An Up Semaphore Stop Signal on the Up Side of the Line about 10 yards from the Loop Facing Points.

A Down Semaphore Stop Signal on the Up Side of the Line about 10 yards from the Loop Facing Points.

UMBERLEIGH.

A Down Semaphore Distant Signal on the Down Side of the Line 800 yards from the Loop Facing Points.

INSTOW.

An Up Semaphore Stop Signal on the Up Side of the Line about 10 yards from the Loop Facing Points.

An Up Distant Semaphore Signal on the Up Side of the Line 800 yards from the Loop Facing Points.

The above mentioned Signals will replace Old Disc and Cross-bar Signals hitherto in use, which will be taken down.

BY ORDER.

Waterloo Bridge Station,
15th March, 1879.

Waterlow and Sons Limited, Printers, London Wall, London.

Exeter & Crediton, although the Act also stated that the broad gauge should be retained until the South Devon could take 'narrow' gauge traffic between Exeter and Plymouth. However, the situation was complicated by the lease of the Bristol & Exeter to the Great Western on 1st January 1876 and their amalgamation on 1st August 1876.

The second South Western lease of the Exeter & Crediton ended on 31st January 1876 and it was renewed again during protracted negotiations. Eventually, after arbitration, the purchase price of the company was valued at £217,687 but since the South Western owned three fifths of the shares it actually paid the Great Western £81,256, the transfer being completed on 26th June 1879. The last meeting of the proprietors of the Exeter & Crediton Railway Company was held at Waterloo station on 20th February 1879, with Capt. J. G. Johnson in the chair. The rent received from the South Western for the second half of 1878 was £3,812 15s 2d, and a 5 per cent

dividend was paid on ordinary shares. Thus ended, on a prosperous note, the 34 years existence of this little company which had had such an eventful early life.

The Last Years of the Broad Gauge

From 1877 the only broad gauge trains to be seen on the North Devon line were the occasional Great Western goods trains between Exeter and Crediton. Both stations were used for the transhipment of goods between 'narrow' gauge and broad gauge wagons but by now the Great Western was busy converting its whole system to the standard gauge. The end came over the weekend of 20th - 23rd May 1892, assisted in part by the South Western. On the night of Sunday 22nd May the Great Western 'narrow' gauge 'down' night mail from Paddington to Cornwall ran along the North Devon line to Coleford Junction on its way to Plymouth. Great Western standard gauge goods trains continued to run between Exeter and Crediton until 1903.

Crediton station in 1880 with Beattie 2-4-0WT No. 181 on a 'down' train. The locomotive water column and 'up' siding were later removed and the platforms extended.

LGRP

Chapter 5
The Later South Western Period

Doubling to Copplestone

Having doubled its Plymouth line the South Western now regarded its North Devon line as commencing at Coleford Junction, but in the 1880s began to double portions of the line, starting with the short section from Coleford Junction to Copplestone. It may have been short in length but included the deep cutting at the summit of the line. Col. Rich made his inspection and reported on 3rd November 1883.

"I have inspected the second line of rails between Yeoford Junction and Copplestone station on the London & South Western Railway.

The new section is about 1¾ miles long. The permanant way is of the London and South Western pattern with the keys outside the rails. The railway is well fenced. The works consist of two new under bridges that have wrought iron girders and there are two of brick and stone, four over bridges, and a viaduct of girders of 30ft span. These works are of sufficient strength and are in good order. The following works are required. Some ballast at Yeoford Junction and on the way to Copplestone. There is a turnout at Copplestone station and a hollow in the platform belonging to the new line in consequence of the broad gauge rails having been removed. The line of rails should be made straight through the station and the platform should be widened. A hollow about the centre of both up and down line platforms which appears to have been made to allow the passengers to step on to the rails and cross the railway should be filled up and made level with the other parts of platforms, and a boarded level crossing for the passengers should be constructed at the west end of the station. The water column at the west end of the down platform should be fenced off and one of the accommodation gates about the centre of the new station which stands far back from the rails should have wooden fences from the gates to within 4 feet of the rails to prevent cattle or sheep running along the railway when they are required to be drawn across the lines.

I submit that the second line of rails from Yeoford to Copplestone may be opened for passenger traffic subject to the above named requirements being attended to at once."

Later, on 8th April 1889, Maj. Gen. Hutchinson inspected and approved a new crossover at Coleford Junction, mentioning that the signal box now contained eleven working levers and one spare lever.

SOUTH WESTERN RAILWAY. | INSTRUCTION No. 378, 1883.

NORTH DEVON AND LIDFORD LINES.

Instructions to Superintendents, Station Masters, Inspectors, Enginemen, Guards, Signalmen, Pointsmen and all concerned,

AS TO

THE OPENING OF THE NEW DOWN LINE BETWEEN COLEFORD JUNCTION & COPPLESTONE STATION.

STATION MASTERS are required personally to distribute this Notice to their Staff; and every person supplied with a copy is held responsible to read it carefully through, to note the general information it contains, and to act up to and to obey the instructions particularly applicable to himself. No excuse of want of knowledge of these Special Arrangements can be admitted for any failure or neglect of duty.

On and after 6.0 p.m. on Sunday, 4th November, the New Down Line between Coleford Junction and Copplestone, will be open for Traffic, thus forming a Double Line Junction at Coleford Junction and a complete Double Line from Exeter to Copplestone.

At the same time the Train Staff and Ticket Working between Yeoford and Copplestone will be abolished, and the Block System in operation between Coleford Junction and Copplestone Station will be in accordance with the Instructions for the working of Double Lines instead of Single Lines as heretofore.

All Down Trains going to Copplestone, will, of course, run on the New Down Line from Coleford Junction to Copplestone.

All Up Trains from Copplestone will run on the present Single Line, which will be the Up Line from Copplestone Station to Coleford Junction.

The Out-door Signals at Coleford Junction and Copplestone Station will remain unaltered.

WATERLOO STATION,   **BY ORDER.**
3rd November, 1883.

H. BESLEY & SON, Printers, "Devonshire Office," 89, South Street, Exeter.

Railway Timetables

These North Devon railway timetables were published in the *North Devon Journal* of 2nd June 1887. The railway developments at this time included services between North Devon and Plymouth, by changing at Yeoford, and the newly instituted service from the GWR to Ilfracombe over the new Barnstaple Junction railway.

RAILWAY TIME TABLES.—JUNE. LONDON AND SOUTH WESTERN RAILWAY

NORTH DEVON TO EXETER AND LONDON

UP TRAINS.—WEEK DAYS.

STATIONS.	Exp. 1 2 3	1 2 3	1 2 3	1 2 3	Fast. 1 2 3	1 2 3	Fast. 1 2 3	1 2 3	1 2 3	SUNDAYS 1 2 3	1 2 3	1 2 3
	1 2 3 a.m.	a.m.	a.m.	a.m.	a.m.	p.m	p.m.	p m	p.m.	a.m.	p.m	p.m.
Torrington......depar.	7 25	7 25	8 30	10 20	10 20	2 40	4 35	6 40	7 40	7 10	1 45	7 40
Bideford .... ,,	7 37	7 37	8 44	10 34	10 34	2 53	4 47	6 52	7 52	7 25	2 0	7 52
Instow .... ,,	7 43	7 43	8 51	10 40	10 40	2 59	4 56	6 58	7 58	7 31	2 6	7 58
Fremington .... ,,	7 51	7 51	8 58	10 48	10 48	3 7	5 3	7 5	8 5	7 39	2 14	8 5
Ilfracombe ...... ,,	7 10	7 10		10 10	10 10	2 25	3 54	—	7 20	—	—	—
Barnstaple ...... ,,	8 3	8 3	9 5	11 3	11 12	3 21	5 18	7 12	8 17	7 50	2 20	8 17
Chappletown .... ,,	8 12	8 12		11 22		5 32		8 26	8 5			8 26
Umberleigh .... ,,	8 18	8 18		11 28	3 33	5 38		8 32	8 10			8 32
Portsmouth Arms ,,	8 27	8 27		11 37	T	5 48		8 42	8 20			8 42
Southmolton Road ,,	8 36	8 36		11 44	3 47	5 57		8 51	8 30			8 51
Eggesford .... ,,	8 45	8 45		11 55	3 55	6 6		9 0	8 42			9 0
Lapford .... ,,	8 54	8 54		12 1	4 3	6 15		9 9	8 55			9 9
Morchard Road .. ,,	9 1	9 1		12 7		6 21		9 15	9 4			9 15
Copplestone .... ,,	9 6	9 6		12 12	4 11	6 26		9 20	9 14			9 20
Yeoford Junction ,,	9 14	9 14		12 18	4 18	6 34		9 26	9 25			9 26
Crediton .... ,,	9 22	9 40		12 25	4 28	—		9 31	9 37			9 34
St. Cyres .... ,,	9 29			12 40	4 35			9 41	9 46			9 41
Exeter, St. David's, arr.	9 35	9 53		12 15 12 50	4 44	6 55		9 50	9 55			9 50
Exeter, Queen-st., depar	10 5	10 15		12 24 12 55	4 44			9 57	10 0			9 57
Yeovil .... arr.	11 28	12 10		2 2	2 44	6 40		—	4 10			—
Salisbury .... ,,	12 23	1 36		3 12	3 52	7 44		—	5 34			—
London .... ,,	2 34	4 43		5 20	6 12	10 9		—	8 2			—

T Stops on Fridays

LONDON TO EXETER AND NORTH DEVON

DOWN TRAINS—WEEK DAYS.

STATIONS.	1 2 3 a.m.	1 2 3 a.m.	1 2 3 a m	1 2 3 a.m.	1 2 3 a.m.	1 2 3 a.m.	Fast 1 2 3	1 2 3	1 2 3 p.m.	Exp 1 2 3	1 2 3	1 2 3 p.m.	1 2 3	SUN. 1 2 3 a.m.
London ....depar.	—					6 25	9 0	11 0	11 0	11 45	3 0	0 0		11 9
Salisbury .... ,,	—				8 20	10 0	11 17	1 5	1 15	3 0	4 7	7 12		2 0
Yeovil Junction.. ,,	—			6 40	9 45	11 20	12 10	1 40	2 10	4 20	5 15	8 15		3 50
Exeter, Queen-st., ,,	—		9 32	12 0	130	1 48	3 25	4 15	6 50	6 55	10 5			6 40
Exeter, St. David's, ,,	—		9 38	12 5	135	154	3 33	4 21	6 55	7 0	10 19			6 45
St. Cyres .... ,,	3 0		9 46	—	144	—	—	4 30	—	7 10	10 19			6 55
Crediton .... ,,	3 10		9 52	—	151	2 8	—	4 36	7 16	7 16	10 25			7 1
Yeoford Junction ,,	3 25		10 2	12 25	2 20	2 20	—	4 45	7 25	7 25	10 33			7 10
Copplestone .... ,,	3 50		10 8	12 34	2 26	2 26	—	4 55	7 32	7 32				7 22
Morchard Road .. ,,	3 59		10 12	12 35	2 30	2 30	—	4 19	7 36	7 36				7 25
Lapford .... ,,	4 3		10 17	12 44	2 35		4 3	5 5	7 43	7 43				7 29
Eggesford .... ,,	4 17	8 55	10 25	12 52	2 41	2 44	4 11	5 13	7 52	7 52				7 35
Southmolton Road ,,	4 20	9 6	10 33	1 0	2 52	2 52	4 18	5 21	8 0	8 0				7 43
Portsmouth Arms ,,		9 17	10 40	1 7	2 59	2 59		5 29	7 7	7 7				7 50
Umberleigh...... ,,		9 25	10 48	1 15	3 8	3 8		5 35	8 17	8 17				7 54
Chapplctown .... ,,		9 30	10 53	1 20	3 13	3 13		5 44	8 26	8 26				8 0
Barnstaple ...... arr	4 57	9 40	11 2	1 30	3 21	3 21	4 45	5 52	8 35	8 35		1 2 3	8 6	
Barnstaple ....depar.	5 10		9 20	11 8	1 34	3 26	3 26	4 45	5 55	8 37		p.n	8 16	
Ilfracombe ...... arr.			12 5	2 22	4 15	4 15	5 32	6 47	7 17			— 2 40	8 40	
Fremington ....depar.	5 25		9 25	11 15	1 40	3 32	3 32		6 2	8 43			2 47	8 47
Instow .... ,,	5 33		9 33	11 24	1 47	3 39	3 39	4 57	6 9	8 50			2 57	8 53
Bideford .... ,,	5 43		9 39	11 31	1 55	3 46	3 46	5 3	6 16	8 57			3 6	8 42
Torrington ...... arr.	6 0		9 51	11 43	2 7	4 0	4 0	5 15	6 29	9 9	9		3 20	8 55

All Trains without exception are 1st, 2nd, and 3rd class

Barnstaple Junction station from Sticklepath Hill in South Western days with the single 'down' platform, and both lines signalled for reversible working. Behind and to the left is the extensive Bartlett Bayliss & Co. timber yard with tall chimney, and beyond it the Shapland & Petters factory and the old 1848 warehouse by now converted into a slaughterhouse. The variety of the wagons in the yard includes vans, cattle trucks and a MR open wagon.

Lens of Sutton

The Barnstaple Junction Railway

The Devon & Somerset Railway, worked by the Great Western and now converted to standard gauge had ambitions to reach Ilfracombe by its own independent route, and promoted a Bill for such a line in 1884.

However, wiser councils prevailed, the Bill was dropped, and the South Western and Great Western agreed to a junction line between their stations at Barnstaple, and for GWR trains or coaches to run through to Ilfracombe. The Great Western Act of 31st July 1885 authorised the

Barnstaple Junction West signal box 1907. Built in 1874 for the opening of the Ilfracombe branch it was replaced by a shorter structure in 1924. The bridges, which carry Sticklepath Road over the two lines, are numbered 97 (in the Coleford Junction to Torrington sequence) and 1 (of the Ilfracombe branch). *F. E. Box courtesy National Railway Museum*

junction line to run for 1 mile 27 chains between the two stations. Work started in December 1885 and the earthworks were constructed for a line to enable trains to run direct between Taunton and Barnstaple Junction, but there was some delay when it was decided to change the route at the eastern end to run into the Great Western station, thus involving a reversal for through traffic. Col. Rich made his inspection in May 1887 and inter alia, reported that the points and signals at the junctions were interlocked and worked from raised cabins. The Barnstaple Junction East signal box may well date from this time. The loop line opened on 1st June 1887, with GWR coaches running through to Ilfracombe. Initially, the Great Western stipulated that the through carriages should be reserved for passengers going to Ilfracombe branch only and that passengers proceeding to other South Western stations should not be allowed to use them. These unfortunate passengers had to continue using the "Galloper" omnibus service between the two stations until the ruling was abolished.

On 8th June 1889 a new siding with the 'up' and 'down' loop lines at Barnstaple Junction was inspected. The connections and signals were worked by existing levers in the junction signal cabin, which then contained 42 working levers and four spare ones. The inspecting officer required three minor changes in signals and interlocking.

Doubling from Umberleigh to Barnstaple

From 1883 the North Devon line was double track from Cowley Bridge to Copplestone and single thence to Barnstaple. Traffic was steadily increasing and after 1887 the South Western and Great Western competed for the London to Ilfracombe traffic, particularly in the summer season. Accordingly, the South Western doubled the Ilfracombe branch between Pottington and Ilfracombe in three stages between 1889 and 1891, and then turned its attention to the single track between Copplestone and Barnstaple. One might have expected the company to extend the existing double line on from Copplestone to Morchard Road and Lapford, but they chose instead the northern end of the line between Umberleigh and Barnstaple. As we saw in Chapter 2, most of the earthworks on this section had been constructed for a double track by William Thorne back in 1847 so that works included many bridges, in particular the long Pill Bridge south of Barnstaple. The double track was inspected and opened in two stages, Col. Rich making his first visit on 14th October 1890.

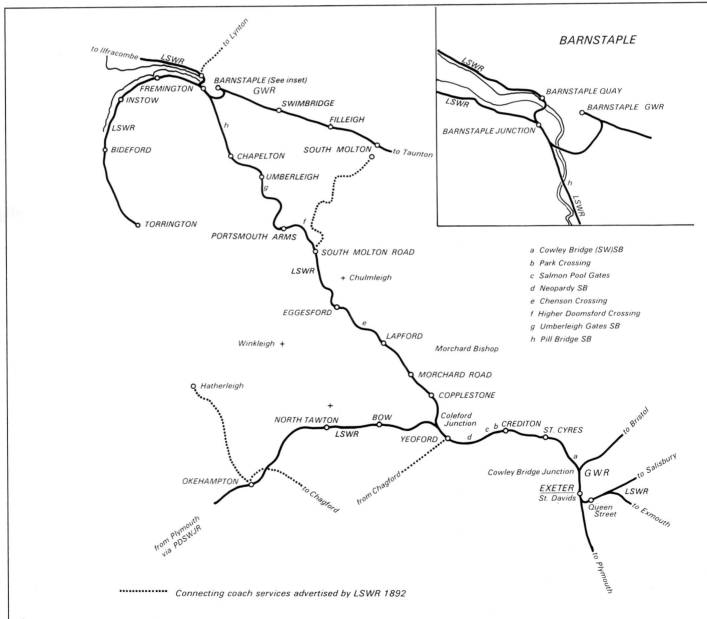

a Cowley Bridge (SW)SB
b Park Crossing
c Salmon Pool Gates
d Neopardy SB
e Chenson Crossing
f Higher Doomsford Crossing
g Umberleigh Gates SB
h Pill Bridge SB

·········· Connecting coach services advertised by LSWR 1892

NORTH DEVON RAILWAY LINES 1892

MAP 2

SOUTH WESTERN RAILWAY.

INSTRUCTION No. 115, 1890.

NORTH DEVON LINE.

Opening of a Double Line

BETWEEN

UMBERLEIGH STATION

AND

PILL BRIDGE SIGNAL BOX,

Situated about three-quarters of a mile from Barnstaple.

AT 3.0 P.M.

On SUNDAY, 19th October, 1890.

Instructions to Superintendents, Station Masters, Inspectors, Enginemen, Guards, Signalmen, and all others concerned,

AS TO THE

ERECTION OF NEW SIGNAL BOXES & SIGNALS

AT

UMBERLEIGH GATES, UMBERLEIGH, & CHAPELTON STATIONS,

AND THE

Opening of a New Block Signalling Section with New Out-door Signals complete at

PILL BRIDGE SIGNAL BOX, BARNSTAPLE,

Between Chapelton and Barnstaple Junction Stations.

Also the Opening of a Double Line of Rails

BETWEEN

UMBERLEIGH STATION AND PILL BRIDGE SIGNAL BOX,

AND

NEW AND ALTERED SIGNALS

in connection with the above.

Revised pages Nos. 98, 99, 100, 101, 102 and 103 of the Service Book containing the NORTH DEVON LINE Train Service, have been issued.

"I have inspected the new second line of rails between Umberleigh and Pill Bridge on the Barnstaple branch of the London and South Western Railway.

The new line is laid with a 6ft interval between it and the original single line of rails. It is 6 miles and 4 chains long. The permanent way consists of the London and South Western Railway standard pattern and is in good order. There is a temporary junction at Pill Bridge which is worked by a frame in which there are seven working levers which are interlocked. The points and signals at the intermediate station at Chapleton are worked from a new cabin, which contains 21 working and two spare levers, which are interlocked, and there is a new cabin at Umberleigh station, which contains 25 working and six spare levers which are interlocked. The works consist of four masonry and brick and one iron and wood over bridges. Fifteen bridges under the railway are constructed with masonry abutments which support wrought iron plates. Two of the over bridges have six openings and two of the under bridges have five openings and there are four viaducts. These are constructed with wrought iron girders carried on stone abutments and piers and consist of thirteen openings. The widest span is about 37 feet. The railway is well fenced and well ballasted with broken stone.

The engineer has promised to attend to the following small detail points. 1st) Connecting the points and signals to the levers in the new cabin. 2nd) To put guide fences for the cattle crossings from the accommodation gates to a place 4ft 6in from the rails where the gates are more than 12 feet from the rails. 3rd) To draw the rails so that there shall not be more than 2½ins between the footboard of the widest carriages to be used on the railway and the edge of the platform at the place where the platform is nearest to the coach.

2

The New Double Line commences at Umberleigh Station and ends at Pill Bridge Signal Box, which is situated three-quarters of a mile East of Barnstaple Junction Station, and about 200 yards East of the Barnstaple Pill Bridge.

The Line from Pill Bridge Signal Box to Barnstaple Junction Station will continue to be a Single Line and will be worked on the Train Staff System, in one section, and all Trains must slacken at Pill Bridge for Train Staff purposes.

The Block System in operation between Umberleigh and Chapelton, and Chapelton and Pill Bridge Signal Box will be in accordance with the Instructions for working of Double Lines of Rails (see revised instructions dated January 5th, 1885) instead of Single Lines as heretofore.

The Block System between Pill Bridge and Barnstaple Junction will be the Single Line Block System now in operation between Chapelton and Barnstaple Junction Stations.

Separate instructions as to the working of the Train Staff System between Pill Bridge and Barnstaple Junction Stations will be issued.

UMBERLEIGH GATES LEVEL CROSSING.

A **New Signal Box** has been erected on the **Up** side of the Line at the Level Crossing, 470 yards east of the Station Signal Box, and from which the Level Crossing Gates, the Umberleigh Station Up Siding Signal Box, and the Left-hand Arm of the Two-armed Bracket Signal described in the next paragraph, will be worked.

A **Two-armed Bracket Signal** on the **Up Line** side, 100 yards from the Umberleigh Gates Signal Box. The **Left hand** or lower arm will be the **Up Siding** at Umberleigh Station Starting Signal, and the **Right hand** or higher Arm will be the **Up Advance Starting Signal** from Umberleigh Station. The Siding Signal will be worked from Umberleigh Gates, and slotted from Umberleigh Station Signal Box.

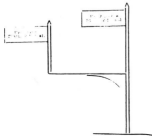

As seen by Drivers of Up Trains

3

UMBERLEIGH STATION

A **New Signal Box** has been erected at the centre of the Up platform and the following Signals will be worked therefrom:

A **Down Distant Signal** on the Down side, 800 yards from the Umberleigh Gates Down Stop Signal.

A **Down Stop Signal** for Umberleigh Gates on the Down side, 11 yards east of the Umberleigh Gates Level Crossing and 481 yards from the Umberleigh Station Signal Box.

A **Down Stop Signal** for Umberleigh Station on the Down side, 219 yards from Umberleigh Station Signal Box.

A **Down Starting Signal** between the Main Lines 60 yards west of the Signal Box.

A **Down Advance Starting Signal** on the Down side 170 yards from the Down Starting Signal.

An **Up Distant Signal** on the Up side 800 yards from the Up Stop Signal.

An **Up Stop Signal** on the Up side 162 yards from the Signal Box.

An **Up Starting Signal** on the Up side 112 yards from the Signal Box.

The existing **Down Starting Signal** will be removed.

CHAPELTON STATION

A **New Signal Box** has been erected in the centre of the Down Platform and the following Signals will be worked therefrom :

A **Down Distant Signal** on the Up side 800 yards from the Down Stop Signal.

A **Down Stop Signal** on the Down side, 184 yards from the Signal Box.

A **Down Starting Signal** on the Down side, 115 yards from the Signal Box.

A **Down Advance Starting Signal** on the Down side, 285 yards from the Down Starting Signal.

An Up Distant Signal on the Up side, 800 yards from the Up Stop Signal.

An **Up Stop Signal** on the Down side, 272 yards from the Signal Box.

An **Up Starting Signal** on the Up side, 26 yards from the Signal Box.

An **Advance Up Starting Signal** on the Up side 313 yards from the Up Starting Signal.

A **Ground Lever Frame** has been fixed on the **Up Line** side at the **West end of the Up Platform** from which the Level Crossing Gates at the West end of the Station will be interlocked and worked in conjunction with the Station Signals.

PILL BRIDGE SIGNAL BOX.

A **New Signal Box** has been erected on the Down Line side, 207 yards the Pill Bridge and the following Signals will be worked therefrom :

a **Distant Signal** on the Down side, 800 yards from the Stop

a **Stop Signal** on the Down side, 200 yards from the Down Starting

A **Starting Signal** on the Down side, 20 yards from the Signal Box.

a **Distant Signal** on the Up side, 800 yards from the Up Stop Signal.

a **Stop Signal** on the Up side, 150 yards from the Signal Box.

A **Starting Signal** on the Up side, 200 yards from the Signal Box.

Subject to these things done I can recommend the Board of Trade to sanction the opening of the second line of rails from Umberleigh to Pill Bridge near Barnstaple".

The South Western Railway quickly attended to these details and the double track was opened according to Instruction No. 115 of 1890 on Sunday 19th October at 3pm. New signal boxes were opened at Umberleigh Gates, Umberleigh, Chapleton and Pill Bridge, the original 1873 signal box at Umberleigh closing at this time.

Meanwhile, work on Pill Bridge continued and on 26th April Maj. Gen Hutchinson inspected and approved new connections at Barnstaple Junction. The following year, Maj. Mandarin inspected the new double track and reported on 6th August 1891.

"I have inspected the widening between Pill Bridge and Barnstaple Junction on the North Devon branch of the L&SW Railway.

The additional line of rails is 75 chains in length, and the permanent way is of the standard L&SW pattern with 82 lbs double headed steel rails. The ballast is of broken stone. The curves and gradient are similar to those on the old single line and the old fences are still used. The line is on an embankment throughout. The superstructures of three small underbridges have been renewed, wrought iron trough flooring having been substituted for the old cast iron girders and the abutments of masonry have been extended. A viaduct over the River Taw at Pill Bridge has been rebuilt, some of the cylindrical piers having been retained. This structure has two spans of 87 feet and one 84 feet, with wrought iron lattice centre and side girders and wrought iron cross girders. The abutments are of masonry and the piers of cast iron cylinders filled with concrete and brickwork. These cylinders are founded upon rock, and are 8ft in diameter at the base and of 6ft diameter above the level of the water. One of the cylinders is very slightly out of plumb, but is quite stable. The whole of the works have been well carried out and the wrought iron girders have ample theoretical strength and were very stiff under test. There are no new stations, no level crossings of public roads and no tunnels on the line.

The signalling at Barnstaple Junction has been slightly altered, and a down siding and several disc signals have been added. The cabin contains 43 working levers, correctly interlocked and 4 spare levers. There is also a block signal cabin at Pill Bridge containing 7 levers of which one is spare. The North Devon branch is now double from Exeter to Copplestone, single from Copplestone to Umberleigh and double from Umberleigh to Barnstaple Junction. The only requirements upon this last piece of doubling which I noted was that outside railguards should be fixed on the new viaduct, and the timber flooring should be covered with gravel so as to protect it from any risk of fire.

Subject to the satisfaction of these requirements I can recommend that the use of the additional line of rails from Pill Bridge to Barnstaple Junction may be sanctioned".

According to South Western Railway Instruction No. 133 of 1891 this line was opened on Monday 27th July 1891.

The Early Life of Ernie Bevin
The quiet station at Copplestone hardly appears to be a hotbed of militant trade unionism and left wing politics, but for five years a boy destined to become one of the leading figures in the labour movement was brought up in the home of a railwayman. Ernest Bevin was orphaned in 1889 at the age of eight on the death of his mother and was brought up by his married half-sister and her husband, Mary and George Pope. George Pope worked for the South Western at Morchard Road and moved to

Crediton station, looking west about 1910, showing many standard South Western fittings and the platforms now extended as far as the level crossing.

Lens of Sutton

Crediton Station

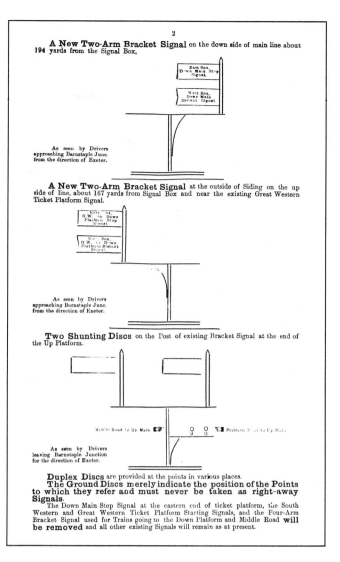

SOUTH WESTERN RAILWAY.

INSTRUCTION No. 133, 1891.

NORTH DEVON LINE.

Instructions to Superintendents, Station Masters, Inspectors, Enginemen, Guards, Signalmen, and all others concerned,

AS TO THE OPENING OF THE

NEW DOWN LINE

Between Pill Bridge Signal Box and Barnstaple Junction Station,

AND

NEW AND ALTERED SIGNALS

AT

BARNSTAPLE JUNCTION STATION

IN CONNECTION THEREWITH.

OPENING OF THE DOUBLE LINE

BETWEEN PILL BRIDGE SIGNAL BOX AND BARNSTAPLE JUNCTION STATION.

On and after **Monday, 27th July, 1891** (commencing with the first Train in the morning), **the new Down Line** between **Pill Bridge Signal Box and Barnstaple Junction Station** will be open for Traffic, thus completing a **Double Line from Umberleigh to Barnstaple Junction Station.**

At the same time, the Train Staff and Ticket working between Pill Bridge Signal Box and Barnstaple Junction Station will be abolished, and the Block System in operation between the same Section will be in accordance with the Instructions for the working of Double Lines (see Revised Instructions, dated November, 1890) instead of Single Lines, as heretofore.

For Particulars of Alterations in Train Service see revised pages, 98, 99, 100, 101, 102 and 103 of the Main Line Service Book.

2

A New Two-Arm Bracket Signal on the down side of main line about 194 yards from the Signal Box,

As seen by Drivers approaching Barnstaple Junc. from the direction of Exeter.

A New Two-Arm Bracket Signal at the outside of Siding on the up side of line, about 167 yards from Signal Box and near the existing Great Western Ticket Platform Signal.

As seen by Drivers approaching Barnstaple Junc. from the direction of Exeter.

Two Shunting Discs on the Post of existing Bracket Signal at the end of the Up Platform.

As seen by Drivers leaving Barnstaple Junction for the direction of Exeter.

Duplex Discs are provided at the points in various places.

The Ground Discs merely indicate the position of the Points to which they refer and must never be taken as right-away Signals.

The Down Main Stop Signal at the eastern end of ticket platform, the South Western and Great Western Ticket Platform Starting Signals, and the Four-Arm Bracket Signal used for Trains going to the Down Platform and Middle Road **will be removed** and all other existing Signals will remain as at present.

Copplestone station, looking north about 1910, showing the offset platforms, water tower and signal box with the goods yard in the background.

Lens of Sutton

Copplestone in 1889, where he and his family lived in a house called "Tiddly Winks", overlooking the station. George Pope's position on the South Western is not known, but platelayers and signalmen were the most numerous posts. At Copplestone, Ernest Bevin attended Colebrook village school and then another school in Crediton, travelling by train, until he was eleven when he left to take a job on a local farm at Chaffcombe for 6d (2½p) a week, a pitifully small wage even at that time. After taking a second job on another farm, Ernie left Copplestone to join his brother Jack in Bristol, at the age of 13 years. He became a full time official of the dockers union at the age of 30 and by 1922 had become the first General Secretary of the newly formed Transport and General Workers Union. Later he became a Labour MP and was Foreign Secretary in the 1945 Labour Government – a long way from his early life at Copplestone.

Signalling Developments

We have seen in Chapter 4 the installation of semaphore signals and signal boxes along the North Devon line in the period 1873-7, but another signal box was opened, probably in the 1880s, at Neopardy. This broke the section of almost four miles between Crediton West and Yeoford, where a small 'down' yard had been built for the re-marshalling of goods trains. The station was extended with a second 'down' platform. At this time, the section between Cowley Bridge Junction and Coleford Junction was becoming increasingly busy with through traffic to Plymouth and the newly opened lines to North Cornwall.

The South Western Railway Instruction No. 163 of 1890 gave details of the closure of certain additional signal boxes on Sundays on and after 3rd January 1891. Through switches had been fitted as an economy measure following an increase in signalmens' wages. Signal boxes affected included St Cyres, Neopardy, Morchard Road, Lapford, South Molton Road, Portsmouth Arms and Chapelton. It would appear from this instruction that through switches had already been fitted at Cowley Bridge (S.W.) and Crediton East. Operation was quite straightforward on the double track sections, but at the passing stations on the single line the station master was responsible for the points and signals being reversed and put right for the passing of each train. How long this system continued on the single line section is not known, but it became common practice on double track sections, for example at Chapelton.

South Western Railway Instruction No. 78 of 1892 concerned the working of the single line between Copplestone and Umberleigh. The existing crossing order system was replaced on Sunday 26th June 1892 by Tyers No. 3 train tablet apparatus, which remained in use for some 70 years.

It is not known when Pill Bridge signal box was taken out of use, but the last known reference to it was in Maj. Mandarin's report of 1891. Likewise, Umberleigh Gates signal box was reduced to a ground frame at some stage, date unknown.

Fast trains between Copplestone and Umberleigh were inevitably delayed by the need to slow down at each station to exchange tablets with the signalmen. One solution to this problem was the provision of mechanical apparatus to enable this exchange to take place at higher speeds. The Railway Magazine of 1905 reported that such mechanical apparatus had been installed at South Molton Road and Portsmouth Arms stations, together with two Adams A12 class locomotives. In fact, four of these locomotives had been fitted with this apparatus in March and April 1903 for working over the Somerset & Dorset

Lapford station, looking north about 1910, with an Adams 460 class 4-4-0 on a train including LSWR 56ft corridor coaches forming an 'up' working. The signalman on the right holds the single line token for the section to Morchard Road, which he will hand to the driver.

Collection A. R. Kingdom

South Molton Road station, looking north about 1905, with platelayers working on the track. The Fortescue Arms advertises Post Horses, and beneath it is a chute used to load stone from a local quarry into railway wagons, one being located under it. There is a locomotive water column, later removed, at the end of the platform, and the turnpike road crosses the line on a stone three-arch bridge, later replaced by a plate girder bridge.

Lens of Sutton

Joint Railway, so it would appear that the Alfred Whittaker design of apparatus was in use. The installation appears to have been experimental and short-lived.

A full account of the signalling at Barnstaple Junction was given in the South Western Gazette of 1907 and gives a good picture of operations at that time.

".... it is probably unique among all other stations on the London and South Western Railway system, as practically every known method of signalling operation (except pneumatic) is in vogue there. It is a double track from Umberleigh to Barnstaple, with Chapleton as an intermediate station and signalling section, but Chapleton is "switched out" at night and is not opened until the arrival of the down mails in the mornings, so that alternately Barnstaple is electrically connected with Umberleigh and Chapleton and the section, whichever it may be, is worked under the "Section clear, but Station or Junction blocked" system, and for this purpose the down line approaching Barnstaple is protected by a distant, an outer and an inner home signal.

The Great Western Railway line is a single track, and worked under the "Absolute Block" system, while the engines carry a train staff or a ticket. The Torrington branch is a single track throughout, and is worked under the train tablet system. The "Permissive" system (as the "Station blocked, but Section clear" is also designated) is in use between Fremington and Barnstaple, and when a train or engine is running to Barnstaple a printed ticket is handed to the driver in addition to the train tablet. This ticket is signed by the Fremington signalman. The "Permissive" system thus allows the Barnstaple signalman to continue necessary work while a down train is approaching from Exeter or an up train from Torrington. Or, what is of more importance, by giving the "Permissive" to a down London and South Western Railway train a Great Western Railway train can be admitted into the station on the down road. The

"Permissive" is, consequently, a great convenience, but it is very properly suspended during foggy weather or snowstorms.

The Ilfracombe branch, as between Barnstaple and Pottington Box, is a single track (and worked under train tablet apparatus), but owing to the curvature approaching Barnstaple it is unsuitable, as the view of the driver is strictly limited. Consequently, when a train has received a tablet for Barnstaple Junction, no other train can be admitted to the up platform road until its arrival.

Then there is the middle road, which is worked under the "Single Line Block" system. It converges on to the up line at each end, and is used principally for up goods trains and also for engines running round their trains from the up platform. In addition to the "Block System" there is a "Release" lever in each signal box so that the signalman who has pulled this lever controls the road, as he would not be able to get his "Ground Signals" without the control of the "Release" lock.

Then there is the wrong road working. When absolutely necessary (and this is frequent), engines or trains may run "up" the down or "down" the up road as required. The advantages of this wrong road working are many. For instance, should a down train be at the down platform an engine can be sent to Torrington or Ilfracombe lines without delay, and similarly pilot-engines or those they have on Great Western Railway trains can as soon as the train is "cleared" return on the down road when it is not possible to allow it to pass on to the up or branch loop.

Then there is what the signalman may do, and what he may not do. He must not let a Great Western Railway train across the down road if an up train is running from Fremington or the Ilfracombe branch into the station. He must stop down trains at his home signals if an up train is running in the section between Fremington and Barnstaple. He must not allow a goods train or engine to leave the goods yard if an up train is in that section. It will be seen that all the roads are well used in each direction, and that there are many rules and regulations which have to be rigidly carried out to ensure safe working."

Copplestone to Umberleigh Doubling authorised and abandoned

In the 1900s the South Western found itself facing keener competition from a re-invigorated Great Western in the west country. The new cut off line between Castle Cary and Langport was first used by express trains on 2nd July 1906, and reduced the distance between Paddington and Taunton by 20 miles in comparison with the old main line via Bristol. In the previous year the Great Western had opened a short eastern spur outside its Barnstaple station to enable through trains to run direct to Barnstaple Junction and Ilfracombe, this opening on 1st July 1905. The Great Western now had shorter and faster routes from London to both Plymouth and Ilfracombe and for a time there was intense rivalry between the companies for this traffic.

On 20th July 1906 the South Western Railway Act conferred further powers for a number of works, including in clause 6F a widening (No. 3) from Umberleigh station to Copplestone station. In connection with this widening clause 7 conferred powers to widen one level crossing in the parish of Chittlehampton, two at Burrington and two at Chawleigh, all over public roads. The firm of Perry & Co. of Bristol was contracted to undertake the work, and navvies employed by the firm were housed in old railway trucks at Eggesford. The earthworks and bridges were completed, but the firm apparently went bankrupt when the LSWR terminated the work after the signing of the

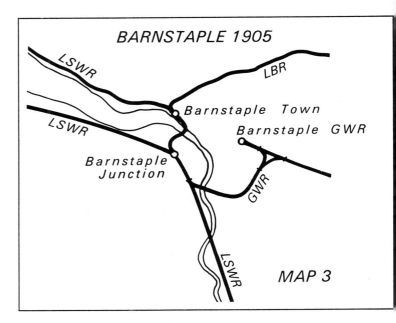

traffic pooling agreement with the Great Western, having spent £75,640 in vain.

Both railways companies had soon found that their competition for traffic was too expensive, and in 1909 negotiations were initiated between Viscount Churchill and Sir Charles Scotter, the chairmen of the Great Western and the South Western respectively. The outcome was an agreement to pool all competitive traffic, signed on 13th May 1910, but excluded cross channel shipping. Receipts were to be shared between the two companies in proportion

NORTH DEVON LINE.

This is a Double Line from Yeoford Junction to Copplestone and Umberleigh to Barnstaple, Single between Copplestone and Umberleigh and Barnstaple and Torrington. It is worked under the Train Tablet system between Copplestone and Umberleigh and between Barnstaple and Torrington.—See separate Instructions.

DOWN TRAINS—SUNDAYS.

STATIONS.	1 Goods & Mail	2 Passenger	3 Passenger	4	5	6	7	8	9	10	11
	a.m.	a.m.	p.m.	p.m.	p.m.						
London (Waterloo)	...	...									
Exeter (Queen Street)	2 50		6 40								
Yeoford Junction	3 36 3 50	7 9 7 11									
Coleford Junction	3 53	7 13									
Copplestone	3 59 4 0	7 17 7 18									
Morchard Road	4 5 4 6	7 21 7 22									
Lapford	4 12	7 26 7 27									
Eggesford	4 20 4 22	7 34 7 35									
South Molton Road	4 30	7 43 7 45									
Portsmouth Arms	4 37	7 49 7 50									
Umberleigh	4 48 4 50	7 57 7 58									
Chapelton	4 56										
Barnstaple Junc.	5 7 5 20	2 40 8 10 8 22									
Fremington	5 27 5 30	2 45 2 48 8 27 8 38									
Instow	5 38 5 40	1 52 2 58 8 34 8 35									
Bideford (Goods)	5 46 5 53										
Bideford (New)	5 56 5 58	2 58 3 0 8 40 8 41									
Torrington	6 10	3 9 8 50									

F No. 1 Train must be limited to 35 Vehicles.
T Blacken for Train Tablet.

For Trains between Exeter and Yeoford, see pages 29 to 45.

The speed of non-stopping trains through Train Tablet Stations must not exceed 8 Miles an hour after dark and both by night and by day the speed of Trains passing Train Tablet Stations must be reduced so that the exchange of tablets by the Enginemen and the Station Staff may be properly and safely performed.
The Guards and the Staff at stations will be held responsible for reporting any infringement of this order.

NORTH DEVON LINE.

This is a Single Line from Torrington to Barnstaple and Umberleigh to Copplestone, and Double from Barnstaple Junction to Yeoford Junction. It is worked under the Train Tablet system between Torrington and Barnstaple and between Umberleigh and Copplestone. See separate Instructions.

UP TRAINS.—WEEK DAYS.

Distance from Torrington	STATIONS.	1 Goods C	2 Passenger	2a Passenger July, Aug. and Sept. only	3 Passenger	4 Express Passenger	5 Passenger	6 Passenger	7 Light Engine	8 Loco. Coal when required.
m.c.		a.m. a.m.	a.m. a.m.		a.m. a.m.	a.m. a.m.			p.m. p.m.	a.m. a.m.
...	Torrington	...	7 45	8 30		10 35	...	...	...	...
5 9	Bideford (New)	7 54 7 56	8 39 8 41		9 39 9 41	10 44 10 47		11 49 11 51	12 24 12 27	...
5 40	Bideford (Goods)									A 12 50
7 50	Instow	8 1 8 3	8 46 8 47		9 46 9 47	10 52 10 53		11 56 11 57	12 32 12 33	T 12 58
11 40	Fremington	8 9 8 10			9 54 9 55	T 10 58		12 4 12 5	T 12 38	1 30
14 09	Barnstaple Jct.	5 50 5 15 8 15 8 56 9	10 0 10 0 5 11 2 11 6				12 10	12 42 12 46	7	T 1 36
18 38	Chapelton	6 2 6 10 8 27 8 29	10 13 10 14							
20 58	Umberleigh	6 18 6 26 8 33 8 35	9 10	10 19 10 20 T 11 16			T 12 56		T 1 48
23 01	Portsmouth Arms	6 40 6 50 8 41 8 42	T 9 16	10 27 10 28 T 11 22			T 1 2		T 1 58
27 73	South Molton Road	6 59 7 25 8 47 8 48	T 9 21	10 33 10 34 T 11 26			1 6 1 7		Cross No. 13
31 67	Eggesford	7 37 8 1 8 55 8 56	T 9 26	10 41 10 42 T 11 32			1 14 1 15		3 33 3 41
35 60	Lapford	8 22 9 4 0 9 2	T 9 32	10 49 10 50 T 11 38			T 1 21		T 2 50
38 09	Morchard Road	8 59 9 20 9 9 9 11	10 55 10 56 T 11 41				T 1 24		T 2 57
39 60	Copplestone	9 27 9 52 9 15 9 16	T 9 37 11 6 11 7 T 11 43				T 1 26		T 3 3
41 59	Coleford Junction	9 19	11 4 T 11 45				1 28		3 8
43 56	Yeoford Junc.	10 0 10 6 9 21 9 22	9 41 11 6 11 7 11 47 11 48				1 30 1 42		3 11 3 16
53 75	Exeter (Queen St.)	10 53	9 52 10 3 10 17 11 32	12 8 12 15			2 3 2 10		4 21
...	London (Waterloo)		1 45	3 35			6 15		...

A A Tablet for this Light Engine to be taken from Bideford (New) to Bideford (Goods) by a competent man provided by the Station Master.
B Arrive 3.30 p.m. during July, August and September.
G The load of No. 1 Train must not exceed equal to 50 Wagons, two loads coal counting as three.
T Blacken for Train Tablet.

For Trains between Yeoford and Exeter, see pages 29 to 45.

The speed of non-stopping Trains through Train Tablet Stations must not exceed 8 Miles an hour after dark, and both by night and by day the speed of Trains passing Train Tablet Stations must be reduced so that the exchange of tablets by the Enginemen and the Station Staff may be properly and safely performed.
The Guards and the Staff at Stations will be held responsible for reporting any infringement of this order.

NORTH DEVON LINE.

This is a Single Line from Torrington to Barnstaple and Umberleigh to Copplestone, and Double from Barnstaple Junction to Umberleigh and Copplestone to Yeoford Junction. It is worked under the Train Tablet System between Torrington and Barnstaple and between Umberleigh and Copplestone.—See separate Instructions.

UP TRAINS—WEEK DAYS.—continued.

STATIONS.	9 Goods A	10 Passenger	11 Passenger	12 Empty Train, Fridays only.	13 Passenger	14 Goods. C	15 Passenger	16 Goods and Cattle when required. F	17 Goods from Barnstaple	18 Passenger	19 Goods H
	p.m.	p.m.	p.m.	p.m.	p.m.	p.m.	p.m.			p.m.	p.m.
Torrington	...	12 55	1 52	2 45	...	3 35	4 25	5 10	...	5 55	...
Bideford (New)	1 7 1 8	1 2	1 2	2 54 2 55	...	3 44 3 47	4 34 4 36	5 19 5 22	...	6 4 6 7	...
Bideford (Goods)	1 10 1 31									Cross No. 16 Down.	
Instow	1 39 1 45	2 9 2 10	2 9 2 10	...	3 52 3 53	4 54 4 56	5 27 5 28			6 20 6 21	...
Fremington	1 55 2 5	2 17 2 18	2 17 2 18	...	4 0 4 2	...	5 35 5 36			6 29 6 31	...
Barnstaple Jct.	3 18 3 50	2 23 2 27	3 18	...	4 7 4 19 5 25	...	5 41 5 50	6 15	...	6 30 6 26	6 47
Chapelton	3 0	2 35 2 36					5 55 5 59			6 41	
Umberleigh	3 5 3 12	2 41 2 42					6 4 6 5	T 6 31	...	6 58 6 53	
Portsmouth Arms	3 23 3 58	2 48 2 50			4 22 4 23	...	6 12 6 10	T 6 43	7 3 7 6	...	
South Molton Road	4 6 4 10	2 55 2 56			4 34 4 35	...	6 22 6 23	6 54	7 16 7 18	...	
Eggesford	4 38 4 54	3 3 3 4			4 42 4 43	...	6 30 6 31	7 13 7 20	7 30 7 35	...	
Lapford	4 5 30	3 11 3 12		4 38	4 50 4 51	...	6 38 T 7 7	7 45	7 59 8	...	
Morchard Road	5 37 5 42	3 17 3 19		4 43 4 46	T 4 6	...	6 44 6 45	7 38 7 45	7 59 8	...	
Copplestone	5 48 5 53	3 23 3 24		T 4 50	T 4 59	...	6 49 6 50	7 50 7 59	8 11 8 16	...	
Coleford Junction	5 59	3 27		4 55	5 1	...	6 53	8 3	8 20	...	
Yeoford Junction	6 1	3 29 3 31		4 56	5 3	...	6 55 6 56	8 6 14	8 24 8 33	...	
Exeter (Queen St.)	7 12	3 54 4 15		5 20	5 35 6 0	...	7 18	8 49	9 0	...	
London (Waterloo)	...	...			10 30	...	...	...	...	...	

A No. 9 Train will convey Coal from Fremington for Barnstaple and G.W. Line only. Its load must be limited to 28 Wagons on arrival at Portsmouth Arms. Cattle for the G. W. Line via St. David's will be put off at Crediton. This Train must not be delayed at Stations after its service time taking on unimportant Wagons or Empty Coaching Stock. C No. 14 Up will take Coal from Fremington for Yeoford and beyond only. F A Notice will be issued when this Train runs. The load must be limited to 30 Vehicles from Barnstaple and it must only be stopped at Stations on the North Devon Line to attach Cattle for Chichester, or important Road Box traffic. All Cattle for Chichester by the 12.47 Goods from Bude, and 11.30 a.m. Goods from Wadebridge will be put off at Crediton and sent forward by it when it runs. H This Train will convey Wagons for all Stations to Copplestone and Ilfracombe. T Blacken for Train Tablet.

NORTH DEVON LINE.

This is a Single Line from Torrington to Barnstaple and Umberleigh to Copplestone, and Double from Barnstaple Junction to Umberleigh and Copplestone to Yeoford Junction. It is worked under the Train Tablet System between Torrington and Barnstaple and between Umberleigh and Copplestone.—See separate Instructions.

	WEEK DAYS—continued.				UP TRAINS—SUNDAYS.						
STATIONS.	20 Pass.	21 Mail and Passengr.	22	23	1 Passenger	2 Passenger	3 Mail and Passengr.	4	5	6	7
	p.m. p.m.	p.m. p.m.			a.m. a.m.	a.m. a.m.	a.m. a.m.				
Torrington	6 25	7 50	...	...	8 18	1 45	7 50	...	...	...	...
Bideford (New)	6 34 6 37	7 59 8 1	...	...	8 27 8 29	1 54 1 56	7 59 8 1	...	...	...	...
Bideford (Goods)											
Instow	6 42 6 45	8 6 8 7			8 34 8 35	2 1 2 2	8 6 8 7				
Fremington	6 52 6 53	8 14 8 15			8 42 8 43	2 9 2 10	8 14 8 15				
Barnstaple Junc.	6 58	8 20 8 25			8 48 8 54 2 15	8 20 8 25					
Chapelton		8 33 8 31			9 2 9	8 33 8 31					
Umberleigh		8 39 8 40			9 8 9	8 39 8 40					
Portsmouth Arms		8 47 8 48			9 18 9 19	8 47 8 48					
South Molton Road		8 53 8 54			9 25 9 26	8 53 8 54					
Eggesford		9 1 9 3			9 36 9 38	9 1 9 3					
Lapford		9 10 9 11			9 46 9 53	9 10 9 11					
Morchard Road		9 16 9 17			9 59 10 0	9 16 9 17					
Copplestone		9 21 9 22			10 8 10 12	9 21 9 22					
Coleford Junction		9 25			10 16	9 25					
Yeoford Junction		9 27 9 28			10 18 10 20	9 27 9 28					
Exeter (Queen St.)		9 57			10 54	9 57					
London (Waterloo)											

For Trains between Yeoford and Exeter, see pages 29 to 45.

The speed of non-stopping Trains through Train Tablet Stations must not exceed 8 Miles an hour after dark, and both by night and by day the speed of Trains passing Train Tablet Stations must be reduced so that the exchange of tablets by the Enginemen and the Station Staff may be properly and safely performed.
The Guards and the Staff at Stations will be held responsible for reporting any infringement of this order.

to traffic carried in 1908, less 25% working expenses on the distances saved. An immediate result was that the South Western ceased running its Ocean Mails specials from Plymouth to London, stopped work on doubling the track between Copplestone and Umberleigh, and competition for the fastest services to Ilfracombe slackened off.

This agreement was to have several unfortunate consequences for the North Devon line over the next half century. Non stop trains had to slow down to exchange tablets at seven stations, and at many stations the passing loops were too short to cross two full length trains. In this situation one train had to be backed into a siding, with points being locked by hand in the absence of facing point locks. The capacity of the line was limited by the single line sections, and one late-running train could delay many others in turn. The line was also very expensive to staff; of the eight stations between Coleford Junction and Barnstaple Junction only Chapelton was situated on a through double track enabling the signal box to be switched out for long periods. Chapelton station was normally manned by just one railwayman, a porter-signalman who attended to all duties; every other station required two signalmen and a porter signalman in addition to station staff. All these signal boxes were manned continuously for two and a half shifts, opening for the 'down' mail train which passed Coleford Junction at about 4am. Consequently, the line had to close early in the evening, the last 'down' train leaving Exeter at about 7pm. Doubling between Copplestone and Umberleigh would have overcome many of these problems, with several signal boxes being switched out for much of the day. In contrast the double track Plymouth main line was open 24 hours a day.

Other Twentieth Century Developments

The First World War affected the North Devon line in a similar way to many other railways. Railwaymen were amongst those who were called away to war service, some of them never to return. There was considerable traffic of servicemen and of war materials, such as quantities of timber loaded at several stations. On the Plymouth line there was much traffic in sailors, munitions and supplies to and from the great naval base at Devonport. German prisoners of war were brought by train to Eggesford

House, vacated by Earl Portsmouth, to wait for the end of hostilities. Extra sidings for 180 wagons were built at Yeoford and a Barnstaple Shipyard siding added.

Some economies were also made at this time arising from the 1910 traffic pooling agreement, with the complete closure of one signal box and the downgrading of two others to ground frames. All were on the Cowley Bridge Junction to Coleford Junction double track section. First, Cowley Bridge (South Western) signal box was closed and replaced with a ground frame on 26th March 1916, Neopardy signal box was completely closed on 7th April 1916, and Crediton East signal box reduced to a ground frame about the same time.

However, the South Western had commenced new works at Barnstaple Junction to ease congestion there, particularly in the summer months. On 23rd June 1922 Maj. Hall reported:

"I have made an inspection on the 21st instant of the new work at Barnstaple Junction, upon the North Devon branch of the London and South Western Railway.

This work consists of a new trailing connection on the up main line, with an up siding. Certain signals have been altered in position and new signals provided in connection with this work. The points and signals concerned are worked from Barnstaple Junction West signal box, which contains an old frame with 31 working levers and 1 spare lever. The existing locking should be altered so that there is a deadlock between No. 18 and No. 16 point levers, unless No. 27 (the points of the new connection) lever is pulled. The interlocking is otherwise correct and the arrangements satisfactory, and subject to this alteration in locking I recommend that this work be finally approved."

Further improvements were put in hand and completed in the Southern Railway period. In 1922 came the end of the independent existence of the London & South Western Railway which had played such an important part in the railway development of North Devon. Starting with the illegal acquisition of shares in 1847 the South Western's trains had arrived at Barnstaple in 1863. By the turn of the century, after considerable expenditure, the company had turned the North Devon line into a well run railway by the standards of the time.

Umberleigh station, looking south about 1920. The goods shed is in the loading dock, on the right. *Lens of Sutton*

The Station, Umberleigh.

126

Chapter 6

Southern Days

The Grouping

The 1921 Railways Act organised the main line railways into four groups. The new Southern Railway comprised the London & South Western Railway, the London, Brighton & South Coast Railway and the South Eastern & Chatham Managing Committee, together with a number of smaller companies including the Lynton & Barnstaple Railway. As from 1923 the Southern Railway owned all the railways in the North Devon with the exception of the Great Western's Barnstaple branch. However, the 1920s was a decade which saw numerous developments on the railways of North Devon, some of which had been initiated in South Western days.

New Developments in North Devon

A new railway, the last of any size built in the west country, was the standard gauge North Devon & Cornwall Junction Light Railway from Torrington to Halwill Junction, built partially along the line of an earlier 3ft gauge line. The first sod was cut on 30th June 1922 and the ceremonial opening was held on 23rd July 1925, with public services starting on 27th July. One effect on the North Devon line was to increase the volume of clay traffic passing between the clay works at Marland and Meeth, both rail connected, and Bristol Docks, the Potteries and elsewhere.

The operation of Barnstaple Junction station had become quite complex with traffic increasing on all four lines. To increase its capacity a considerable quantity of rock was excavated to enable a second 'down' track to be constructed behind the 'down' platform, thus converting it to an island platform. More complicated pointwork and crossings had to be installed at the west end of the station at the junction of the Torrington and Ilfracombe lines.

Maj. Hall made his inspection and reported on 23rd July 1924.

"I made an inspection on the 18th instant of the new work at Barnstaple Junction on the Southern Railway. The work under inspection consist of a new down running loop behind the existing platform, which has been converted into one of the island type. The footbridge has also been extended on the down side of the station with a new staircase to an approach path on this side.

The new down loop diverges from the down main line at the east end of the station at a facing connection, and trailing connections have been laid at the west end between the down loop and the down main to Torrington and down branch to Ilfracombe respectively. Track circuiting has been installed throughout on the down loop line, with a lock on the down loop block switch. The facing connection and the necessary signals at the east end of the down loop are worked from Barnstaple East signal

A magnificent study of Barnstaple Junction from the East signal box early in Southern Railway days. The second 'down' platform commissioned in 1924 can be seen on the left, but some wagons remain in pre-Grouping lettering, including MR, GE, CL and LSWR. Behind the standard South Western 50ft turntable is Adams X6 class 4-4-0 No. 658, a Barnstaple locomotive, with Drummond boiler and dome. A Drummond 4-4-0 is on an 'up' passenger train, with at least one M7 class 0-4-4T on shed.

British Railways

box, which contains 36 working levers and three spare levers, and the interlocking is correct. At the west end the connections and signals are worked from Barnstaple West signal box, which contains 37 working and 3 spare levers. The junction point locking presents some difficulty at this end of the yard owing to the nature of the layout, but after discussion with the company's officers, I came to the conclusion that the manner in which this had been carried out was in the circumstances that were most suitable to the traffic.

At the trailing points on the down main of the new crossover from the down loop to the down main is placed a ground Signal No. 9 for movements in the facing direction along the down main or down loop line for train connecting purposes. The signal is not slotted or controlled from the East Junction and no reference to the signalman at the latter place is necessary on the part of the signalman at the West Junction before this signal is pulled. In the circumstances therefore a limit of wrong line shunt on both loop and main lines should be erected at some point which represents the furthest extent of these train-connecting movements. In respect of the down loop, this limit of shunt will also apply to movements authorised by No. 8 signal from the down siding into the down loop in the facing direction. Subject to compliance with the foregoing requirements in respect of limit of shunt, I recommend that this new work be approved."

Comparing Maj. Hall's reports of 1922 and 1924 it would appear that the old tall stone-built Barnstaple Junction West signal box of 1874 was at this time replaced by the second signal box, constructed in brick and concrete, the old frame of 32 levers being replaced by one of 40 levers. When Barnstaple Junction was re-signalled in 1924 the junction signal posts indicated that the main line was to Torrington with Ilfracombe the branch. However, within a year the roles had been reversed, as when the summer timetable was introduced on 12th July 1925 the through trains from Exeter were diverted to Ilfracombe with the Torrington line becoming the branch. More passenger traffic was handled on the Ilfracombe line than the Torrington line, but the 1 in 36 gradients on Morthoe bank required new motive power. This arrived new in July 1925 in the shape of the N class 2-6-0s which took over the principal passenger services to Ilfracombe, although freight trains continued to run through to Bideford and Torrington.

The Southern Railway also re-built the two passenger stations between which the North Devon trains ran. The old 1860 South Western station at Exeter Queen Street, with its dark wooden train sheds, was extensively re-built between 1927 and 1933 and on completion of the work was renamed Exeter Central on 1st July 1933. The new layout provided more adequate facilities for the re-marshalling of through expresses between Waterloo and the west country. The old 1874 station at Ilfracombe was limited in extent and was re-built in 1928 and 1929, the short platform being extended to accommodate full length trains, a new locomotive shed and turntable provided, and more carriage sidings added. This new accommodation enabled both the Southern and Great Western to run more summer holiday trains to the resort. At about this time the Great Western considered a scheme for re-building Exeter St Davids, with independent high level tracks for Southern trains, but the scheme was dropped.

At this time the Southern Railway gained two important customers at intermediate stations on the North Devon line, where local traffic was limited. In 1927 the dairy firm

NORTH DEVON LINE.

(Timetable of Down Trains, Week-Days — Exeter Queen Street to Torrington, dated 25th July, 1921.)

A—Put out News Parcels at Stations Copplestone to Umberleigh inclusive if required.
B—Call at Bideford (Goods) to detach Nine Elms to Bideford Vacuum Wagon.
C—Leave Exeter at 2.20 a.m. on Mondays.
D—Worked by G.W.Co.'s engine and guard.

NORTH DEVON LINE.

(Timetable of Down Trains, Week-Days — Exeter Queen Street to Torrington, dated 25th July, 1921.)

A—Stops at Lapford and Eggesford for crossing purposes only.
B—Stops at Barnstaple Town. Not to be advertised.
C—Stops at Copplestone for crossing purposes only.
D—Permissive stop at Portsmouth Arms to set down passengers (from Salisbury or London).
E—Worked by G.W.R. engine and guard.

(T.T. 1656.)

NORTH DEVON LINE.

This is a Single Line from Coppleston to Umberleigh, from Barnstaple Junction to Torrington, and from Barnstaple Junction to Pottington Signal Box, between which points it is worked under the Regulations for working Single Lines by the Electric Train Tablet Block System.

For Special Instructions as to the working and load of Trains and List of Catch Points between Braunton and Ilfracombe, see pages 101 and 102 of the Appendix of the Book of Rules and Regulations and Working Time Tables dated 25th July, 1921.

DOWN TRAINS. SUNDAYS.	Pass.	Pass.	Pass.	Pass.	Pass.	Pass.
	arr. dep.	arr. dep.	arr. dep.	arr. dep.	arr. dep.	arr. dep.
	a.m. a.m.	a.m. a.m.	p.m. p.m.	p.m. p.m.	p.m. p.m.	p.m. p.m.

Exeter (Queen Street)

For times of Trains at intermediate Stations between Exeter (Queen Street) and Yeoford, see Exeter and Plymouth Line pages.

Yeoford						
Coleford Junction						
Coppleston						
Morchard Road						
Lapford						
Eggesford						
South Molton Road						
Portsmouth Arms						
Umberleigh						
Chapelton						
Barnstaple Junc.	10 20		1 55		6 30	
Barnstaple Town	10 24 10 25	1 26	2		6 33 6 35	
Pottington Box	10 26		2 1		6 36	
Wrafton	10 32 10 33	2 7 2		6 42 6 43	
Braunton	10 35 10 37	2 10 2 12		6 45 6 47	
Heanton Mill Crossing	10 41		2 16		6 51	
Mortehoe	10 52 10 54	2 27 2 29		7 2 7 4	
Ilfracombe	11 4		2 39		7 14	

Barnstaple Junc.	9 0		12 35		3 40	8 20
Fremington	9 7 9 8		12 39	3 47 3 48		8 27 8 28
Instow	9 14 9 15		12 40 12 50	3 54 3 55		8 34 8 35
Bideford (Goods)						
Bideford (New)	9 20 9 21		12 55 12 56	4 0 4 1		8 40 8 41
Torrington	9 30		1 5	4 10		8 50

This is a Single Line from Pottington Signal Box to Barnstaple Junction, from Torrington to Barnstaple Junction and from Umberleigh to Coppleston, between which points it is worked under the Regulations for working Single Lines by the Electric Train Tablet Block System.

For Special Instructions as to the working and load of Trains and List of Catch Points between Braunton and Ilfracombe see pages 101 and 102 of the Appendix to the Book of Rules and Regulations and Working Time Tables, dated 25th July, 1921.

Distances.	UP TRAINS. WEEK-DAYS	Goods. FO	Goods to Crediton NF	Engine.	Pass.	G.W.R. Empty. SO	Pass.	G.W.R. Empty. SO	Pass.	Pass. to Waterloo

For times at Intermediate Stations between Yeoford and Exeter (Queen Street) see Plymouth and Exeter Line pages.

Exeter (Queen Street)

B.—Not to convey passengers for Mortehoe from Ilfracombe from 27th July to 15th Sept., inclusive, except on Fridays and Saturdays. On Fridays and Saturdays will not convey passengers from Ilfracombe for stations east of Yeoford. Through carriages Ilfracombe to Brighton attached to this train Monday to Thursday inclusive. Torrington portion to be attached in front at Barnstaple Junction.

C.—Permissive stop at Portsmouth Arms to take up passengers for Salisbury or London. (T.T. 1650).

D.—Worked by G.W.R. Co.'s Engine and Guard.

NORTH DEVON LINE.

This is a Single Line from Pottington Signal Box to Barnstaple Junction, from Torrington to Barnstaple Junction and from Umberleigh to Coppleston, between which points it is worked under the Regulations for working Single Lines by the Electric Train Tablet Block System.

For Special Instructions as to the working and load of Trains and List of Catch Points between Braunton and Ilfracombe, see pages 101 and 102 of the Appendix to the Book of Rules and Regulations and Working Time Tables, dated 25th July, 1921.

UP TRAINS. WEEK-DAYS.	Pass. NFS	Pass. FSO Commencing on Friday 24th July.	Goods.	Goods.	Pass. G.W.R.	Pass. to Waterloo	Pass. to Waterloo	Engine.

For times at intermediate Stations between Yeoford and Exeter (Queen Street) see Plymouth and Exeter Line pages.

Exeter (Queen St.)

UP TRAINS. WEEK-DAYS.	G.W.R. Excursion FO	Pass.	Goods.	Pass.	Pass. Exeter.	Goods or Engine. Q	Pass. Waterloo	Pass. Eastleigh.

For times at intermediate Stations between Yeoford and Exeter (Queen Street) see Plymouth and Exeter Line pages.

Exeter (Queen St.)

A—Arrives Queen Street at 2.23 on Saturdays.   B—To convey a through coach for the G.W. Line, to be attached to the rear leaving Ilfracombe.   C—Barnstaple (Town) times not to be advertised. Through carriages Ilfracombe to Brighton attached to this train.   D—Worked by G.W. Co.'s engine and Guard.

NORTH DEVON LINE.

This is a Single Line from Pottington Signal Box to Barnstaple Junction, from Torrington to Barnstaple Junction and from Umberleigh to Coppleston, between which points it is worked under the Regulations for working Single Lines by the Electric Train Tablet Block System.

For Special Instructions as to the working and load of Trains and List of Catch Points between Braunton and Ilfracombe, see pages 101 and 102 of the Appendix to the Book of Rules and Regulations and Working Time Tables, dated 25th July, 1921.

UP TRAINS. WEEK-DAYS.	Goods.	Goods.	Pass.	Mail and Pass.	Pass. G.W.R.	G.W.R. Excursion FO	G.W.R. Excursion FO	Pass. G.W.R.	G.W.R. Excursion FO	G.W.R. Excursion FO	Excursion to Waterloo Fridays

For times at intermediate Stations between Yeoford and Exeter (Queen Street) see Plymouth and Exeter Line pages.

Exeter (Queen St.)

UP TRAINS. SUNDAYS.	Pass.	Pass.	Pass.	Pass.	Pass.	Pass.
	arr. dep.	arr. dep.	arr. dep.	arr. dep.	arr. dep.	arr. dep.
	a.m. a.m.	a.m. a.m.	p.m. p.m.	p.m. p.m.	p.m. p.m.	p.m. p.m.

For times at intermediate Stations between Yeoford and Exeter (Queen Street) see Plymouth and Exeter Line pages.

Exeter (Queen Street)

A—Worked by G.W. Company's engine and guard, and to leave Barnstaple Junction 8.45 p.m. for Taunton.
B—Worked by G.W. Company's engine and guard.

---

of Ambrosia commenced construction of its factory at Lapford station, and the production of milk products commenced in 1928. The firm already had a factory at Lifton and considered several sites in the area for its expansion. Col. Stephens had hoped to bring Ambrosia to a site on his new North Devon & Cornwall Junction Light Railway, and indeed, the company had bought shares in the line, but eventually decided on Lapford. Further down the line at Chapelton, the local firm of Chappell & Walton established their sawmills in the station yard in 1930. The operations of both firms were described in Chapter 1, but in both cases they brought considerable new business to the railway.

General Progress in the 1920s and '30s

The General Manager of the Southern Railway, Sir Herbert Walker, initiated a competition for his railwaymen to find a name for the principal West of England express, the 11am from Waterloo. For most of the year, the express conveyed through carriages to Sidmouth, Exmouth, Ilfracombe, Torrington, Bude, Padstow and Plymouth, but in the summer season was expanded to three or four trains. A Woking guard, Frank Rowlands, won the competition with his suggestion of "The Atlantic Coast Express" (the "ACE") and shortly afterwards he transferred to Torrington where, incidentally, he became a town councillor. Sadly, he died from injuries received in a shunting accident at Marland in 1932, but the "Atlantic Coast Express" continued to run along the North Devon line until 1964.

The Southern Railway made a number of economies on the line, particularly at the southern end. At Cowley Bridge the ground frame and crossover were taken out of use on 1st April 1928, and all movements were controlled

An 'up' goods train hauled by Drummond 700 class 0-6-0 No. 350, as rebuilt by Urie, passes Bishops Tawton, about a mile south of Barnstaple Junction on the double track section.

A. Halls courtesy R. J. Sellick

A lengthy 'down' passenger train hauled by Maunsell N class 2-6-0 No. A860 passes Bishops Tawton.

A. Halls courtesy R. J. Sellick

Drummond T9 class 4-4-0, No. 283, at Yeoford on an 'up' train in Southern days.

F. E. Box courtesy National Railway Museum

Barnstaple Junction on a busy summer day in the 1930s, with GWR 2-6-2T No. 5542 on a through train from the Taunton line to Ilfracombe, and an N class 2-6-0 on an 'up' train, the first three vehicles being an ex-LSWR three-coach non-corridor set.

Lens of Sutton

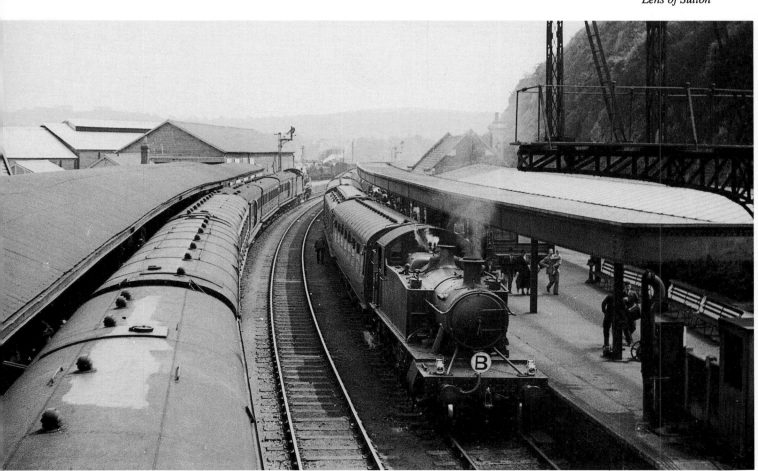

by the Great Western signal box. At Newton St Cyres the 1875 signal box was closed and replaced by a new one in the booking office, the change taking place on 17th August 1930. Situated on a double track main line the signal box could be switched out at slack traffic periods, and the staff establishment reduced to two porter signalmen who could attend to all station and signalling duties. At about this time Coleford Junction was provided with an outer home signal on the Plymouth line, enabling the signalman to accept 'up' trains from Plymouth even when a North Devon line train was also accepted. Previous to this an 'up' Plymouth train had to be halted at the 'up' home signal before a North Devon train could be accepted. The effect was to enable Bow signal box to be switched out for much of the day without adversely affecting traffic. At Chapelton the 'up' refuge siding and a crossover were removed in 1930-1 as an economy measure. At Barnstaple Junction several wagon turntables in the yard were taken out and replaced with conventional pointwork with more siding accommodation.

The 1930s saw a considerable slump in the national economy which reduced railway business. The Southern Railway closed the Lynton & Barnstaple line in 1935, and traffic on the North Devon line had fallen away to the extent that when the need arose the double track section between Barnstaple and Umberleigh could be reduced to a single line, the second track being used as a siding. In the late 1930s the Royal Air Force commenced the construction of its new airfield at Chivenor, served by Wrafton station. However, the yard at Wrafton comprised only two short sidings which could not accommodate the large number of wagons loaded with construction materials. Initially single line working was instituted between Umberleigh and Chapelton, and later between Umberleigh and Barnstaple, using the 'down' line. Loaded wagons were stored on the 'up' line, and special trains were then run with loaded wagons to Wrafton as and when required.

World War Two
The Second World War brought more incidents and changes to the North Devon line than the First World War. There was similar heavy traffic in servicemen and materials on the Plymouth line, but this time, there was heavy bombing at Exeter and particularly Plymouth. Again, many railwaymen joined the forces, some never to return. After the Dunkirk evacuation of 1940 many soldiers were brought by train to army camps at Okehampton, and the signalmen worked very long hours to cope with the extra traffic. Siding accommodation was very limited, so the empty stock was worked back to Yeoford and thence down the North Devon line where the 'up' line between Umberleigh and Barnstaple was again used as a siding. Here, for some considerable time, was a long line of assorted coaching stock from all parts of the country. In their haste or weariness many of the troops had left behind in the carriages all sorts of military equipment including rifles, revolvers, ammunition, helmets and food. Sand from the beach at Dunkirk found its way on to the office desk at Umberleigh. Some of the rifles were still loaded, and this led to at least one near accident.

During the period of the Dunkirk evacuation some six locomotives of classes N, L11 and T9, all coupled together, were sent to Copplestone for stabling away from Exeter. Here they had water available and could be sent to North Devon, North Cornwall or Plymouth and were clear of the congestion and vulnerability to bombing at Exeter.

Another airfield was constructed at Winkleigh, for which Eggesford station was most convenient. Considerable quantities of construction materials were brought to Eggesford station by train and delivered to the airfield by road. There was considerable passenger traffic involving servicemen travelling to and from their units including RAF Winkleigh, RAF Chivenor and numerous others. American servicemen and tanks were also taken through to Bideford. Troop traffic was often very heavy. For example, on one occasion six trains of American servicemen were run in one day from Scotland to Braunton for billeting in camps in the area. There was even an armoured train hauled by ex-GER F4 class 2-4-2T No. 7077, which shuttled around the coastal lines between Barnstaple, Bideford and Braunton. Considerable numbers of women and children were evacuated from London and other large cities to North Devon towns and villages, some being accommodated in the homes of the railwaymen themselves.

Considerable work was carried out on the railways in the west country to provide new connections between the Great Western and Southern lines to facilitate more flexibility of operation, particularly if one route was shut by enemy action. Such new connections were built at Yeovil, Lydford, St Budeaux and Launceston, and at times there were more Great Western than Southern trains running between Coleford Junction and Cowley Bridge Junction. As we have seen siding accommodation was very limited and a number of yards were built or considerably extended, including Exeter Riverside, Lydford, Halwill Junction and Yeoford. During 1942-3 the 'down' yard at Yeoford was enlarged by widening from four to six sidings and greatly lengthened, extending back almost to Neopardy. The enlarged yards, particularly at Exeter Riverside and Yeoford, were invaluable for many years, facilitating the handling of the heavy post-war goods traffic. On the debit side of the Great Western's Barnstaple East Loop was closed at the end of the summer season, on 4th September 1939, and all through trains had to reverse at the Great Western station.

During the wartime blackout several incidents occurred. On one occasion, a cattle special train ran right through Lapford station without exchanging the single line tablets, the locomotive crew not knowing where they were!

Wartime and post-war food rationing caused the closure of livestock markets, and changes in production of dairy products at factories such as Ambrosia. Between 1940 and 1954 special trains of cattle trucks were run for the Meat and Livestock Commission who bought direct from the farmers and forwarded fatstock to several destinations. Cream, canned by Ambrosia was a luxury, and its production was replaced by dried milk and yeast extract, some of which went to British prisoners of war camps run by the Japanese.

The Post-War Period
For more than a decade after the war the railways were very busy indeed, and the North Devon line was handling more traffic than ever before. Freight traffic was particularly heavy and caused operating difficulties at several places. At Yeoford freight trains requiring re-marshalling were sometimes so long that shunting could not start until the signalman could allow part of the train to be left on the running line. At Barnstaple Junction the same thing happened with the yard full of wagons, so shunting continued right through the night after the passenger trains stopped running, wagons being shunted on the running lines. At some of the intermediate stations the small yards were often completely filled with wagons so, for example,

loaded wagons for Ambrosia had to be held at Yeoford until there was room for them at Lapford. Another major construction project was started after the war in North Devon when the Central Electricity Generating Board built its new East Yelland Power Station. It incorporated extensive sidings and much of the construction materials including boilers, transformers and steelworks was delivered by rail along the North Devon line.

As if to celebrate the end of the war in 1945, the Southern Railway introduced its new streamlined 'West Country' class 4-6-2 locomotives on the principal Exeter to Ilfracombe services. It also tried to lift public morale during the period of past war austerity by introducing the all-Pullman "Devon Belle" express in 1947, the Ilfracombe coaches being hauled initially by 'West Country' class No. 21C117 *Ilfracombe*. But at the end of the year, the Southern Railway era ended when the new nationalized British Railways was formed.

On 24th May 1935 Maunsell N class 2-6-0 No. 1407, of Exmouth Junction depot, departs from Barnstaple Junction with an 'up' train, possibly the 11.18am "Atlantic Coast Express".

H. C. Casserley

Chapter 7

British Railways

Nationalization

Under the terms of the 1947 Transport Act the new British Railways came into existence on 1st January 1948 with high hopes of a new era for the railways. Initially, all the Southern lines west of Salisbury were administered by the Western Region, but the day to day operation was still the responsibility of the Southern management at Exeter Central, and in 1958, the lines were transferred to the Southern Region. The Western Region regained control in 1963 and in 1964 initiated the first of a number of major changes on the North Devon line.

Rationalization at Barnstaple

Both the Southern Railway and Great Western Railway had their own considerable establishments at Barnstaple, including passenger stations, goods yards, locomotive depots, management structures and railwaymen. One early achievement of British Railways was to quietly rationalize many of these facilities to eliminate duplication and make the best use of resources. The first item to be dealt with in 1948 was the freight services, where traffic was very heavy and the immediate concern was the efficient conduct of business rather than economies. Full wagon loads were concentrated on Barnstaple Junction while the Great Western station, renamed Barnstaple Victoria Road on 11th March 1950, dealt with sundries and general merchandise. The large fleet of collection and delivery road vehicles and their drivers were based at Victoria Road station, but they also served Barnstaple Junction station for the passenger train parcels traffic. For some years, the freight traffic handled was very heavy, a decline setting in during the late 1950s.

Next, in 1952, the Great Western locomotive depot was closed. The locomotive and footplate staff were transferred to Barnstaple Junction depot, where locomotives of Southern, Great Western and later, London, Midland & Scottish origin were to be seen. Numerous light engine workings were introduced between the two stations to position locomotives at the start and end of their duties. Great Western locomotives now regularly worked through to Ilfracombe on their trains. When Torrington shed closed in 1959 more locomotives and men were transferred to Barnstaple Junction depot and there were more corresponding light engine workings. At one stage the depot had 28 locomotives, compared with its previous sixteen or so, and there were more than a hundred men employed at the locomotive depot.

It was, however, surprising that separate passenger stations were retained for some time, and that the Barnstaple East Loop was not re-opened after its closure in 1939. Traffic congestion at Barnstaple Junction may have been responsible but eventually, on 12th June 1960, Victoria Road station was closed to passenger traffic. Passenger trains from Taunton now ran along the re-opened East Loop direct to Barnstaple Junction, to where all passenger guards and booking staff were transferred. The north side of the Great Western triangle was closed, together with all the Great Western signal boxes, and the line from the former South Loop signal box to Victoria Road retained for freight services. Access to Victoria Road Sidings was by means of a new ground frame released by the electric token from Barnstaple Junction to Swimbridge, and only the freight staff remained at Victoria Road.

N class 2-6-0 No. 31846 at Barnstaple shed on 14th September 1952. On the right is the Barnstaple Breakdown Train coach, an old South Western vehicle.

R. J. Sellick

The Early British Railways Period

The lessons learned during the Second World War of the value of the two routes to Plymouth were put to good use in early British Railways days, and Southern and Western Region locomotives and men regularly worked over each others routes. Due to weight restrictions on Meldon Viaduct the largest Western Region locomotives usually seen were 2-6-0s, which also almost monopolized the Taunton-Barnstaple-Ilfracombe services. On the North Devon line only the section between Coleford Junction and Barnstaple Junction did not see Western Region locomotives on a regular basis. On this section South Molton Road station was renamed King's Nympton on 1st March 1951, the village being only some three miles away!

Soon after Nationalization the Western Region District Officers Inspection Saloon visited the North Devon line, hauled by 2-6-2T No. 4581. During the aftermath of the Lynmouth flood disaster in August 1952 the line was closed on the Saturday morning to check on suspected flood damage to bridges. No trains left North Devon until early afternoon, whilst every 'down' loop from Copplestone to Portsmouth Arms held a waiting train.

At this time, with heavier traffic then ever before, the resources of the North Devon line were stretched to the limit, particularly, with the longer trains then running. The capacity of the crossing loops at the five intermediate stations on the single line section varied between 15 and 41 wagons, together with engine and brake van. Freight trains often exceeded this and had to be shunted into sidings for crossing purposes. On half a dozen summer Saturdays numerous full length restaraunt car trains ran between Waterloo and the North Devon seaside resorts. When they crossed at stations like King's Nympton one train had to be backed into a siding, the points being

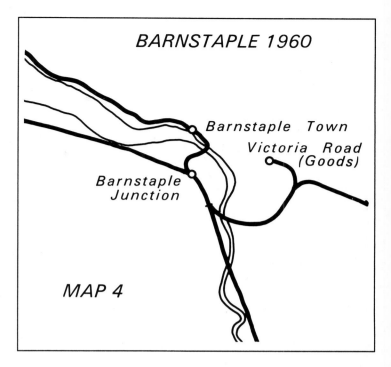

locked with a piece of wood by a porter under the supervision of the signalman. On other occasions very close co-operation between the signalman and the two drivers was required to ease one train past another with only inches to spare at each end of the crossing loop. Up to five minutes was allowed for such crossing purposes, and delays sometimes accumulated of up to half an hour, but even this compared well with the performance on the Western Region main line where delays of two or three hours were not uncommon.

M7 class 0-4-4T No.30250 with a rake of three ex-GWR coaches in carmine and cream livery at Barnstaple Junction on 6th April 1953. The 577 duty disc involved this Barnstaple locomotive in three return trips daily to Torrington, together with shunting duties.

R. J. Sellick

The 'up' "Devon Belle" passes Crediton 'down' distant signal on 28th August 1954. Bulleid Pacific No. 34058 *Sir Frederick Pile* has a heavy load of nine Pullman cars, including the Observation Car which was turned on the Ilfracombe turntable.

S. C. Nash

Non-stop trains were required to slow to 10mph when exchanging single line tablets, but with heavy passenger trains this was impossible if schedules were to be maintained. The unofficial practice became that two men were on the platform, one to collect one tablet from the fireman, the other to hand over the next tablet to the driver. Trains ran through the stations at speeds considerably in excess of 10mph.

There were a number of accidents and incidents on the line at this period. On 11th October 1950 a wagon of a

King's Nympton on 4th July 1953, showing the laborious manoeuvre necessary to cross two full length trains in the short passing loop. The 'down' train has been reversed into a siding, with points locked by hand with a block of wood, to enable it to cross the 'up' "Devon Belle".

R. J. Sellick

K22 WEEKDAYS YEOFORD TO ILFRACOMBE AND TORRINGTON

DOWN

Mileage from Nine Elms M	C	Station		No.		2.6 am Mail and Freight Exeter Central	SO (Until 14th September inclusive)	SX until 13th September inclusive, Daily commencing 16th September		LE (SX until 13th September inclusive. Daily commencing 16th September)		12.35 am MO, 12.30 am MX Salisbury to Torrington (SX until 13th September inclusive. Daily commencing 16th September)	SO 12.30 am Salisbury to Torrington (Until 14th September inclusive)			Q	
						am	am	am		am		am	am			am	
181	37	YEOFORD	arr	1		3 26						6 41	6 41				
			dep	2		3 45						7 9	7 9				
182	34	Coleford Jn.		3		3 49						7 13	7 13				
184	33	Copplestone	arr	4													
		Ⓚ	dep	5		3 56						7 24	7 24				
186	5	Morchard Road Ⓚ	arr	6													
			dep	7		4 0						7 28	7 28				
187	34	Lapford Ⓚ	arr	8													
			dep	9		4 5						7 33	7 33				
192	26	Eggesford Ⓚ	arr	10		4 13											
			dep	11		4 15						7X40	7 40				
196	22	Kings Nympton Ⓚ	arr	12		4 23						7X48	7X48				
			dep	13		4 24						8 8	8 8				
199	13	Portsmouth Arms Ⓚ	arr	14													
			dep	15		4 30						8 14	8 14				
203	25	Umberleigh Ⓚ	arr	16		4 39											
			dep	17		4 41						8 21	8 21				
205	55	Chapelton	arr	18													
			dep	19													
210	1	BARNSTAPLE JN.	arr	20		4 55						8 35	8 35				
		ⓉⓀ	dep	21		5 15	5 30	6 38				9 27	9 12			9 45	
210	57	Barnstaple Town Ⓣ🅃		22			5 34	6 42									
210	70	Pottington Sig. Box 🅃		23			5 35	6 43									
215	3	Wrafton	arr	24													
			dep	25													
215	77	Braunton	arr	26													
			dep	27			5 44	6 52									
218	19	Heddon Mill Crossing		28			5 50	6 58									
221	67	Mortehoe and W'combe	arr	29			6 1	7 9									
			dep	30			6 4	7 12									
224	77	ILFRACOMBE	arr	31			6 14	7 22									
212	53	Fremington Ⓚ	arr	32								9 33	9X18			9 53	
			dep	33		5 22						9 43	9 41				
216	34	Instow Ⓚ	arr	34		5 29						9 51	9X49				
			dep	35		5 30						10 5	10 0				
218	44	Bideford Goods ⒾⓀ	arr	36		5 38						10 11	10 6				
			dep	37		5 48				9‖50		10 58	10 52				
219	4	Bideford New Ⓚ	arr	38		5 51						11X 1	10X55				
			dep	39		5 56				9 52		11 7	11 13				
219	47	Bartletts Siding ⒾⓀ	arr	40								11 9	11 15				
			dep	41								11 25	11 31				
224	13	TORRINGTON Ⓚ	arr	42		6 8				10‖ 2		11 35	11 41				

WEEKDAYS BARNSTAPLE JUNCTION AND BARNSTAPLE VICTORIA RD.

Mileage M	C	Station		SO (Until 14th September)	LE (Work 8.0 am Ft. Commencing 16th September)	(SX until 13th September incl. Daily commencing 16th Sept.)	LE (SX until 13th September. Daily commencing 16th September)	(SX until 13th September. Daily commencing 16th Sept.)		LE SO (Until 14th September inclusive)	EBV SX Q	(SX until 13th September inclusive. Daily commencing 16th September)
				am	am	am	am	am	am	PM	PM	PM
0	0	Barnstaple Vic. Rd. Ⓢ	dep	7 18	7‖45	8 10	9‖15	9 45	10 50	2‖12	4 30	5 50
1	61	Barnstaple Jn. Ⓢ	arr	7 23	7‖50	8 15	9‖20	9 50	10 55	2‖17	4 35	5 55

Mileage M	C	Station		SO (13th July to 24th August inclusive.)	(Daily until 6th July, SX from 8th July to 23rd August inclusive. Daily commencing 26th August)	LE (SX until 13th September. Daily commencing 16th September)	(SX until 13th September. Daily commencing 16th September)	SO (Until 14th Sept. incl.)	LE SO (Until 14th Sept. incl.)	SX Q	(SX until 13th September. Daily commencing 16th Sept.)	LE FO (Until 13th September inclusive)	LE SO (Until 14th Sept. incl.)	
				am	am	am	am	am	PM	PM	PM	PM	PM	
0	0	Barnstaple Jn. Ⓢ	dep	6 28	8 0	8‖45	11 5	11 30	2‖39	4 5	5 10	7‖ 0	7‖30	
1	61	Barnstaple Vic. Rd. Ⓢ	arr	6 33	8 5	8‖50	11 10	11 35	2‖44	4 10	5 15	7‖ 5	7‖35	

WEEKDAYS YEOFORD TO ILFRACOMBE AND TORRINGTON — SUNDAYS K23

No.	SX until 13th September inclusive. Daily commencing 16th September		SO (Until 14th September inclusive)		6.30 am Exmouth Jn. Sidings (SX until 13th September inclusive. Daily commencing 16th September)		9.15 am Exmouth Jn. Sidings (SX until 13th September inclusive. Daily commencing 16th September)	LE SX Q	LE SX	SO (Commences 21st September)		SX	SUNDAYS	(Until 15th September inclusive)					
	am		am		am		am	PM	PM	PM		PM		am					
1					8 40		11 47												
2					9 6		12 32												
3					9 10		12 36												
4					9 22		12 44												
5					9 30		1 0												
6					9X38		1 6												
7					9 47		1 32												
8					9X55		1X40												
9					10 22		2 30												
10					10 30		2 39												
11					10 55														
12					11X 1														
13					11 40														
14					11 46														
15					12 0														
16					12 7														
17					12 20														
18					12 26														
19					12 36														
20					12 45														
21	10 45		11 53					2‖ 0		4 5		4 25		7 55					
22	10 49		11 57							4 20		4 29		7 59					
23	R55		11 58							4 21		4 30		8 0					
24	11 3																		
25	11 18																		
26	11 20		12 6							Barnstaple Town arrive 4.9 pm									
27	11 53		12 21											8 9					
28	12 0		12 28											8 15					
29	12 11		12 39											8 26					
30	12 26		12 50											8 29					
31	12 36		1 0											8 39					
32	Pollington Signal Box arrive 10R50 am							2‖ 5											
33									2‖24										
34									2X30										
35									2 36										
36									2‖42										
37																			
38																			
39																			
40																			
41																			
42																			

AXMINSTER AND LYME REGIS WEEKDAYS

Mileage M	C	Station		No.		(Available SX until 13th September. Daily commencing 16th Sept.)	Mixed Q		
					am		am		
0	0	AXMINSTER Ⓣ	dep	1	7 29		10 40		
4	21	Combpyne	arr	2	7 41				
			dep	3	7 47		10 53		
6	59	LYME REGIS Ⓣ	arr	4	7 55		11 0½		

Mileage M	C	Station		No.	LE	(Available SX until 13th September. Daily commencing 16th September)	Mixed
					am		am
0	0	LYME REGIS Ⓣ	dep	1	6‖15		8 11
2	38	Combpyne	arr	2			8 19
			dep	3			8 19½
6	59	AXMINSTER Ⓣ	arr	4	6‖30		8 32

K24 WEEKDAYS TORRINGTON AND ILFRACOMBE TO YEOFORD

UP

M	C	M	C	Station		No.	LE	To Exmouth Jn. Sidings (SX until 13th September inclusive. Daily commencing 16th September)		Freight or LE (SX until 13th September inclusive. Daily commencing 16th September)	LE Q	LE SO (Runs 22nd June to 10th August, also 14th September)		(SX until 13th September inclusive. Daily commencing 16th September)		LE Q	To Crediton SX	SO (Commences 21st September)
							am	am		am	am	am		PM		PM	PM	PM
0	0			TORRINGTON Ⓚ	dep	1	6‖40			10 55								
5	9			Bideford New Ⓚ	arr	2				11X 6								
					dep	3	6X49			11 7								
5	49			Bideford Goods ⒾⓀ	arr	4	6‖52			11 10								
					dep	5						11‖40		12 40				
7	59			Instow Ⓚ	arr	6						11X46						
					dep	7						11 49		12 47				
				East Yelland Sdg.	arr	8								12 51				
					dep	9								1 6				
11	40			Fremington Ⓚ	arr	10								1 11				
					dep	11					11‖30	11 56				1‖35		
		0	0	ILFRACOMBE	dep	12												
		3	10	Mortehoe and W'combe	arr	13												
					dep	14												
		6	58	Heddon Mill Crossing		15												
		9	0	Braunton	arr	16												
					dep	17												
		9	74	Wrafton	arr	18												
					dep	19												
		14	7	Pottington Signal Box 🅃		20												
		14	20	Barnstaple Town 🅃	arr	21												
				Ⓣ	dep	22												
		14	58	Shapland and P. Sdg.	arr	23												
					dep	24												
14	12	14	76	BARNSTAPLE JN. ⓉⓀ	arr	25					11‖35	12‖ 1				1‖40		
					dep	26		5 45										
		19	22	Chapelton	arr	27												
					dep	28												
		21	52	Umberleigh	arr	29		6 0										
				Ⓚ	dep	30		6 40										
		25	64	Portsmouth Arms Ⓚ	arr	31												
					dep	32		6 51										
		28	55	Kings Nympton Ⓚ	arr	33		6 59										
					dep	34		7 6										
		32	51	Eggesford Ⓚ	arr	35		7X18										
					dep	36		7 48									3 17	3 17
		36	43	Lapford Ⓚ	arr	37											3 27	3 27
					dep	38		7 58									3 55	3 53
		38	72	Morchard Road Ⓚ	arr	39												4 0
					dep	40		8 8									4 2	4 14
		40	44	Copplestone Ⓚ	arr	41												4 21
					dep	42		8 14									4 8	4 52
		42	43	Coleford Jn.		43		8 18									4 12	4 56
		43	40	YEOFORD	arr	44		8 21									4W15	4 59
					dep	45		9 7									4 20	

TORRINGTON AND ILFRACOMBE TO YEOFORD WEEKDAYS K25

No.	SF To Feltham SX	SF To Nine Elms SO (Commences 21st September)	(SX until 13th September inclusive. Daily commencing 16th September; Set down churns of water at Willingcott Crossing)	SO (Until 14th September inclusive; Set down churns of water at Willingcott Crossing)	XF To Nine Elms SX	LE SX Q	SO (Commences 21st September)	SX (Barnstaple Jn. arrive 7.9 pm when not required to call at Shapland and Petter's Sdg.)	SF To Nine Elms SO (Until 14th September inclusive)		SF To Nine Elms (SX until 13th September inclusive. Daily commencing 16th September)	SX Q	Q (Available SX until 13th September inclusive, Daily commencing 16th September)	Q (Available SX until 13th September inclusive. Daily commencing 16th September)	To Exmouth Jn. Sidings Q	SUNDAYS XF To Nine Elms		
	PM	PM	PM	PM	PM	PM	PM	PM	PM		PM	PM	PM	PM	PM	PM		
1	12 45	12 45							4 5		5 25	6 0						
2																		
3	12 57	12 57							4X17		5 39	6X14						
4	1 0	1 0							4 20									
5	1 55	1 55			4 15				4 58									
6	2 2	2 2							5X 5									
7	2 6	2 6			4 21				5 14		5 47	6 21						
8																		
9																		
10	2 13	2 13			4X29				5 21		5X55	6X29						
11	2 21	2 21			4 48	4‖55			5 31		6 3	6 48		8 37				
12			3 14	3 40									7 0					
13			3 28	3 54														
14			3 33	4 0														
15			3 44	4 11														
16			3 52	4 19									7 28					
17			4 10	4 38									7 38					
18			4 13	4 41														
19			4 24	4 51														
20			4 33	5 0			5 26	6 50					7 49					
21							5 27	6 52										
22			4 34	5 1			5 35	7 5					7 50					
23							5 37	7R 7										
24							5 51	7R20										
25	2 29	2 29	4 38	5 5	4 54	5‖ 0	5 53	7 22	5 39		6 11	6 54	7 54	8 45				
26	3 20	3 20			5 8				6 12		6 41				9 2	6 30		
27		3R29																
28		3R33																
29	3 35	3 40							6 27						9 17			
30	3 40	4 9			5 19				6 35		6 54				9 27	6 41		
31		4 20			5X25				6 46									
32	3 50	4 25			5 28				6 53		7 2				9 37	6 47		
33		4 33							7 1									
34	3 58	4 43			5 34				7 10		7 11				9 47	6 52		
35	4 8	4X53							7X20		7X20							
36	4 43	5 17			5 40				7 48		7 54				9 56	6 58		
37					5X46													
38	4 52	5 26			5 55				7 57		8 3				10 5	7 4		
39	4X59																	
40	5 4	5 33			6 0				8 4		8 10				10 12	7 8		
41	5 11	5 40			6 5											7 13		
42	5 22	5 50			6 16				8 10		8 16				10 18	7 25		
43	5 26	5 54			6 21				8 14		8 20				10 22	7 31		
44	5 30								8 17		8 23				10 25			
45	5 48	5 56							8 30		8 50				10 48			

freight train was derailed near St Cyres, damaging a length of track. On 30th September 1960, after a day of torrential rain the level of the River Yeo rose rapidly and it washed away a bridge and section of embankment at Downes, just east of Crediton. Fortunately the driver of an 'up' train sensed the danger and halted the train, avoiding an accident. A bus services was operated between Exeter and Crediton until the track could be reinstated and traffic resumed on 12th October.

There was another accident at Yeoford station which was potentially very serious, but which caused no major injury. The 2am 'up' freight from Plymouth Friary had hit and killed a pony straying on the line near Bow, the carcase being responsible for uncoupling the train into two parts which was unknown to the train crew. The Coleford Junction signalman, Eddie Clapp, noticed the 'West Country' class locomotive passing with only two oil tankers and no tail lights, so immediately put detonators on the track to warn the guard that the remainder of the train was running down the bank out of control at increasing speed. Eddie Clapp had already notified the Yeoford signalman, Bill Keat, but the driver made his booked stop at Yeoford, not seeing the signal to proceed from the signal box. The inevitable collision took place

The 10.48am Torrington to Waterloo express at speed near Crediton on 28th August 1954, behind N class 2-6-0 No. 31841.

S. C. Nash

outside Yeoford signal box when the rear portion of the divided train crashed into the oil tanks and locomotive. The two tank wagons were damaged and their load of paraffin poured out. They in turn stove in the tender of the locomotive, which, having lost its water, caused the driver to drop the fire. Thankfully, the paraffin did not catch fire and the fire brigade arrived quickly to damp things down.

Railway Reports

By 1960 the whole British Railways system was losing considerable traffic to road transport - private cars, buses and lorries, and railway deficits were increasing. The

King's Nympton, 20th June 1959 as N class 2-6-0 No.31832 heads an 'up' passenger train of Bulleid stock.

R. J. Sellick

Umberleigh, 20th June 1959 and the signalman prepares to hand over the single line token to the driver of Bulleid Pacific No.34079 *141 Squadron*, on a long 'up' train.

R. J. Sellick

N class 2-6-0 No. 31843 on a 'down' train of mixed passenger stock, 20th June 1959.

R. J. Sellick

At Barnstaple Junction on 7th April 1953 M7 class 0-4-4T No. 30256 waits outside the shed whilst an N class 2-6-0 shunts the yard.

R. J. Sellick

government brought in Dr Richard Beeching from ICI to be the new Chairman of British Railways, and in March 1963 he published his recommendations in "The Reshaping of British Railways", popularly known as the Beeching Report. This recommended the development of freight and fast passenger services on the main lines, concentrating on the profitable bulk flows of traffic, and

the elimination of large numbers of unprofitable stations and branch lines. A series of maps illustrated the situation, showing the minimal level of passenger and freight traffic of less than 5,000 passengers and 5,000 tons per week on all the North Devon lines north of Coleford Junction. Every intermediate station between Exeter and Barnstaple had passenger receipts less than £5,000 per annum and all

In the earlier British Railways period Lapford station was flooded on 1st October 1960 when the River Yeo burst its banks. The river passes under both road and railway towards the top of the photograph, and to the right, above the flood level, can be seen the cattle pens and auctioneers hut of the Lapford Periodical Auction Market. Permanent way materials lie on the 'up' road.

D. Pearce

On 30th September 1960 following torrential rain the River Yeo rose and washed out a bridge near Downes, a mile east of Crediton. Permanent way staff inspect the damage.
E. Clapp

but three handled less than 5,000 tons of freight. Only between Cowley Bridge Junction and Coleford Junction was traffic at a higher level, but west of Okehampton this again fell to a minimum level.

The recommendations for North Devon's railways were devastating, with the withdrawal of passenger services in three of the four lines to Barnstaple, leaving only the Barnstaple to Exeter line with all the intermediate stations closed with the exception of Crediton, Lapford and Eggesford. The line from Barnstaple to Torrington and Meeth was to be retained for freight services only. The only public goods station to be retained in North Devon was at Barnstaple, although a few private sidings were to be kept, such as that for Ambrosia at Lapford. Further afield all Southern lines west of Meldon Quarry, near Okehampton, were to be closed completely.

Later in 1963 the North Devon Railway Report, written by David St John Thomas and sponsored by the Dartington Hall Trustees was published. It accepted that receipts for passenger and goods traffic covered less than half of the running cost of the railway system in North Devon, with many stations and trains covering less than a fifth of their costs, and carried the results of an extensive traffic survey taken on 7th May 1963. It recommended that King's Nympton station be retained as a railhead for South Molton, that the Exeter - Barnstaple services be reduced to about six trains a day, one or two running through to London with all making better connections at Exeter St Davids with Western main line trains, and that double track sections be singled with full length passing loops. Other recommendations included the retention of the Ilfracombe line passenger service, a skeleton passenger service to Bideford and numerous economies including dieselization and automatic level crossings.

Rationalization of the Railways of North Devon

At the end of 1962 the Western Region again took over all the Southern lines in the west country, this time for good. There were few visible changes until on Sunday 5th September 1964 the last "Atlantic Coast Express" and other through trains ran from Waterloo. Diesel locomotives had already begun to share duties with steam engines, but the new era really began on Monday 6th September 1964 when a new semi-fast diesel hauled service was inaugurated between Waterloo and Exeter St Davids, but there were no onward connections. Instead diesel trains ran between Exeter St Davids, Ilfracombe and

Plymouth via Okehampton connecting with the Paddington express service. Only one principal express passenger train continued to run on the Southern west of Exeter, the Plymouth to Brighton restaurant car train, which ran until 4th March 1967. There were connecting trains from Barnstaple Junction to Torrington, and a diesel service from Barnstaple Junction to Taunton. Both multiple unit and locomotive hauled trains were used, but in several cases, the service was already doomed.

The last passenger service between Torrington and Halwill Junction ran on 27th February 1965, and the last between Barnstaple Junction and Torrington on 2nd October 1965, the line from Barnstaple to Meeth being retained for freight only. The Barnstaple to Taunton line saw its last passenger service on 1st October 1966 and the whole line was closed with the exception of the Victoria Road freight branch. So, by the end of 1966, North Devon had only a passenger service between Exeter and Ilfracombe, together with the two goods branches from Barnstaple.

After publication of the Beeching Report there was much concern and rumour about the condition of the old viaducts across the River Exe at Cowley Bridge. As we

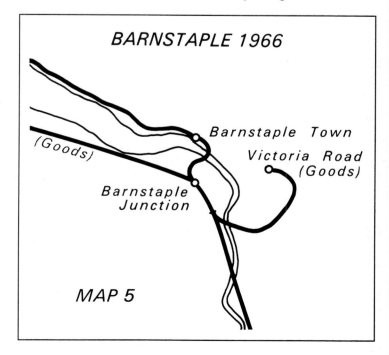

BARNSTAPLE 1966

(Goods)

Barnstaple Town

Victoria Road (Goods)

Barnstaple Junction

MAP 5

Table 59 — **Weekdays**

Exeter St David's to Plymouth (via Okehampton) and Ilfracombe

			K	A	B				C	D	E	[symbol]		B		B
EXETER ST DAVID'S	d			5 18	5 31				8 22	9 00	10 48	11 47		13 24		13 32
NEWTON ST CYRES	d								8 29		10 57					13 39
CREDITON	d				5 45				8 34	9 11	11 02					13 44
YEOFORD	d				5 53				8 41	9 18	11 09	12 03				13 51
BOW	d									9 26	11 18			13 44		
NORTH TAWTON	d									9 33	11 24			13 50		
SAMPFORD COURTENAY	d									9 39	11 29					
OKEHAMPTON	a			5 57						9 46	11 36			14 01		
	d			6 05			7 02			9 50	11 40				14 15	
BRIDESTOWE	d			6 19			7 22			10 03	11 53					
LYDFORD	d			6 26			7 30			10 10	11 58				14 33	
BRENTOR	d			6 30			7 34			10 14	12 02					
TAVISTOCK NORTH	d	6 00		6b47		7 15	7c50	9 00		10 25	12 13		14 00		14 45	
BERE ALSTON	d	6 12		7 00		7 26	8 04	9 11		10 37	12 25		14 10		14 56	
BERE FERRERS	d	6 17		7 06		7 32	8 10	9 17		10 42	12 30		14 17		15 02	
ST BUDEAUX, VICTORIA ROAD	d	6 25		7 14		7 39	8 18	9 24		10 50	12 38		14 25		15 10	
KEYHAM	d	6 28		7 18		7 42	8 22	9 27		10 54	12 41		14 29			
DOCKYARD HALT	d	6 30		7 20		7 45					12 43		14 33			
DEVONPORT, ALBERT ROAD	d	6 33		7 23		7 47	8 26	9 31		10 58	12 46		14 36		15 16	
PLYMOUTH	a	6 37		7 28		7 56	8 30	9 35		11 02	12 50		14 40		15 20	
COPPLESTONE	d				6 00				8 46			12 08				13 57
MORCHARD ROAD	d				6 04				8 50			12 12				14 01
LAPFORD	d				6 09				8 55			12 17				14 06
EGGESFORD	d				6 16				9 01			12 23				14 12
KING'S NYMPTON	d				6 23				9 07			12 30				14 18
PORTSMOUTH ARMS	d				6 29				9 13			12 35				14 24
UMBERLEIGH	d				6 36				9 21			12 42				14 30
CHAPELTON	d								9 27			12 47				14 35
BARNSTAPLE JUNCTION	a		6 04		6 46				9 35			12 54				14 42
	d		6 12		7 12				9 38			12 55				14 44
BARNSTAPLE TOWN	d		6 17		7 15				9 42			13 00				14 47
WRAFTON	d		6 25		7 23				9 50			13 07				14 55
BRAUNTON	d		6 29		7 28				9 52			13 10				14 57
MORTEHOE & WOOLACOMBE	d		6 43		7 43				10 06			13 23				15 10
ILFRACOMBE	a		6 52		7 52				10 15			13 32				15 19

		L	G			E	H		B	E	J			E [symbol]	
EXETER ST DAVID'S	d	14 22	15 10	15 35		15 45	16 35		17 22	17 50	19 38			20 15	20 20
NEWTON ST CYRES	d			15 42			16 46			17 57	19 47				20 28
CREDITON	d			15 47		15 55	16 53		17 35	18 02	19 52				20 33
YEOFORD	d			15 54			17 00			18 09				20 32	20 40
BOW	d			16 02						18 17					20 49
NORTH TAWTON	d			16 08						18 23					20 55
SAMPFORD COURTENAY	d			16 14						18 29					21 00
OKEHAMPTON	a		15 43	16 21						18 35					21 07
	d		15 45	16 22						18 40					21 09
BRIDESTOWE	d			16 35						18 54					21 21
LYDFORD	d			16 41						19 00					21 27
BRENTOR	d			16 45						19 05					21 30
TAVISTOCK NORTH	d		16 11	16 55				17 40		19 15		20 00			21 40
BERE ALSTON	d		16 25	17 07				17 52		19 27		20a11	20 31		21 52
BERE FERRERS	d			17 12				17 58		19 32			20 37		21 58
ST BUDEAUX, VICTORIA ROAD	d			17 20				18 05		19 42			20 44		22 05
KEYHAM	d			17 23				18 08		19 44			20 47		22 08
DOCKYARD HALT	d			17 26											
DEVONPORT, ALBERT ROAD	d		16 45	17 29				18 14		19 49			20 52		22 13
PLYMOUTH	a		16 50	17 33				18 18		19 53			20 55		22 16
COPPLESTONE	d					16 05	17g13		17 46		20 02				
MORCHARD ROAD	d					16 10	17 18		17 50		20 06				
LAPFORD	d					16 14	17 22		17 54		20 10			20 45	
EGGESFORD	d					16 20	17 29		18 00		20 17			20 50	
KING'S NYMPTON	d					16 27	17 35		18 07		20 24			20 58	
PORTSMOUTH ARMS	d					16 33	17 40		18 13		20 29				
UMBERLEIGH	d					16 40	17 47		18 20		20 35				
CHAPELTON	d					16 45	17 52		18 24		20 40				
BARNSTAPLE JUNCTION	a	15 18				16 52	17 58		18 31		20 47			21 19	
	d	15 23			16 15	16 53	18 00		18 33		20 49				
BARNSTAPLE TOWN	d	15 27			16 18	17 00	18 04		18 37		20 53				
WRAFTON	d	15 35			16 26	17 07	18 12		18 44		21 00				
BRAUNTON	d	15 38			16 29	17 10	18 14		18 47		21 03				
MORTEHOE & WOOLACOMBE	d	15 22			16 43	17 24	18 28		19 00		21 17				
ILFRACOMBE	a	16 00			16 52	17 32	18 37		19 10		21 25				

Heavy figures indicate through carriages
For general notes see page 3

A Through train from London Waterloo
B Through train from Exeter Central
C Through train from Exmouth
D Through train from Axminster
E Through train from Salisbury
G Through train from Brighton
H Through train from Sidmouth
J Through train from Honiton
K Through train from Exeter Central dep 5.05
L From 24 May. [symbol] from London Paddington
b Arr 6.39
c Arr 7.43
g Arr 17.07

Table 59—continued — **Weekdays**

Ilfracombe and Plymouth (via Okehampton) to Exeter St. David's

			E [symbol]	E	D		A	C		A		D	G ⊗	L	D			D
ILFRACOMBE	d				7 00			8 05	9 50					11 00	11 50			13 50
MORTEHOE & WOOLACOMBE	d				7 12			8 17	10 03					11 13	12 02			14 02
BRAUNTON	d				7 23			8 28	10 13					11 24	12 13			14 12
WRAFTON	d				7 25			8 30	10 16					11 27	12 15			14 15
BARNSTAPLE TOWN	d				7 33			8 38	10 24					11 36	12 24			14 24
BARNSTAPLE JUNCTION	a				7 36			8 42	10 27					11 39	12 27			14 27
	d		7 05		7 37			8 44		10 38				11 44	12 30			14 33
CHAPELTON	d				7 43			8 50							12 36			14 39
UMBERLEIGH	d				7 49			8 55							12 41			14 45
PORTSMOUTH ARMS	d				7 55			9 00							12 48			14 51
KING'S NYMPTON	d		7 25		8 01			9 07		10 58					12 54			15 00
EGGESFORD	d		7 32		8 07			9 15		11 05					13 00			15 07
LAPFORD	d		7 38		8 14			9 23							13 07			15 14
MORCHARD ROAD	d				8 19			9 28							13 12			15 20
COPPLESTONE	d				8 24			9 33							13 16			15 24
PLYMOUTH	d	6 00				7 30	7 50				9 50		10 55			12 20	13 15	
DEVONPORT, ALBERT ROAD	d	6 04				7 34	7 54				9 54		11 00			12 24	13 19	
DOCKYARD HALT	d	6 06				7 36	7 56									12 26	13 21	
KEYHAM	d	6 08				7 38	7 58									12 28	13 23	
ST BUDEAUX, VICTORIA ROAD	d	6 11				7 42	8 02				10 00					12 32	13 26	
BERE FERRERS	d	6 20				7 49	8 10				10 08					12 39	13 33	
BERE ALSTON	d	6 32				7 57	8 16				10 15					12 47	13 41	
TAVISTOCK NORTH	d	6e45		7 10		8a09	8 28				10 26		11 25			12 58	13a52	
BRENTOR	d			7 19												13 06		
LYDFORD	d			7 24			8 42				10 38					13 10		
BRIDESTOWE	d			7 30			8 48				10 45					13 16		
OKEHAMPTON	a			7 46			9 00				10 57		11 52			13 28		
	d			7 48			9 03					11 10	11 54			13 32		
SAMPFORD COURTENAY	d			7 54								11 16				13 38		
NORTH TAWTON	d			7 59			9 13					11 21				13 42		
BOW	d			8 04								11 28						
YEOFORD	d		7 53	8 13	8 30		9 25			11 24		11 38			13 22			15 30
CREDITON	d		7 59	8 19	8 35		9 33			11 29		11 44			13 28	14 00		15 35
NEWTON ST CYRES	d			8 24						11 34					13 33			15 40
EXETER ST DAVID'S	a		8 10	8 34	8 50		9 45	9 51		11 42		11 58	12 25	12 43	13 45	14 12		15 47

			H			K	SX	D		E		D	
ILFRACOMBE	d		15 50					17 20		18 15		19 45	
MORTEHOE & WOOLACOMBE	d		16 02					17 33		18 28		19 57	
BRAUNTON	d		16 12					17 45		18 38		20 08	
WRAFTON	d		16 15					17 48		18 40		20 13	
BARNSTAPLE TOWN	d		16 23					17 57		18 48		20 23	
BARNSTAPLE JUNCTION	a		16 27					18 00		18 52		20 27	
	d		16 29					18 06		18 55		20 31	
CHAPELTON	d		16 35					18 13		19 00		20 38	
UMBERLEIGH	d		16 40					18 20		19 06		20 43	
PORTSMOUTH ARMS	d		16 46					18 28		19 13		20 50	
KING'S NYMPTON	d		16 52					18 33		19 19		20 56	
EGGESFORD	d		16 58					18 42		19 25		21 04	
LAPFORD	d		17 05					18 50		19 33		21 11	
MORCHARD ROAD	d		17 10					18 55		19 38		21 17	
COPPLESTONE	d		17 14					19 00		19 42		21 22	
PLYMOUTH	d	15 15		16 10	16 48	17 15	17 39		18 13		19 42		21 35
DEVONPORT, ALBERT ROAD	d	15 19		16 14	16 52	17 19	17 43		18 17		19 47		21 40
DOCKYARD HALT	d	15 21		16 16	16 55	17 21			18 19		19 49		21 42
KEYHAM	d	15 23		16 18	16 57	17 23	17 47		18 21		19 51		21 43
ST BUDEAUX, VICTORIA ROAD	d	15 27		16 23	17 02	17 29	17 52		18 24		19 54		21 47
BERE FERRERS	d	15 35		16 31	17 08	17 36	17 59		18 32		20 02		21 55
BERE ALSTON	d	15 42		16 38	17 18	17 44	18a06		18 39		20 10		22 03
TAVISTOCK NORTH	d	15 54		16a49	17 30	17 55			18a51		20 23		22a14
BRENTOR	d	16 04			17 40						20 33		
LYDFORD	d	16 08			17 45						20 37		
BRIDESTOWE	d	16 15			17 52						20 43		
OKEHAMPTON	a	16 27			18 05	18 22					20 56		
	d	16 29				18 28					21 00		
SAMPFORD COURTENAY	d	16 35				18 35					21 05		
NORTH TAWTON	d	16 40				18 41					21 10		
BOW	d	16 45				18 47					21 16		
YEOFORD	d	16 54						19 08		19 48	21 24	21 30	
CREDITON	d	16 58						19 14		19 53		21 38	
NEWTON ST CYRES	d	17 04						19 20		19 58		21 44	
EXETER ST DAVID'S	a	17 11	17 37			19 08		19 30		20 05	21 40	21 53	

Heavy figures indicate through carriages
For general notes see page 3

A Through train to Salisbury
C Through train to Kingswear
D Through train to Exeter Central
E Through train to Exmouth
G Through train to Brighton
H Through train to Honiton
K Through train to Eastleigh
L From 24 May. [symbol] to London Paddington

saw in Chapter 4, new viaducts were built in 1875 in connection with track doubling and replacing earlier structures. However, between November 1965 and January 1967, two viaducts were rebuilt for a single line of track, the new works being brought into use on 15th January 1967.

Even before the publication of the Beeching Report small goods yards had been closed. starting with Newton St Cyres in 1960 and Portsmouth Arms in 1961. By the end of 1965 only three intermediate yards remained open, those at King's Nympton, Lapford and Crediton, and these mainly for coal traffic. When the new coal concentration depot at Exmouth Junction opened on 4th December 1967, these three yards were shut for public traffic, but private sidings were retained at King's Nympton and Lapford, mainly for fertilizer traffic.

A gradual process of withdrawing the posts of station staff was also initiated, and eventually every intermediate station became an unstaffed halt. Waiting shelters and electric lights were installed and when available, the station houses were sold off into private use. In many cases a single platform now sufficed, but at Eggesford a new 'down' platform was constructed after the subsidence of the original one. From 30th September 1968, the guards on the diesel trains were responsible for collecting the fares from passengers joining the trains at all intermediate stations.

At about this time, there was a fatal accident just north of Coleford Junction. A self-propelled ditching machine working for a local farmer attempted to cross the line on an occupation crossing, when it was in collision with an evening diesel train up from Barnstaple. The ditcher driver was killed, the multiple unit derailed, and the train driver and passengers shaken. The local ganger had instructed the driver of the ditching machine not to cross unless railway engineers were present, but the driver disregarded the instruction and paid for his error with his life. By this time crossover points at Coleford Junction had been removed, so signalman Bill Keat was called out to act as pilotman between Yeoford and Copplestone, all North Devon train using the 'down' road between these station. The next day, the other Coleford Junction signalman, Sam Ponsford, counted forty separate pieces of the ditching machine scattered along the track. Along the same stretch of line one summer a tractor and trailer loaded with bales of hay ran out of control down the embankment and blocked the track. Fortunately, the railway authorities were informed and single line working was again instituted until the Exmouth Junction 45 ton Ransomes & Rapier crane arrived next day to clear the wreckage.

Another aspect of rationalization, was the closure of signal boxes, associated with taking out passing loops, goods yards, double track sections and junctions. First to go in 1964 was Morchard Road, and when the last four closed in 1971, only Crediton, Eggesford and Barnstaple Junction A remained. In fact, the original 1873 signal box at Eggesford literally collapsed into the mill leat below and was closed on 21st November 1967, but was replaced with a new box which opened on 28th September 1969. Crediton and Eggesford signal boxes also supervised level crossings, converted to the lifting barrier type, but other crossings such as Umberleigh Gates were converted to automatic operations, Salmon Pool Gates was similarly converted as late as 1980.

By the end of 1965 the only full public goods services in North Devon were operated from the yards at Barnstaple. Full loads were dealt with at Barnstaple Junction with parcels and sundries at Victoria Road. However, when the parcels and sundries depot came under the management of National Carriers Limited there were disagreements about which parcels should proceed by goods trains or by NCL, and the costs of rail haulage were disputed. Eventually NCL commenced using road transport between its depots at Barnstaple and Exeter, and the Victoria Road goods station was closed on 5th March 1970, and the branch on 30th May.

All general goods services on the Ilfracombe line had been withdrawn on 7th September 1964, but despite economy measures, including track singling, the last train

ran on Saturday 3rd October 1970. Despite a recommendation in the Beeching Report the surviving service on the Plymouth line, between Exeter and Okehampton, already severed between Meldon and Bere Alston on 6th May 1968, was also withdrawn when the last train ran on 3rd June 1972. This closure was in contrast to the fate of two other Southern lines in Devon, the Exmouth branch and the Plymouth to Gunnislake line, which were proposed for closure in the Beeching Report but remained open. However, the Okehampton line has remained open for the stone trains from Meldon Quarry.

In 1971 there were two major track singling operations. First, on 21st May, the line between Barnstaple and Umberleigh was singled and the layout at Barnstaple simplified, and then on 17th October a major change occurred in the south. The physical junction between the Barnstaple and Meldon lines was moved to Crediton and two single lines ran parallel west from there, giving the appearance of double track as far as their divergence at Coleford. The old South Western and Southern signalling at Crediton, Eggesford and Barnstaple was largely swept away in favour of Western Region semaphore signals which looked somewhat incongruous in their South Western setting.

So by the summer of 1972 the North Devon railway situation had stabilised and did not change significantly for a decade. Starting from Cowley Bridge Junction there was a short length of single track over the new viaducts opening out into a conventional 'up' and 'down' double track to Crediton. Here a pair of crossovers formed a junction for the two single lines to Meldon and Eggesford, the only crossing place on the way to Barnstaple. From here another freight line continued on to Torrington and Meeth. There was an engineers siding at Crediton and other sidings at Lapford and King's Nympton. The line was kept open for longer in the evening with the last trains leaving Exeter at about 9pm and Barnstaple about 10pm.

On 21st November 1967 the 'down' platform which supported the signal box at Eggesford collapsed into the mill leat below. Signalman Mr W. Butt could only get out of the signal box through the windows, assisted by signalman Mr W. McMath.

North Devon Journal Herald

Barnstaple Junction about 1971, showing the remaining connection to the then closed Ilfracombe line. From left to right, diesel multiple unit set No. P581, Class 08 shunter and van in the middle siding and a Class 25 locomotive with a train of empty clay wagons for Marland and Meeth.

Lens of Sutton

143

The North Devon Railway Line Development Group

In 1978 the North Devon Railway Line Development Group was formed to encourage the fullest possible use of the Barnstaple to Exeter line by both passengers and freight and to promote improvements to the line and its services, by assisting British Rail in publicising train services and facilities on the line. The inaugural meeting was held in Barnstaple on 28th April and a committee of local men established to run the group, with Mr Alan Rushton of Bideford as secretary and treasurer later succeeded by Mr Ian Dinmore at the Barnstaple Travel Centre. The regular newsletter contained a number of suggestions for the improvement of services including speeding up trains by eliminating some intermediate stops, better connections at Exeter, more through services to London and improvements of bridges to allow larger locomotives to run through to Barnstaple. A very successful "Ride the North Devon Line" promotional booklet was produced in conjunction with British Rail and other bodies.

Eggesford on Saturday 23rd August 1980. An 'up' train formed by a three-coach diesel multiple unit crosses a locomotive-hauled 'down' train. The new 1969 signal box and lifting barriers of the level crossing can be seen.

Author

Barnstaple on 28th August 1980. Class 25 No. 25058 shunts a van on to the rear of the two diesel multiple units forming the 16.11 'up' train.

Author

144

The ceremonial opening of Barnstaple Travel Centre on 12th November 1981 performed by Mr George Creber, chairman of Devon County Council (right), supported by Mr Tony Speller MP for North Devon and Sir Peter Parker, chairman of British Rail (centre).

North Devon Journal Herald

The Group also produced a plan for a Bideford to Exeter passenger train service, written by Roger Joanes, and published in July 1979. The plan was well documented and proposed the opening of the Barnstaple to Bideford line to passenger trains catering for long distant passengers using the InterCity network at Exeter. One major difficulty in such a reopening of the passenger service between Barnstaple and Bideford was that under existing legislation, if the new service was unsuccessful, it would take several years to close it again. This would involve a very large expense which was a great discouragement to any possible re-opening. However, the Member of

Parliament for North Devon, Mr Tony Speller, took the matter up in the House of Commons in 1981 and his private member's Amendment to the 1962 Transport Act, to facilitate such re-openings without these penalties, was passed with widespread support. Several re-openings have been made under this legislation, but not in North Devon.

An important event for the North Devon line occurred on 10th November 1981, when a Travel Centre was opened at Barnstaple station by Mr George Creber, the Chairman of Devon County Council, assisted by Sir Peter Parker, the Chairman of British Rail. The County Council had contributed £30,000 towards the total cost of £108,000

The 12.25 train from Barnstaple to Exeter arrives at Crediton on 26th August 1981, the driver handing over the single line token to signalman J. Vinsen. The crossing is now protected by lifting barriers operated from the signal box.

Author

and British Rail's new 1981 timetable had provided more and faster trains between Barnstaple and Exeter, several of them calling only at Crediton and Eggesford. At the opening there was considerable support for the re-opening of the line to Bideford for passenger services if financial support were forthcoming, but it was not. In the same year the manager of the Barnstaple Travel Centre, John Ware, introduced very attractive fares to Barnstaple on market days, Tuesdays and Fridays. Passengers on the two morning trains, from Crediton downwards, could travel to Barnstaple for 50p return and fill up seats on two lightly loaded trains. The public response was excellent with passengers travelling in their hundreds on the two services. Subsequently the promotion was repeated in slightly different but still attractive terms which continued to fill the trains.

During this period there were a number of incidents and mishaps on the North Devon line. On several occasions, such as February 1978 and January 1982, heavy falls of snow blocked the line for several days until a snow plough could clear it. Occasionally, such as in March 1981, there was heavy flooding of the River Exe which closed both the Western Region main line and the North Devon line at Cowley Bridge. Freight trains were at times in difficulty, often damaging the track until the train crew realised that there had been a derailment and were able to stop. Such an accident occurred on 24th April 1980 at Copplestone, and twice with Meldon stone trains, once at Yeoford when spilled ballast blocked both lines, and in August 1984 at Bow when that line was shut for a week. On 5th April 1982 a locomotive was derailed whilst shunting at Lapford sidings, and in July 1984 a train hit a car crossing the line at Salmon Pool Crossing.

Developments in the 1980s

As the 1980s unfolded a number of further developments occurred. Hopes of extending passenger services to Bideford were dashed when the Barnstaple to Meeth line closed completely. The last clay wagons were hauled over the line on 13th September 1982 and the "Last Train to Torrington" ran on 6th November. One effect of this closure was to reduce significantly the payload of the daily freight train running between Barnstaple and Exeter which for many years had included a dozen or so clay wagons.

The Western Region's West of England main line was one of the last major main lines in the country to be controlled by semaphore signalling. In the mid-1980s a programme of replacement with multiple aspect colour light signalling was initiated, based on power signal boxes at Westbury and Exeter. The North Devon line was affected by this at Cowley Bridge Junction, but it was also decided, as an economy measure, that the existing traffic to Crediton could be accommodated on a single track. On the weekend of 15th-16th December 1984 the line was closed completely for the commissioning of a new layout and signalling at Crediton. The line to Cowley Bridge was singled, a long passing loop installed, and new colour light signalling controlled from a panel in the old 1875 signal box brought into use. For a short time all North Devon and Meldon trains had to slow at Cowley Bridge Junction for single line token exchange, but in 1985 Cowley Bridge Junction signal box was closed when the new power signal box took over the control of the Exeter area.

The railway lorry collection and delivery service from Barnstaple was withdrawn as part of a national British Rail policy change in mid 1981, but in late 1982 a limited service was introduced for parts of North Devon in and

The 16.07 train from Barnstaple to Paignton, comprising four BR Mk 1 coaches behind No. 31213, awaits its departure on 24th August 1984. This train ran to Post Office requirements, and two PO vans had off-loaded mailbags into the guards van.

Author

Right and below: On the night of Saturday 18th and Sunday 19th August 1984 engineers installed a point to the east of Crediton station, to be used for a crossing loop when the line was singled the following December. The two photographs show, above, ballast being spread from a slowly-moving train of 'Sea Cow' and 'Sea Lion' wagons and, below, the new point and ballast, with the ballast train heading away to Exeter.
Author

near Barnstaple, contracted out to the private firm of City Link. But sadly the mail contract for the Post Office ceased in January 1985, when the traffic was transferred to road transport. However "Red Star" and "Night Star" parcel services were encouraged and developed. Newspaper traffic ceased in July 1988 and soon the 4.05am service from Exeter ceased, together with the 5.50am from Barnstaple which had provided on early London connection.

In may 1986 a fleet of lightweight two-car multiple units, the 142 class or 'Skippers' were introduced on all branch line services in Devon and Cornwall, including the North Devon line. The new trains were fast and economical to operate, but their four-wheel chassis gave a rather bumpy and sometimes, noisy ride. At busy times there was insufficient accommodation either for the increasing numbers of passengers wishing to travel, or for large parcels, prams and bicycles. Sometimes special buses had to be run for passengers unable to get on the crowded trains. These problems, together with mechanical difficulties, led to the transfer of the fleet to Lancashire and Yorkshire from October 1987, the replacements being conventional two and three-car diesel multiple units from the Cardiff and Birmingham areas.

In the first half of 1987 the freight traffic handled at Barnstaple, mainly in cement, glue, timber and RAF stores, dwindled away and in September most sidings in the disused yard were lifted, with BR hoping to redevelop the site as a hypermarket. This left only Lapford siding to handle Speedlink traffic, mainly in grain, timber and fertilizers.

Barnstaple and Eggesford signal boxes closed on 1st

147

TRAIN SERVICES UNTIL 11 MAY 1980

Exeter — Barnstaple
Mondays to Saturdays

London Paddington	Birmingham New Street	Bristol Temple Meads	Plymouth	Exmouth	Exeter Central	Exeter St David's	Newton St Cyres	Crediton	Yeoford	Copplestone	Morchard Road	Lapford	Eggesford	King's Nympton	Portsmouth Arms	Umberleigh	Chapelton	Barnstaple	Ilfracombe	Lynton
00 05d	21 37f	02 20d	00 30	→		04 05		04 17	→	→	→		04 39		→	04 56	→	05 07		07 12n
—	02 02c	06 35	07 25	08 00	08 39	08 50	→	09 03	09 11	09 18	09 22	09 27	09 33	09 40	09 45	09 53	09 58		12 29	14 12r
08 30	08 15	10 07	10 10	11 02	11 30	11 35		11 46				12 06			→	15 07	→	15 17	16 25	—
11 40	10 15	11 55	13 11	13 18	13 44	14 14		14 25	14 32	→	14 42	14 50	14 57	→			15 17	16 25		18 52
13 30	12 15	13 55	14 36	15 15	15 41	16 08	→	16 19	→	→	16 33	16 41	16 47	→		16 58	→	17 10	18 25	
15 30	15 15	17 08	16 50	18 13	18 41	18 46	18 54	19 00	19 07	19 13	19 16	19 21	19 29	19 36	19 41	19 48	19 52	20 01	21 25	—
17 40	17 15	19 10	18 35	20 00	20 27	20 45	→	20 56	21 03	→			21 13	21 21		21 36	→	21 46	23 25	

Sundays

London Paddington	Birmingham New Street	Bristol Temple Meads	Plymouth	Exmouth	Exeter Central	Exeter St David's	Newton St Cyres	Crediton	Yeoford	Copplestone	Morchard Road	Lapford	Eggesford	King's Nympton	Portsmouth Arms	Umberleigh	Chapelton	Barnstaple	Ilfracombe	Lynton
—	—	—	09 45z	—		11 20	→	11 31	→	→	→	11 46	11 52	11 59	→	12 09	→	12 20	13 25	
D 10 30D	07 25D	11 35D	12 30D	—		13 55D	→	14 06D	→	→	14 21D	14 27D	14 34D	→	15 09C	17 25D		14 55D	17 25D	
C 10 30C	07 25C	11 05C	12 30C	—		14 20C	→	14 31C	→	→	14 46C	14 52C	14 59C	→	15 09C		15 20C	17 25C		
14 30	13 15	15 40y	15 55	17 23	17 50	18 00	→	18 11	→	→	18 26	18 32	18 39	→	18 49	→	19 00	21 25	

Barnstaple — Exeter
Mondays to Saturdays

Lynton	Ilfracombe	Barnstaple	Chapelton	Umberleigh	Portsmouth Arms	King's Nympton	Eggesford	Lapford	Morchard Road	Copplestone	Yeoford	Crediton	Newton St Cyres	Exeter St David's	Exeter Central	Exmouth	Plymouth	Bristol Temple Meads	Birmingham New Street	London Paddington
—	—	06 17	→	06 26	→	06 37	06 45	06 52	→	→	07 02	07 09	07 14	07 23	07 29	07 55				
—	06 40	07 50	08 00	08 05	08 13	08 19	08 27	08 35	08 40	08 45	08 50	08 58	09 03	09 13			10 45	08 51	10 40	10 27
07 15t	08 45	10 15	→	10 25	→	10 40	→	→	→	→	11 00	11 11	11 25	11 51			12 26	12 54	14 40	12 29
09 55	10 45	12 37	→	→	→	13 02	→	→	→	→	13 22	13 33	13 55	14 20			14 53	15 03	16 45	16 25
14 20r	14 45	16 10	→	16 20	→	16 32	16 40	16 47	→	16 59	17 06	17 18	18 00	18 41	18 40		18 53	20 48	20 25	
16 30	15 45	17 45	17 54	17 59	18 07	18 13	18 21	18 28	→	18 39	18 46	18 59	19 32	19 57	20 18	21 12	23 34g	22 30	
19 00	19 45	20 50	→	21 00	→	21 12	21 22	21 30	→	→	21 46	21 58	→	23 47	23 54h	03 45f	—			
	20 45	21 50				22 15			→	→	22 35	22 45	22 53	23 18	00 25	03 20j	05 48k			

Sundays

Lynton	Ilfracombe	Barnstaple	Chapelton	Umberleigh	Portsmouth Arms	King's Nympton	Eggesford	Lapford	Morchard Road	Copplestone	Yeoford	Crediton	Newton St Cyres	Exeter St David's	Exeter Central	Exmouth	Plymouth	Bristol Temple Meads	Birmingham New Street	London Paddington
—	—	12 28	→	12 37	→	12 48	12 55	13 02	→	→	13 17	13 28	→	14 51m	14 58e	16 07	18 40	16 40v		
	15 45	16 50	→	16 59	→	17 10	17 17	17 24	→	→	17 39	17 51	18 02	18 27	19 27b	→	→	21 17w		
	17 45	19 06	→	19 15	→	19 26	19 33	19 40	→	→	19 55	20 07	20 56	21 21	21 50	23 45		03 00q		

C   From 13 January
D   until 6 January
🚌 By Western National bus (to and from Barnstaple Station approach road)

b   arrive 19 33 from 13 January
c   Tuesday to Saturday mornings
d   Tuesdays to Saturdays and Mondays 8 October to 7 January
e   15 22 from 13 January
f   Monday to Friday nights, Sunday night depart 22 10
g   Mondays to Fridays arrive 23 27
h   On Saturdays until 6 January arrive 00 37. From 13 January arrive 00 28
j   Tuesdays to Saturdays. No service Saturday night/Sunday morning until 6 January. Sundays from 13 January arrive 04 44.

k   Tuesdays to Saturdays. Sundays until 6 January arrive 06 05, from 13 January arrive 07 10
m   from 30 March
n   on Saturdays arrive 07 07
p   From Barnstaple Bus Station
q   Not on 7 April and 5 May
r   Saturdays only
t   On Mondays to Fridays depart 07 20
v   Arrive 17 15, from 13 January
w   Arrive 21 38, from 13 January
y   Depart 15 29, from 13 January
z   Depart 09 40, from 13 January

The British Railways Board accept no liability for any inaccuracy in this folder. All fares and facilities may be altered or cancelled.

Published by British Rail Western   W2309/1179
Printed by Deanery Press Ltd., Stratford, London E15 2HU.

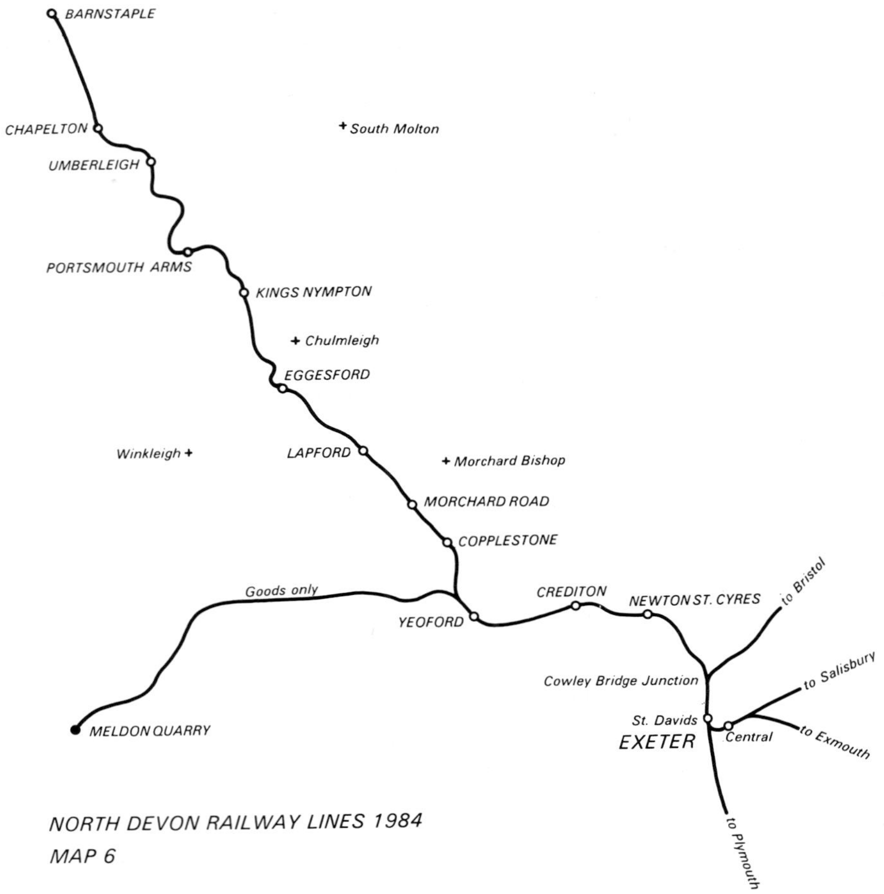

NORTH DEVON RAILWAY LINES 1984

MAP 6

Wednesday 13th August 1986 sees the 14.25 Barnstaple to Exeter train, a 'Skipper' Class 142 unit, approaching Nymet Bridge.

Author

Tuesday 12th August 1986 with the 14.25 Barnstaple to Exeter train, a 'Skipper' Class 142, pauses at Umberleigh. On the right is the wooden building and van used by the permanent way gang based here, who maintain this end of the line.

Author

November 1987. No Signalman Key Token (NSKT) apparatus was to be used west of Crediton, with train crews operating the token apparatus and the level crossing at Eggesford. This NSKT system, already in use on the Central Wales line, is designed to improve the economics of the line. The need for economy was underlined by construction work on the North Devon link road crossing the line south of Barnstaple station, which started in 1987, the completion of which in 1989 produced more competition for the line.

In 1988 the Transport Users Consultative Committee for Western England awarded its Superstaff Award to Ian Dinmore of the Barnstaple Travel Centre, having received many letters of support. However the following year, as another economy measure, the Travel Centre was reduced to a Booking Office and several railwaymen lost their jobs. On a more positive note in 1990 the line was heavily promoted as the Tarka Line to attract more use, an eleven-point development plan being funded by British Rail and local councils with £80,000.

In August 1990 engineers laid a new run-round loop south of Barnstaple station, capable of taking only four carriages, but took out the remaining sidings in the yard, together with the 'down' platform road which had previously provided the run-round loop. Plans were also in preparation to relocate Barnstaple station to the south, thus freeing the rest of the site for more commercial re-development. Meanwhile Speedlink announced the withdrawal of its wagonload service from mid-1991, when the Lapford siding was likely to close, thus completely ending rail freight operation in North Devon, although the Meldon stone trains are not affected.

In 1992 the veteran diesel multiple units are due to be replaced by Class 153 single unit 'Sprinter' vehicles, formed by modifying earlier Class 155 2-car units.

The driver of the 12.15 Exmouth train uses the new signalling facility at Eggesford to telephone the Crediton signalman for permission to use the Key Token machine to continue the journey to Barnstaple, after the 'up' service token is returned to the corresponding machine on the 'up' platform, Tuesday 28th March 1989. *Author*

Pathfinder Tours ran a special, the "Taw & Tor Tourer" through to Barnstaple on 16th September 1990 'top and tailed' by Class 50s Nos 50032 *Courageous* and 50031 *Hood*. From here, the twelve-coach train went to Exmouth, Newton Abbot and the Heathfield branch. The 'down' road at Barnstaple had been lifted only the previous month and the platform line reduced in length.

Steve Widdowson

Chapter 8

Traffic and Train Services

A Survey of Passenger Traffic

Passenger traffic on the North Devon line has always fallen into two distinct categories, a limited amount at each of the intermediate stations and a far greater volume of through traffic. Of the eleven intermediate stations only one, Crediton, directly served a community of more than a thousand people. The other stations served communities of only a few hundred, the larger villages of Morchard Bishop, Winkleigh and Chulmleigh being badly served by the railway. Few people commuted by train but local passenger traffic developed in other ways.

Serving an agricultural area the railway quickly developed its market business. Livestock markets were held at both Barnstaple and Exeter on Fridays. Cheap market tickets were issued to enable farmers and their wives to attend these markets, and this became a very important traffic. Farmers wives travelled to market with large baskets loaded with produce, including butter, eggs, cheese, poultry, rabbits, fruit and vegetables. At their market stalls they often had regular customers for their wares. As early as 1853 the Exeter & Crediton Railway was running an extra Market Train, and the North Devon Railway promoted this traffic with cheap market tickets. For many years this was the only cheap travel that was encouraged, the one parliamentary train with third class accommodation running at very inconvenient times early in the morning or late at night.

Apart from regular train services excursions were organised from an early stage by Robert Ogilvie in the 1850s. Broad gauge excursion trains ran from Bideford, picking up at the other stations and ran through to destinations including Torquay and Plymouth. Excursions by both scheduled and special trains continued to be a feature of the North Devon line, with the Southern Railway running a large number in the 1930s. Between 1977 and 1982 a considerable number of excursion trains organised by Mr Roger Joanes ran from Torrington, Bideford and Barnstaple to Paddington, South Devon and other destinations. Back in 1857 a fortnight's excursion was run from Paddington to North Devon to give

Londoners two weeks holiday in the area, thus starting another important traffic.

Often local events stimulated extra traffic, such as the annual Barnstaple Fair, the Bath and West Show held in 1859, a Barnstaple Flower Show or the North Devon Races at Barnstaple. Elsewhere on the line, there were the periodic livestock markets held at the Fox and Hounds Hotel at Eggesford and at many other stations, and horse racing at Crediton. Nowadays, the annual Chapelton Steam Fair in August serves the same function. In more recent years, there have been have large numbers of excursion trains run for railway enthusiasts over lines without regular passenger services or about to close. The "Last Train to Torrington", from Bristol, on 6th November 1982, loaded to 843 passengers in 15 coaches.

At two stations on the line passengers often had to change trains. This happened at Barnstaple Junction and also at Yeoford, where through passengers between the Plymouth line and North Devon changed trains. There was always considerable activity when trains were being divided or connected up, this being a regular activity at Barnstaple Junction and happened occasionally at Yeoford.

Passenger train traffic also included parcels, newspapers, mailbags, milk churns and other items carried in the luggage compartments and vans. For many years the first 'down' and last 'up' trains of the day carried the mails, making connections at Exeter and elsewhere. Postmen from more remote villages such as Winkleigh brought their mailbags to the station at Morchard Road or Eggesford in the evening for the 'up' mail, slept briefly in accommodation provided at the station, and rose early to collect the village mail the next morning. At one time the evening 'up' mail train from Torrington to Exeter carried post office staff who franked and sorted letters on board. Every station had an office for the parcels traffic, which was sometimes more numerous than the passengers. For many years another early morning 'down' train brought the London newspapers to North Devon, collecting the Plymouth morning papers off another train at Yeoford.

Passenger Traffic Statistics

Table 1
Passenger Tickets Issued and Collected
Southern Railway 1930

Exeter Queen Street	940,953
Exeter St Davids	28,605
Newton St Cyres	15,383
Crediton	34,453
Yeoford	22,817
Copplestone	8,275
Morchard Road	9,212
Lapford	13,119
Eggesford	16,473
South Molton Road	11,354
Portsmouth Arms	9,370
Umberleigh	20,205
Chapelton	16,131
Barnstaple Junction	156,032
for comparison	
St Cyres - Chapelton (11 stations)	176,792
Ilfracombe line (5 stations)	561,005
Torrington line (4 stations)	279,894
St Cyres - Ilfracombe/Torrington (21 stations)	1,173,723

The volume of passenger traffic carried by the Southern Railway on the North Devon line is illustrated by the 1930 statistics of tickets issued and collected in *Table 1*. Of the 21 stations between St Cyres, Ilfracombe and Torrington, the eleven between St Cyres and Chapelton accounted for less than one sixth. The stations nearest Barnstaple and Exeter did most business, with journeys to the markets, shops and entertainments being shorter and cheaper.

Table 2
North Devon Railway Census 7th May 1963
Passengers joining and leaving trains

Yeoford	46
Copplestone	10
Morchard Road	21½
Lapford	67½
Eggesford	40½
King's Nympton	39
Portsmouth Arms	26½
Umberleigh	25½
Chapelton	22
Barnstaple Junction	618
Total	**916½**

(1 child = ½ passenger)

On 7th May 1963, a Tuesday before the summer season started, the North Devon Railway Action Committee carried out a census of passenger traffic on all lines in North Devon, north of Crediton. Fifty-six passengers arrived in the area on long distance journeys via Exeter, and 78 departed. An average of 22.09 passengers used each train between stops, although the elimination of two under-employed trains would have increased this to about 30.

Devon County Council carried out a survey of passenger use of the North Devon line in 1976-7. The statistics are given in *Table 3*, but the Barnstaple figures here relate only to the Exeter trains, whereas, in *Tables 1* and *2* there were four lines to Barnstaple Junction. However the table illustrates several features which have been a characteristic of the line for many years, the big difference in traffic handled in winter and summer, the overwhelming predominance of passengers using Barnstaple and the minimal use of some other stations.

Similar surveys were undertaken in July 1988 by John Smith for the User Group and in July-August 1989 by Ian Sankey, showing broadly similar results to the Summer 1977 survey, Smith's total journeys for the week being 5,407 in comparison with 5,573 eleven years earlier. However in 1989 an additional 85 return journeys daily were made by students travelling to college, mainly at Barnstaple, but some at Exeter, including 30 from King's Nympton and 17 from Eggesford.

Table 3
Passenger use on the North Devon Line
Devon County Council Survey

	summer week 1977	winter week 1976
Newton St Cyres	6	1
Crediton	218	62
Yeoford	63	39
Copplestone	1	3
Morchard Road	0	0
Lapford	46	37
Eggesford	160	95
King's Nympton	72	40
Portsmouth Arms	11	7
Umberleigh	80	52
Chapelton	13	5
Barnstaple	4,903	1,738
Total	**5,573**	**2,079**

Passenger Train Services

Table 4
Number of Weekday Passenger Trains from Barnstaple to Exeter

September 1854	4
March 1863	5
August 1874	6
June 1887	6
Summer 1909	10
Summer 1932	11
Summer 1958	9
June 1965	11
Summer 1983	10
Summer 1990	10

Table 5
Fastest passenger train service from Barnstaple to Exeter and London

	Exeter St Davids		London		
	hr	min	hr	min	
September 1854	2	0	9	35	P
March 1863	1	50	7	47	W
August 1874	1	25	6	58	W
June 1887	1	12	6	17	W
Summer 1909		59	4	30	W
Summer 1932	1	0	4	28	W
Summer 1958		59	4	22	W
June 1965	1	5	3	50	P
Summer 1983		54	3	12	P
Summer 1990		55	3	8	P

P Paddington   W Waterloo

Table 6
Earliest and latest services between Barnstaple and London

		Earliest arrival in London	Latest departure from London
September 1854	P	5.5pm	12.50pm
March 1863	W	5.30pm	11.00am
August 1874	W	4.46pm	2.10pm
June 1887	W	2.34pm	2.30pm
Summer 1909	W	1.47pm	3.30pm
Summer 1932	W	2.09pm	3.00pm
Summer 1958	W	1.50pm	3.00pm
June 1965	P	10.55am	4.30pm
Summer 1983	P	9.30am	5.45pm
February 1985	P	9.30am	7.00pm
Summer 1990	P	11.05am	6.35pm

An immaculate N class 2-6-0, No. A857, new to Barnstaple shed in 1925, with a three-coach 'up' passenger train leaves Pill Bridge, just south of Barnstaple, and passes the site of the 1890 Pill Bridge signal box.

A. Halls Courtesy R. J. Sellick

Bulleid Pacific No. 34075 *264 Squadron* emerges from Downes cutting, east of Crediton, on 22nd August 1959 with the 10am Morthoe to Waterloo express.

S. C. Nash

The development of passenger train services on the North Devon line is illustrated in *Tables 4, 5* and *6*. *Table 4* illustrates how the frequently of weekday services built up from four trains daily in 1854 to about ten throughout this century. It should be noted however that there were considerably more trains at the peak of the summer season, for example in the summer of 1958 there were 15 trains in Saturdays compared with nine on weekdays. *Table 5* illustrates the very slow early train service which was gradually speeded up as the South Western modernised the track and rolling stock, then for half a century journey times remained about the same. The 1983 fastest time of 54 minutes is partly due to only two stops for single tablet exchange in comparison with

seven exchanges for many years. The considerable improvements in journey times to London in recent years are due to connections with fast diesel hauled Paddington expresses at Exeter St Davids, most recently operated with InterCity 125 units. The value of these connections is also brought out in *Table 6* which shows that only in very recent years it has been possible for North Devonians to go to London and back in a day, particularly important for the business community. The service is provided by good connections into the "Golden Hind" express, although in 1985 an even later departure from Paddington was available.

Although the passenger service to Waterloo provided by the South Western and Southern between 1863 and 1964 may have lacked the speed of today, they did have one big advantage. On most weekdays there were four or five services with through carriages between Barnstaple and Waterloo, a great advantage to those travelling with quantities of luggage, the very young or the very old. As the summer season reached its peak the through carriages were expanded into through trains, the 11am "Atlantic Coast Express" from Waterloo running in three or four parts, and restaurant cars worked right through, first to Torrington and then to Ilfracombe. For some years the Western Region did run one Paddington to Barnstaple through train in Summer Saturdays but this was withdrawn at the end of the 1980 summer season, and in 1982 the remaining Barnstaple to Waterloo summer Saturday service was withdrawn.

The "Atlantic Coast Express" was not the only train to run non stop along the North Devon line from Exeter to Barnstaple right round the year, the overnight newspaper train from Waterloo being another. Between 1947 and 1954 the "Devon Belle" also ran, but in the summer season only, and only for three, four or five days a week in

each direction. On summer Saturdays for many years there were several more trains with no advertised stops which had to wait at stations for crossing purposes. However occasionally, some trains did omit some smaller station calls, such as Chapelton, Morchard Road, Copplestone and Newton St Cyres. Another principal train which used the southern end of the line was the Plymouth Friary to Brighton through train, which normally comprised ten coaches including a restaurant car, and which ran daily throughout the year.

For many years, the principal expresses from Waterloo were divided at Exeter Central into Plymouth and North Devon sections which ran as far as Coleford Junction within minutes of each other. Sometimes through carriages for Bude or Padstow were detached at Okehampton, and the whole process also worked in reverse in the 'up' direction. The result was that Newton St Cyres, Crediton and Yeoford had about double the train service enjoyed by stations from Copplestone downwards. Occasionally the division took place not at Exeter, but at Yeoford. For example in 1913 the 6.35am stopping train from Waterloo

The 'down' "Devon Belle" approaches Crediton on 28th August 1954 behind Bulleid Pacific No. 34058 *Sir Frederick Pile*. The train, comprising seven Pullman cars is passing a milk tank wagon in the yard, left.

S. C. Nash

to Torrington was overtaken at Yeoford by the 8.50am express from Waterloo to Plymouth, and a through carriage for Ilfracombe was shunted on to the stopping train which arrived at 1.30pm and left at 1.48pm. Later, in the 1950s the 11.39am 'down' train from Exeter Central was double headed to Yeoford, where it was divided, the Ilfracombe train leaving first, followed by the Plymouth train. There were corresponding arrangements in the 'up' direction.

There were a number of trains which, over the years, terminated at intermediate stations. These were mainly connected with market traffic on Fridays and included an 8.55am from Eggesford to Barnstaple in 1887, and a 3.42pm from Exeter Queen Street to Lapford in 1906 which became a 3.49pm to Eggesford in 1909. There were other short daily workings including in 1909 a 8.10am from Crediton to Exeter which filled a gap in services and was used by commuters. In the 1950s and 1960s the second 'up' train of the day, the 6.48am from Ilfracombe, terminated at King's Nympton and returned as the 8.20am to Barnstaple Junction for the benefit of commuters and school children. Although most North Devon line trains ran between Exeter and Torrington up to 1925, and to Ilfracombe after 1925, there have always been through workings to and from other destinations. Back in the 1870s there was a return working from Yeovil to Torrington, and in the 1950s two morning 'down' trains ran from Yeovil Town to Ilfracombe. In the 1930s there were through trains from Salisbury to Torrington and Salisbury to Ilfracombe, with 'up' workings from Ilfracombe to Salisbury and Ilfracombe to Eastleigh. In the 1950s there were occasional through trains to or from Exmouth.

Dieselization in 1964 brought numerous through workings including 'down' trains from Salisbury,

Below: The principal 'down' train of the day, on Saturday 23rd August 1980, the 09.48 from Paddington to Barnstaple, consisting of ten BR Mk 1 coaches hauled by Class 25 No. 25206, passes the derelict 'down' platform and siding at Lapford. Although this train loaded on average more than 300 passengers it was withdrawn at the end of the 1980 summer season. *Author*

The 11.39am 'down' train from Exeter Central was double headed as far as Yeoford where it was divided into Plymouth and Ilfracombe trains. On 18th July 1959 the locomotives were Bulleid Pacific No. 34030 *Watersmeet* and N class 2-6-0 No. 31830, seen here passing Crediton 'down' distant signal.

S. C. Nash

Sidmouth, Honiton and Exmouth to Ilfracombe, 'up' trains from Ilfracombe to Kingswear, Honiton and Exmouth and from Torrington to Salisbury. Since then, through workings have varied to include Plymouth, Paignton, Exmouth, Axminster, Newton Abbot, Basingstoke and Penzance.

There have also been occasional through coach workings for special occasions. For example in the early 1930s the Copplestone Methodist Sunday School took their annual outing by train to Exmouth or Teignmouth. In both cases a through coach was provided, and when the outing went to Teignmouth the coach was shunted from the Southern to the Great Western train at Exeter St

Davids, with a corresponding movement in the return direction.

In the Summer 1992 timetable several extra trains terminating at Crediton are scheduled, their purpose being to encourage motorists to park their cars here and use the train to avoid road traffic congestion in Exeter.

Coach Services

Road vehicles have always been used to extend passenger services into towns and villages not directly served by the railway. Between 1851 and 1854 two coaches *Hero* and *Royal Mail* ran between Bideford and Crediton station, and *Queen* and *Ruby* coaches ran between Barnstaple and

The same 11.39am 'down' train from Exeter Central five years earlier, on 29th August 1954, near Newton St Cyres but this time triple headed. Locomotives are T9 class 4-4-0 No. 30717, Bulleid Pacific No. 34036 *Westward Ho* and N class 2-6-0 No. 31849. The T9 is probably on a balancing working.

S. C. Nash

(Copyable Ink.)
[644]

Refer to No. 211 in your reply.

Bar/125

LONDON & SOUTH WESTERN RAILWAY.

GOODS DEPARTMENT,

From L. & S. W. R. BARNSTAPLE GOODS **to** Barum G.W. STATION.

Jan 8 1889

GOODS NOT INVOICED.

By Truck No. ✓ arriving Jan 10 30. 8 1889 we received

Tucker Ilfracombe 1 Box

Weight ___ Tons ___ cwt. ___ qrs. ___ lbs. The above was not Invoiced.

Please send an Invoice early,

Mr. Gray

C. Heather

ADDITIONAL ACCOMMODATION BETWEEN

CHAGFORD, EXETER, LONDON, &c.,

Via YEOFORD JUNCTION. The distance from Yeoford to Chagford is only 11 miles.

From CHAGFORD.

On every Week Day, until further notice, a well-appointed **OMNIBUS** Will leave the MOOR PARK HOTEL, CHAGFORD, at 8.20 a.m. (Fridays excepted), meeting the Up Train leaving Yeoford at 11.54 a.m., arriving at Exeter at 12.21, Yeovil 1.58, Salisbury 2.49, Southampton 5.26, Portsmouth 6.27, and London (Waterloo) 5.0 p.m.: and the Down Train leaving Yeoford at 2.15 p.m., arriving at Holsworthy (for Bude: by Coach) 3.49 p.m., Tavistock 3.12 p.m., Devonport 3.37 p.m., Plymouth (North Road) 3.42 p.m. and Plymouth (Friary) 3.56 p.m., also the Down Train leaving Yeoford 12.15 p.m., arriving at Barnstaple 1.15 p.m., Bideford 1.44 p.m., and Ilfracombe 2.25 p.m.

On FRIDAYS only, the Omnibus will leave Chagford at 7.0 a.m., meeting the Up Train leaving Yeoford at 9.35 a.m., arriving at Exeter at 10.10 a.m., London (Waterloo) 2.30 p.m., Yeovil 12.12 p.m., Salisbury 12.25 p.m., Southampton 1.38 p.m., and Portsmouth 2.31 p.m.; and the Down Train leaving Yeoford at 9.36 a.m., arriving at Holsworthy 11.12 a.m., Tavistock 10.44 a.m., Devonport 11.16 a.m., Plymouth (North Road) 11.22 a.m. and Plymouth (Friary) 11.35 a.m., also the Down Train leaving Yeoford at 10.4 a.m., and arriving at Barnstaple 11.5 a.m., Bideford 11.33 a.m. and Ilfracombe 12.10 p.m.

To CHAGFORD.

The Omnibus will return each week day from Yeoford at 5.5 p.m. on the arrival of the Trains leaving London (Waterloo) at 11.0 a.m., Portsmouth 10.40 a.m., Southampton 11.33 a.m., Salisbury 1.15 p.m., Yeovil 2.15 p.m., and Exeter at 4.30 p.m., Ilfracombe 2.5 p.m., Bideford 2.33 p.m., Barnstaple 3.0 p.m., Plymouth (Friary) 2.15, Plymouth (North Road) 2.30 p.m., Devonport 2.35 p.m., Tavistock 3.19 p.m., and Holsworthy 2.45 p.m.

The Omnibus will pass through or near the following places:—Sandypark, Gidleigh, Whiddon Down, Throwleigh, South Tawton and Hittesleigh; Drewsteington is only distant about 2 miles from Whiddon Down, where the 'bus could be met.

THROUGH FARES.

CHAGFORD AND EXETER.					CHAGFORD AND LONDON.				
Single Journey.			Return Tickets.		Single Journey.			Return Tickets.	
1st Class.	2nd Class	3rd Class.	1st Class.	2nd Class.	1st Class.	2nd Class	3rd Class.	1st Class.	2nd Class
s. d.	s. d.	s. d.	s. d.	s. d.	s. d.	s. d.	s. d.	s. d.	s. d.
3 4	2 10	2 4½	5 9	5 0	38 6	27 10	16 8½	61 0	45 0

On FRIDAYS (Exeter Market Days), Through 3rd Class Tickets will be issued from Chagford to Exeter at 3s. 4d. for the Double Journey.

Cheap Excursion Tickets to London on Saturdays and Mondays will be issued from Chagford by the above Coach, arriving in London at 5.0 p.m., and will be available to return on the Saturday or Saturday week following.

The return Train will leave Waterloo at 11.0 a.m.

Similar Excursion Tickets will also be issued from London to Chagford on Saturdays by the 11.0 a.m. Fast Train, and will be available to return on the following Monday, Saturday, Monday week, Saturday week or Monday fortnight only.

FARE:—Third Class 18s. 6d.

All Goods and Parcels for Chagford should be addressed to L. & S. W. Railway via Yeoford.

Crediton stations. The coaches, timed to connect with the trains, used the old roads running respectively via Winkleigh, Beaford and Torrington and Chulmleigh and South Molton.

When the North Devon Railway opened there were a number of coach services operated at various times in connection with the trains. From Copplestone station there were two coach routes, the *Royal Mail* running to Launceston via North Tawton and Okehampton, and *Queen* to Holsworthy via North Tawton, Hatherleigh and Black Torrington. From Eggesford station *Torrington* ran via Winkleigh and Beaford to Torrington, and from South Molton Road station Saunders bus ran to South Molton. From Barnstaple station there was a whole range of coach services including the *Sea Bather* to Lynton, the *Queen* and *Mail* to Ilfracombe, *Mail Monarch* and *Hero* to Bideford, together with a horse omnibus service to the Golden Lion Hotel in connection with every train. As the railway system expanded to serve more towns and villages the coach services were modified, but at Barnstaple the *Galloper* omnibus, which plied between Barnstaple Junction and the Great Western station, continued to run after the opening of the loop line in 1887, its use being initially restricted to passengers for the Ilfracombe branch.

By 1892 the South Western was advertising three coach services in connection with trains on the North Devon line, between Yeoford station and Chagford, South Molton Road station and South Molton and Barnstaple Junction station and Lynton. The Lynton service was withdrawn when the Lynton & Barnstaple Railway opened in 1898, and reinstated after its closure in 1935. The Yeoford station to Chagford service was later replaced in 1904 by a South Western Motor Bus service from Exeter Queen Street, but when the three Milnes-Daimler 16-seaters were replaced by two Clarksons steam buses the road was damaged and the service reverted back to Yeoford station for a while.

We have already considered the 8.20am passenger train from King's Nympton to Barnstaple Junction in the 1950s and 1960s. The train connected with a bus from South Molton to give an earlier arrival at Barnstaple than the first train of the day from Taunton. In the 1990s bus services operated by Bow Belle coaches and Western National are more convenient than the trains for local journeys from Newton St Cyres, Crediton, Copplestone and Morchard Road, but the trains provide the only public transport for all the other villages along the line. By 1990 the County Council provided buses from several villages in connection with re-timed trains to enable students to attend college at both Barnstaple and Exeter.

A Survey of Freight Traffic

Early traffic from 1848 on the original Taw Vale line included coal and lime from Paddington. In 1851 Thomas Ward advertised that Peruvian guano, super phosphate, other manures, tiles, coal, lime and salt were available from his new depot at Crediton station. Iron rails and chairs and other construction materials were brought over both lines for construction of the North Devon Railway, and after its opening early traffic included coal, lime, livestock, manure and general merchandise.

As the railway age developed, the freight traffic settled into a pattern, illustrated quantitively in *Table 7*. Of the twenty goods stations between Newton St Cyres, Ilfracombe and Torrington, the eleven between Newton St

Above: In Southern days K10 class 4-4-0 No. E153 departs from Barnstaple Junction with a heavy 'up' freight train.
A. Halls courtesy National Railway Museum

In Southern days, another 'up' freight train passes Bishops Tawton behind Drummond 700 class 0-6-0 No. E306, carrying Exmouth Junction duty disc 531.
A. Halls courtesy R. J. Sellick

Drummond T9 class 4-4-0 No. 30717 waits in Barnstaple Junction yard with an 'up' goods train on 14th April 1954. The first two wagons are loaded with containers of meat.

R. J. Sellick

Cyres and Chapelton accounted for less than a quarter of all loaded wagons forwarded and received. Barnstaple Junction was by far the most important in the area, accounting for almost a third of all loaded wagons. Beyond Barnstaple, the Torrington line produced far more freight traffic than the Ilfracombe line, in contrast to the passenger traffic. Some freight traffic was short distance, including clay from Torrington to Fremington, house coal from Fremington to numerous local stations, and livestock to Barnstaple and Exeter markets. Even so, much of the freight traffic running between Exeter and Barnstaple was through traffic, but what the intermediate stations may have missed in quantity they usually made up for in variety.

Freight Traffic Statistics

Table 7

Loaded wagons (including livestock) forwarded and received
Southern Railway 1930

Exeter Queen Street	49,922
Newton St Cyres	549
Crediton	4,518
Yeoford	983
Copplestone	1,666
Morchard Road	1,559
Lapford	2,434
Eggesford	2,122
South Molton Road	1,889
Portsmouth Arms	1,002
Umberleigh	930
Chapelton	536
Barnstaple Junction	23,684
for comparison	
St Cyres - Chapelton (11 stations)	18,188
Ilfracombe line (4 stations)	10,235
Torrington line (4 stations)	28,348
St Cyres - Ilfracombe/Torrington (20 stations)	80,455

The most important traffic forwarded was livestock, followed by meat, milk, timber and many other agricultural traffics and the produce of small local factories. Traffic received included coal, minerals, fertilisers, animal feedstuffs and agricultural machinery. There was a considerable volume of general merchandise in and out, but in general the goods yards received more loaded wagons than they forwarded. We now consider each of these in turn.

Livestock Traffic

The most important industry of North Devon is its agriculture and for a century the North Devon line facilitated the transport of livestock from local stations to customers and markets near and far. Livestock was usually the most important single traffic forwarded from all North Devon line stations, sometimes accounting for a half of all the loaded wagons forwarded over a year. For example, of the 6,710 loaded wagons forwarded from stations between Newton St Cyres and Chapelton, 1,920 were loaded with livestock in 1930. Every station, except Chapelton, had livestock facilities, but the traffic was occasional, running only on particular days. A considerable amount of livestock traffic ran on Friday mornings to market at Exeter and to a lesser extent to Barnstaple. Much livestock was loaded after the periodic auctions held at or nearby the stations. Also during and after the Second World War, when meat rationing was in force, numerous livestock trains were run for the Ministry of Food.

The most important livestock auction market for the North Devon line was that at Exeter. The early morning goods train from Barnstaple ran early on Friday mornings, collecting loaded cattle trucks from many intermediate stations, to arrive at Queen Street station where the livestock was unloaded and herded through the streets to the market. In Southern days, this was the 4.25am freight from Barnstaple Junction which usually arrived at Exeter Queen Street at 12 noon, but on Fridays was accelerated to arrive at 9.45am. The livestock included cattle, pigs and sheep and continued for a century, interrupted occasionally by a local outbreak of foot and mouth disease which shut the markets. A similar situation, on a smaller scale, occurred at Barnstaple Junction where again the market was on a Friday. As we have already seen there was considerable extra passenger traffic on market days provided by the farming community.

For many years almost every intermediate station, excepting only Newton St Cyres and Chapelton which were close to the large weekly markets, had their own periodic livestock auction markets, held in pens set up in a field or yard adjacent to the station. The Eggesford market was established shortly after the opening of the North Devon Railway in 1854, causing the nearby Chulmleigh market to close, but an annual chartered fair has since been established at Chulmleigh. Other markets were also established at an early stage.

Many of the livestock auctions were operated by the Chulmleigh firm of Hannaford, Ward & Southcombe, later Southcombes, on a monthly basis. The auction at Eggesford took place on the second Wednesday of the month, Portsmouth Arms on the second Thursday, Lapford on the third Wednesday and South Molton Road on the fourth Wednesday. Copplestone market was operated in conjunction with Dobbs and Stagg on a Monday and Messrs Staggs ran the Umberleigh market. This was the situation in the 1940s and 1950s, but in previous years there were also cattle auctions at the stations at Yeoford and Morchard Road, with Hannafords later operating an occasional market at Morchard Bishop.

Market day at one of the stations began with the farmers and drovers herding livestock, cattle, sheep and pigs, along the country lanes to the auction pens, while, in later years, some arrived by rail or by road vehicles. The station master would ensure that a sufficient supply of empty cattle trucks had been ordered previously and shunted into the yard. The local inn was open all day and the farmers and their families, buyers and local butchers would enjoy a day out which had both a commercial and a social purpose for the local community. Prices obtained by the auctioneer, for many years Mr A. J. Bussell of Chulmleigh, were always keenly watched to ascertain the state of the market. Sometimes there was an Annual Market Day Prize when the champion cup was presented to the owner of the champion steer or bull.

At the end of the auction the buyers and their men, together with the railwaymen, herded the livestock into the cattle loading pens and thence into cattle trucks. This was quite straightforward at Eggesford where the Fox and Hounds siding terminated adjacent to the auction market, but more difficult at some other stations such as South Molton Road or Lapford where the livestock had to be herded across the main road into the station yard. Usually there were only sufficient pens for two or three cattle trucks to be loaded and then they were shunted out of the dock to be replaced by more empty trucks. Years ago the shunting was performed by horse, but later a shunting engine was used. Sometimes as many as twenty trucks were loaded after an auction, and they were usually forwarded on the 'up' market goods, the 12.45pm from Torrington to Nine Elms, many of the trucks being destined for Maiden Lane.

During the wartime and post-war period of meat rationing the usual auctions were suspended and the Meat and Livestock Commission of the Ministry of Food took control of all fatstock marketing. Instead of receiving auction prices the farmers were paid for their fatstock on a standard grading system. The North Devon markets were notified by the Meat and Livestock Commission at Cardiff of the destination of their fatstock, which was forwarded by road or rail to Maiden Lane, Brynmawr and Maesycwmmr and other destinations. By this time the enlarged yard at Yeoford was the base for a large fleet of about two hundred cattle trucks and, every day, three or four cattle specials of up to fifty wagons would be run from stations in North Devon and North Cornwall. An Exmouth Junction locomotive, often an N class 2-6-0 or T9 class 4-4-0, would collect the empty cattle trucks from Yeoford and run to various country stations including Torrington, Portsmouth Arms, Eggesford, Lapford, South Molton Road and Morchard Road to load livestock. During the afternoon and evening up to four loaded cattle specials ran on the North Devon line bound for Maiden

Prize Day at South Molton Road cattle market, with a Devon Steer gaining the Champion Cup. Auctioneer Mr A. J. Bussell, who conducted many of these cattle auction markets at several stations on the line, rests his hand on the ledge of the rostrum.
Collection A. J. Bussell

In South Western days a loaded meat van was recorded in Lapford yard with the North Devon Railway bridge behind. Mr Snell's slaughterhouse was to the left.

Collection H. V. Tumilty

Lane or one of the other destinations.

Maiden Lane goods station in North London, on the old LNWR, was the railhead for the major Caledonian Road cattle market. After unloading and cleaning the cattle trucks were worked back to Yeoford yard to await their next turn of duty. As an example of the traffic, on one Wednesday the grading centre at Thelbridge Cross forwarded large numbers of sheep by road to Lapford station. They were loaded into cattle trucks, 35 at a time, and 72 loaded cattle trucks were forwarded in the day from the station in two cattle specials, one in the early afternoon and the second in the early evening.

Loading livestock was not always a straightforward task. One winter's day at Morchard Road several railwaymen were loading bullocks into cattle trucks, but the animals had been out in the fields for months and were quite wild. Suddenly one jumped right out of the cattle pen and ran down the platform approach road to freedom, being lost in a snowstorm. The livestock traffic declined in the late 1950s and disappeared completely in the early 1960s, together with the station auction markets.

Meat Traffic

Meat was another important traffic on the North Devon line, with almost every station yard boasting its own slaughterhouse at one time. These provided some incoming and much forwarded traffic. Locally grown fatstock was purchased at one of the local cattle auctions and brought to one of the slaughterhouses to meet its fate. Some of the slaughterhouses were specialised, with Gunn's at Morchard Road dealing only in sheep, Mr Snell at Lapford in sheep and pigs, and that at Eggesford in horses. The methods used were often primitive and would not conform with modern regulations. For example, when pigs were slaughtered at Lapford their blood ran out over the tiled yard and turned the River Yeo red. The premises used invariably consisted if a wooden or stone shed, while that at Lapford occupied the spare arch in the North Devon Railway three-arch over bridge. After their use as a slaughterhouse had ceased, the buildings were often converted to other uses, the Lapford slaughterhouse has now lost its wooden end walls but the tiled yard and meathooks fixed in the masonry arch are still visible.

Although some of the meat produced was for local consumption much was forwarded by rail. The South Western had a fleet of meat vans equipped with hooks for hanging the carcases, and one of these was photographed at Lapford, illustrating the loading. These vans were ventilated, but not refrigerated, so a speedy transit up the main line to Nine Elms yard, and hence Smithfield Market, was an important consideration. At many stations a siding ran to a loading dock adjacent to the slaughterhouse for ease of loading, and at Barnstaple Junction the siding ran inside the slaughterhouse itself. However at Lapford it was less convenient since all carcasses had to be carried or carted across both running lines from the slaughterhouse to the yard opposite. In later years, much of this meat was carried in containers loaded on flat wagons, which were express fitted. The containers were convenient for onward road transit at the London end, but also facilitated the use of rail transit by slaughterhouses distant from the line. After the installation of a new 10-ton crane at Eggesford station, containers of meat from a slaughterhouse at Winkleigh were brought to the station by road and loaded on to flat wagons, and later photographs of Eggesford yard often show a flat wagon waiting under the crane.

The slaughterhouses also forwarded other produce, skins and hides were usually loaded in ordinary open wagons, and offal and bone meal was packed in steel drums which were also loaded into open wagons. Smaller consignments of meat and hoof and horn bone meal were forwarded by passenger train services. One such customer was Tellams of Cheriton Bishop who forwarded from Yeoford station, the staff always being pleased to see the back of these smelly parcels. Meat traffic remained heavy until the mid 1960s, a train running even on Sundays, but it was taken over by road transport. Only at Copplestone does the slaughterhouse in the station yard remain in business.

Milk Traffic

For many years the milk traffic on the North Devon line was comparitively light. There was some milk churn traffic, carried in the luggage compartments of passenger trains, but the South Western milk churn trains to London originated no further west than Yeovil. Initially it was the establishment of processing factories that converted milk into several dairy products which led to an increase in the milk traffic. When Ambrosia opened its factory at Lapford in 1928 milk was supplied initially from the Honiton area where the company had existing contracts, and subsequently the firm's own lorries collected churns from farms in the area. However much of the milk from Honiton came by rail, and a number of farmers forwarded

GREAT WESTERN RAILWAY.
From _Bridgwater_
To _Beoford_
Route via _____
Date _16 - 10 - 189 0_ Train _____
Wagon No. _4078_   Sheet No. _____
Consignee _____
(1,000,000—4-96.)

MIDLAND RAILWAY Co. G F 155
13517   10 - 11 - 1894
FROM AVONSIDE WHARF STATION, BRISTOL,
To _Yeoford_
Company _____
Route _Bath_
Wagon No. _____
Consignee _Cornish_

(999-D) **GREAT WESTERN RAILWAY.**
BUCKFASTLEIGH
From _____
To _Yeoford_
Route via _Exeter_
Date _13/8 - 89_ Train _9. 10pm_
Wagon No. _7495_   Sheet No. _____
Consignee _____
(1,000,000—6-95.)

(999-1) **GREAT WESTERN RAILWAY.**
From BRISTOL HARBOUR
To _Yeoford_
Route via _____
Date _4 - 1 - 1896_. Train _____
Wagon No. _44624_   Sheet No. _____
Consignee _____

milk churns to Ambrosia from other intermediate stations.

Liquid milk for the London market was forwarded with the introduction of glass-lined and later stainless steel tanker wagons from the 1940s to the 1960s. At Lapford rail tankers were shunted into the Ambrosia factory and loaded directly from storage tanks, up to six tankers a day being forwarded, depending on local levels of milk production and the requirements of the Ambrosia factory. At Crediton a tanker lorry from the local firm of Miloko was driven to the station yard where the load was pumped into a rail tank wagon, usually one a day being forwarded. Loaded milk tanker wagons were forwarded to a variety of destinations in the London area including Mottingham, Stewarts Lane, Vauxhall and Morden.

Timber Traffic
Timber was forwarded from time to time from most stations on the line. Often this consisted of wagons of pit

props cut from local woods and from the extensive Eggesford Forest established in 1919, and forwarded to collieries. Sometimes there was widespread tree felling as happened during and after the First World War when large numbers of mature trees were brought to the station yards at South Molton Road and Eggesford stations. Local hauliers used horses to bring in timber from the woods, and in the station yards steam powered saws were used to cut the timber to size for loading and onward transit.

However the timber traffic was most extensive and regular from established timber yards and sawmills at or adjacent to the station yards. In South Western days there were extensive timber yards at Barnstaple Junction and Crediton stations, but they later closed. In Southern and British Railway days the major firms were Yeoford Sawmills, and Chapelton Sawmills established in 1930 by the firm of Chappell & Walton. The later firm forwarded almost all its products by rail, including timber cut for all

Posed for the camera on the main road outside Lapford station in the 1930s was a fleet of Ambrosia lorries employed to collect milk in churns from local farms, for the milk processing factory. The entrance to Lapford 'down' platform is on the extreme left of the picture.
Collection W. Sutton

London and South Western Ry. 787
FROM WATERLOO TO
EGGESFORD

London and South Western Ry. 787
From WATERLOO TO
Copplestone

London and South Western Ry. 787
FROM WATERLOO TO
SOUTH MOLTON ROAD

There was a considerable volume and variety of traffic forwarded under the general merchandise heading. Ambrosia at Lapford forwarded van loads of butter, skimmed milk powder, cream, yeast extract and other products to destinations including Bristol, Birmingham, Manchester, Glasgow, Swansea and London. Up to ten loaded wagons a day were forwarded by Ambrosia alone. At Crediton the sweet manufacturers Arthurs, Bristows & Jacksons forwarded their produce which for many years was brought to the goods shed where it was loaded into vans, but later the produce was packed into containers which were loaded on to flat wagons using the yard crane. Incidentally, this use of the yard cranes to transfer containers between road and rail vehicles was done entirely by hand and was very hard physical work for the railwaymen. Other traffic forwarded included, in the very early days, bricks, tiles and pipes from the Morchard Road brickworks, a lace van from Barnstaple, and later some stone forwarded from South Molton Road station by a local quarry.

Traffic Received

Every station received coal for local merchants and businesses. Household coal came from Fremington, and from other coalfields direct by rail. Steam coal for Ambrosia and Chappell & Walton came direct from the collieries. Merchants stored coal in the station yard and distributed it by road to their customers. The traffic declined in the 1960s and ended when, on 4th December 1967, the coal concentration depot opened at Exmouth Junction and merchants received their coal by road. However some merchants, such as Ward & Co. of Crediton, still operate from their depots in the old goods yards.

All stations received some mineral traffic of various descriptions including some materials for road construction and maintenance, although much stone was quarried locally. Bricks, tiles and pipes were received from a number of suppliers including brickworks at Marland and Morchard Road. Bags of cement came in and in British Railway days a Blue Circle Cement depot was established in the yard at Barnstaple Junction. Presflo wagons brought cement in bulk to a large hopper from where it was distributed by road, the traffic ending in 1987.

Fertilisers have always been an important traffic, lime being carried from the start and manure for many years. For a long period every station received considerable tonnages of fertilisers from manufacturers including Fisons, ICI and UKF. After the Beeching yard closures,

types of fencing. But a most interesting feature was the production of high quality timber used in railway wagon construction and repair, Chapelton Sawmills supplying most of the main line wagon workshops. In the mid 1980s timber for paper-making was again forwarded from Barnstaple and Lapford.

Other Traffic Forwarded

More agricultural produce was forwarded on an occasional or seasonal basis, including wagon loads of hay, straw, reeds and manure. Many stations forwarded apples in season both for jam making and the manufacture of cider, and soft fruit including tubs of blackcurrants from Umberleigh. At one time there was a traffic in farmhouse cider from Yeoford to the dockyard at Devonport, the stoneware jars being loaded on to passenger trains. Until the arrival of myxamotosis, which reduced their population, rabbits by the hamper were loaded from several stations. Most stations produced some business in horseboxes and carriage trucks, the former particularly around Eggesford when Earl Portsmouth's hunt met.

The 6.30am freight from Exmouth Junction Sidings to Barnstaple leaves Chapelton behind an 0-6-0 goods engine. The wagons of pit props for South Wales have been collected from Chapelton Sawmills, the yard here being served only by 'down' trains.
Collection J. A. W. Parkman

sidings at Lapford and King's Nympton were retained for this traffic, and although King's Nympton has since shut UKF, now Kemira, still bring air-braked wagons loaded with fertilisers to Lapford. Animal feedstuffs such as cow cake were also received in considerable tonnages. At some stations, a merchant had his own depot to store and distribute numerous commodities including coal, fertilisers and animal feedstuffs, examples being Ward & Co. at Crediton and J. Cole & Co. at South Molton Road. At some other stations, such as Crediton, Messrs Silcocks had their own stores which were run entirely by the railwaymen who were responsible for all the work done.

As farms became more mechanised agricultural machinery, tyres and spare parts were received at most stations. However the agricultural engineering firm of Murch Brothers at Umberleigh developed a considerable business in the area, and many tractors and other agricultural machinery were received by train. Indeed, the firm still flourishes and utilises some of the station yard for its stock, although now it all arrives by road.

General Merchandise Received

General merchandise received was unloaded in the goods shed, but provision was very varied on the line. Only four yards, at Crediton, Copplestone, South Molton Road and Barnstaple Junction enjoyed the luxury of the conventional goods shed with a siding passing right through it where vans could be loaded and unloaded in shelter. Most other yards had a goods shed built adjacent to a siding or loading dock, but at both Portsmouth Arms and Lapford the goods shed was built on the 'up' platform, and goods trains had to pull up there for the loading and unloading of consignments.

Up to about 1960, when road transport took over, the general merchandise received included almost every item required by local shops and industries. Perishable items normally travelled by passenger train and from every station deliveries were made by horse or motor transport over the area served. Sometimes railway provided the transport, at other times an agent or local firm was responsible. Crediton provides an interesting example of the goods involved, although the scale of the operation at Barnstaple was more extensive and at other stations less. Deliveries from Crediton station included the full range of groceries sold at Lee's Stores and Bricknells, paints, nails, screws, tools and so on for the ironmongers H. R. Adams, clothing for gents outfitters Summerwells and A. E. Lee. Wet fish from Hull and Grimsby was delivered to several fishmongers. Four delivery lorries were based at Crediton goods yard for these deliveries, the general merchandise totalling as much as 10,000 tons per year.

Other goods received on the line included supplies of tin cans for Ambrosia and bitumen for Devon County Council at Lapford, and oil at Eggesford. After the widespread yard closures of the 1960s the yard at Barnstaple Junction inherited several traffics previously handled elsewhere, including steel plate for Appledore Shipyard, previously handled at Bideford, and stores for RAF Chivenor, previously handled at Wrafton. In the mid 1980s traffic received also included imported grain at Lapford and glue at Barnstaple.

As we have seen there was much more traffic running on the North Devon line through to, and from, stations beyond Barnstaple, particularly on the Torrington line. Much of this traffic was very similar to that described for the intermediate stations, but there were some others.

On 9th June 1960 Drummond 700 class 0-6-0 No. 30691 passes Cowley Bridge Junction with a long 'up' North Devon line freight, probably the 'Market Goods', the 12.45pm from Torrington to Nine Elms which was rostered for a member of this class between Barnstaple and Exeter.

S. C. Nash

Later the same day Bulleid Pacific No. 34096 *Trevone* passes Cowley Bridge Junction on the 4.15pm from Bideford to Nine Elms, most of the vehicles carrying meat containers.

S. C. Nash

These included clay from Marland and Meeth running to the Potteries and ports at Bristol and later Fowey, milk tankers from Torrington bound for London and trainloads of locomotive coal from Fremington to Exmouth Junction and other Southern locomotive depots. On the section from Cowley Bridge Junction to Coleford Junction there were considerable volumes of freight mainly on the Plymouth line, but also bound for Bude and North Cornwall. Ballast trains from Meldon Quarry continue to this day.

The 3.17pm goods from Eggesford to Crediton pauses at Copplestone to shunt the yard behind BR Class 2 2-6-2T No. 84020. Here the two milk tankers behind the engine were often shunted into the yard to be collected by the next 'up' passenger train.

Lens of Sutton

Friday 22nd August 1980 sees the 17.15 goods from Barnstaple to Exeter approaching Umberleigh Gates behind Class 25 Bo-Bo diesel electric No. 25058.

Author

Freight Train Services

Table 8

Number of weekday freight trains from Barnstaple to Exeter

February 1865	2 (1 standard gauge, 1 broad)
Summer 1913	3
Summer 1932	3 (plus 1 from Eggesford)
Summer 1957	4 (plus 1 from Eggesford)
1984	1 (plus 1 from Lapford Q)

Table 8 covers freight services north of Coleford Junction and illustrates the provision of freight trains. In general terms, up to 1965 or so, there were two early morning freight trains which ran through from Exeter to Barnstaple Junction and thence shunted the yards to Torrington. Then there was a third which left Exmouth Junction about 6.30am and shunted all the yards to Barnstaple, arriving about lunchtime. A corresponding 'up' freight left

No. 25058 shunts the yard at Barnstaple on 28th August 1980. Wagons include low-sided air-braked vehicles used for steel traffic, standard 13-ton wagons loaded with clay and sheeted over, and some empty clay wagons are visible on the far line.

Author

Class 33 No. 33042 passes Cowley Bridge Junction with a train of empty 'Sea Cow' ballast wagons bound for Meldon Quarry on 4th June 1982.

Author

Class 47 No. 47282 approaches Park Crossing, just west of Crediton, with the 15.00 ballast train from Meldon Quarry to Bristol East Depot, 13th August 1984.

Author

Barnstaple Junction early in the morning, shunted all the yards and arrived at Exeter about lunchtime, followed in the afternoon and evening by two or three more freight trains. One or two of these ran straight through but the 12.45pm from Torrington to Nine Elms, the "Market Goods", shunted several yards on the way. It was this train which often collected meat vans and loaded cattle trucks, so by the time it reached Lapford and Morchard Road it was often too long to pass another train in the crossing loop, and had to be shunted into the yard.

As traffic grew in Southern days, particularly from Ambrosia at Lapford, another freight train was put on, the 9.15am from Exmouth Junction to Eggesford and 3.17pm return. If Eggesford had no traffic this train was turned round at Lapford where the yard was awkward to shunt for 'up' trains. In the late 1940s and early 1950s this freight train collected between one and six loaded milk tankers from the Ambrosia siding and took them on to Copplestone where they were shunted into the yard. Shortly afterwards the 3pm passenger train from Ilfracombe arrived, reversed into Copplestone yard to attach the tankers, and took them on to Exeter. The times given are from the 1957 working timetable, but varied a little over the years. By 1957 an express fitted-freight train was running to accommodate perishable traffic, particularly meat and also milk. On weekdays this was the 4.15pm from Bideford Goods to Nine Elms, and on Sundays the 6.30pm from Barnstaple Junction to Nine Elms.

As yards closed a single daily freight covered most requirements. Times varied over the years but by 1981 this left Exeter Riverside yard at 5.15am for Barnstaple, shunted the yard, left about 8.30am to deliver empty clay wagons to Marland and Meeth sidings returning with loaded wagons at about 11.30am. After performing station pilot duties in the afternoon it left Barnstaple for Exeter at 4.50pm. After closure of the Meeth line in 1982 this changed and in 1984 left Exeter Riverside at 5.30am and returned from Barnstaple at 9.10am. In addition to this there was an Exeter to Lapford Sidings trip departing at 4.45am on Mondays Only when required. In addition some five ballast trains run daily to and from Meldon Quarry.

By 1986 only one or two freight trains a week reached Barnstaple, that on 21st August comprising six cement wagons, five UKF fertiliser vans and three loaded timber wagons.

Railfreight Class 47 No. 47361 shunts Lapford sidings on 22nd May 1991, delivering three loaded fertiliser wagons and taking away empties. This occasional freight service, the last on the North Devon line, ended a couple of months later with the demise of Speedlink.

Peter Knottley

Chapter 9
Locomotives and Rolling Stock

Contractors' Locomotives and Rolling Stock

Apparently the first items of rolling stock used in North Devon were the examples of standard gauge equipment employed by William Thorne on the Taw Vale Nos 1 and 2 contracts. This was sold at two auctions, the second on 6th February 1851 at Barnstaple station. The sale included a locomotive and tender by Chapman, the locomotive being a 2-2-2 with 6ft driving wheels and 4ft leading and trailing wheels, together with 82 wagons and a variety of timber and other equipment.

During 1852-4 Brassey is believed to have employed standard gauge Bury 0-4-0s *Fairfield* and *Manchester* and broad gauge 2-4-0 *Venus* on the construction works, although some records suggest that the latter was not acquired until 1856. The firm of W. J. Pickering employed a standard gauge Hunslet 0-6-0ST on a contract at Barnstaple, but the date or nature of the contract is not known.

The Bristol & Exeter Railway

From 1851 the Crediton branch was usually worked by a small 2-2-2 tank engine designed by Pearson, two being built by Longridge and three by Wilson & Co, Nos 30-34. According to Col. Yolland in 1859 the Crediton line was usually worked by 2-2-2 and 4-4-0 tank engines, but when 4-2-2s with a rigid wheelbase were put on they regularly came off on the sharp curve at Cowley Bridge. The 4-2-2 in question was one of the series Nos 1-10. The broad gauge goods service to Crediton from 1862 to 1892 was maintained with various 7ft 0¼in gauge locomotives of the period.

In the period 1854-5 the Bristol & Exeter is known to have employed several locomotives on the North Devon. There was No.19, a 4-2-2 built by Longridge, an express passenger type, No.25, an 0-6-0 goods built by Stothert & Slaughter, and 2-2-2Ts Nos 31 and 32. Doubtless other Bristol & Exeter locomotives worked on the North Devon, but certainly not the 2-2-2 tender locomotive depicted in the engraving of the opening ceremony at Barnstaple - the Bristol & Exeter had none of this type!

The North Devon Railway

Brassey and Ogilvie took over the operation of the North Devon Railway from the Bristol & Exeter on 28th July 1855, using a variety of broad gauge rolling stock. Although three new locomotives were supplied much of the locomotive and carriage stock was acquired second hand. Much of this was purchased from the Midland Railway where it had become surplus to requirements on the Bristol & Gloucester line, broad gauge since 1844 but converted to 'narrow' gauge in June 1854. Brassey acquired twelve locomotives and 24 items of coaching stock in the period 1855-7.

First to be considered are three locomotives built at Brassey's Canada Works, Birkenhead; a 2-4-0 *Creedy* and 2-2-2s *Yeo* and *Dart*. These were 'Crewe' type locomotives, originally intended for the 5ft 6in gauge Grand Trunk Railway of Canada, and widened for the 7ft 0¼in gauge. *Creedy* worked the first train to Bideford on 2nd November 1855. Next are a group of eight locomotives built for the Bristol & Gloucester Railway by Stothert & Slaughter in 1844, of which six were renamed on arrival in North Devon. There were five 2-2-2s, *Star*,

Barum, *Exe*, *Tite* and *Mole*, a 2-4-0 *Venus* and two 0-6-0s, *Dreadnought* and *Defiance* which retained their original names on their splashers. Finally, there was a 2-2-2 *Taw* built by Robert Stephenson as a standard gauge locomotive and later converted to broad gauge by Stothert & Slaughter. *Taw* was derailed at Yelland after breaking a tyre on 4th January 1859, and Lt Col. Yolland subsequently gave a full description and history of the locomotive in his report, but *Taw* was disposed of shortly afterwards. North Devon Railway locomotives were painted brown with yellow bands and lining, and carried plates inscribed 'North Devon Railway Works, Barnstaple'.

When the South Western took over on 1st August 1862 the broad gauge locomotive situation was as follows:

Good Order (in service) *Creedy*, *Dart*, *Star*
Fair Order (spare engine) *Yeo*
Serviceable, but in store *Barum*, *Tite*, *Venus*
Not serviceable, in store *Defiance*, *Exe*
Derelict *Mole*, *Dreadnought*

However Brassey also had a number of standard gauge locomotives which were repaired or stored at Barnstaple on occasions between contracts. These included Bury 0-4-2s *Fairfield* and *Manchester* used during construction in 1852-4, but by 1863 *Fairfield* was lying derelict at Barnstaple. *Junction* and *Birkenhead* were Sharps 0-4-2s and *Penzance* a Sharps 2-2-2T. Apparently none of these locomotives were converted to the broad gauge.

Brassey also acquired all his passenger rolling stock from the redundant Bristol & Gloucester Railway broad gauge stock. The 24 items comprised of six composite carriages (first and second class), three composite carriages (first and third class), four second class carriages, three third class carriages with guards compartment, three carriage trucks, three horse boxes and two guards vans. All these vehicles were passed on to the LSWR, together with 81 goods wagons, some of which had also come from the Bristol & Gloucester stock.

After the South Western had extended its standard gauge services to Bideford in 1863 there was far less work available for the broad gauge rolling stock. This was principally coal traffic from Fremington and the Crediton to Bideford mixed train, for which *Creedy* was usually shedded at Crediton. To assist *Creedy* the 2-2-2 *Dart* was rebuilt as a 2-4-0 between 1867 and May 1868 at a cost of £300, using parts supplied by Nine Elms works. As for the 0-6-0 goods engines, *Defiance* was badly damaged by fire at Crediton on 8th October 1862 but was repaired and returned to service, whilst *Dreadnought* was sold to a Mr Sharp, a contractor at Falmouth, in June 1863. Meanwhile in 1866 the South Western authorised the appointment of two additional carpenters to be employed in repairing broad gauge wagons, and in 1869 accepted a tender from Mr Clarke for painting and varnishing five broad gauge carriages.

The South Western reconsidered its broad gauge rolling stock situation on 25th August 1870. The engineer, Joseph Beattie, recommended that *Defiance*, *Mole* and *Exe*, being worn out, should be scrapped and that *Barum*, *Tite* and *Venus* not being required, should be sold or scrapped. This left four engines, *Creedy*, *Dart*, *Yeo* and *Star* to cover the broad gauge services after Beattie's recommendations were accepted. Only *Venus* found a buyer, but in April 1871, *Star* was kept in working order by cannibalising parts from *Barum* and *Tite*. Beattie also recommended that 24 carriages be sold or scrapped and that six broken broad gauge wagons be replaced with six standard gauge wagons. However, on 8th September 1870, the LSWR decided to retain the broad gauge carriages, which presumably could be used for market and excursion traffic.

After the demise of the broad gauge on the North Devon in April 1877 the redundant locomotive and rolling stock were collected at Barnstaple. *Star* was sold but the other three locomotives were broken up, their boilers being used in a stationary capacity. On 20th September 1877 the South Western decided that the broad gauge wagons and carriages should be broken up at Barnstaple.

one was photographed at Bideford, No. 196 involved in a collision at Fremington in 1869 and No. 181 photographed on a train at Crediton in 1880. In 1887-8, Nos 195, 196, 200 and 204 were working in North Devon and as late as 1894-5 Barnstaple shed had Nos 0257 and 0266, although they were scrapped shortly after.

Numerous examples of the different classes of Beattie 2-4-0 tender locomotives were employed over the years. When the Torrington extension opened in 1872 two of the first locomotives shedded there, working to Exeter and back, were 'Eagle' class No. 30 *Vulture* and 'Volcano' class No. 89 *Saturn* with sister locomotive No. 61 *Snake* working the line from the Exeter end. In 1872-3 the Yeovil to Torrington train was worked by Yeovil locomotives 'Volcano' class No. 84 *Styx* and 'Falcon' class No. 25 *Reindeer*. The latter was joined on the roster

Locomotives of North Devon Railway							
Name	Previous No. and Name	Type	Builder	Building Date	Date of Purchase by Brassey	Withdrawal Date	Notes
New Locomotives							
Creedy	–	2-4-0	Brassey	6/1855	6/1855	4/1877	
Yeo	–	2-2-2	Brassey	12/1857	12/1857	4/1877	
Dart	–	2-2-2	Brassey	8/1855	8/1855	11/1867	rebuilt 1867
	rebuilt to 2-4-0	–	rebuilt 1867/8	–	4/1877		
Ex-Bristol & Gloucester Railway Locomotives							
Star	4 Bristol	2-2-2	Stothert & Slaughter	7/1844	6/1855	4/1877	Sold
Barum	5 Gloucester	2-2-2	Stothert & Slaughter	7/1844	11/1855	7/1870	
Exe	6 Berkeley	2-2-2	Stothert & Slaughter	7/1844	4/1856	7/1870	
Tite	8 Cheltenham	2-2-2	Stothert & Slaughter	7/1844	8/1856	7/1870	
Mole	9 Stroud	2-2-2	Stothert & Slaughter	12/1844	11/1855	7/1870	
Venus	2 Industry	2-4-0	Stothert & Slaughter	9/1844	3/1856	9/1870	Sold
Dreadnought	10 Dreadnought	0-6-0	Stothert & Slaughter	7/1844	5/1856	6/1863	Sold
Defiance	11 Defiance	0-6-0	Stothert & Slaughter	12/1844	8/1857	1/1867	
Other Locomotives							
Taw	–	2-2-2	Robert Stephenson	1838-40	8/1855	pre 1863	

The North Devon Railway had engine sheds, provided with coal, water and turntables at Crediton, Barnstaple and Bideford, and substantial locomotive workshops at Barnstaple. Brassey built up the workshops here not just to maintain his North Devon locomotives, but also the locomotives he used on other contracts. The South Western used the workshops for several substantial jobs, including the re-building of *Dart* and the lifting of locomotive boilers. Equipment installed included a wheel lathe, screw lathe and smith's shops, and the workshop staff were recorded for posterity in August 1863 with *Creedy* on the Barnstaple turntable. All carriage and wagon maintenance was also carried out here. The sidings at Barnstaple were used for storing several dumped or worn out locomotives before they were scrapped here. The South Western continued to use the Barnstaple workshops for repairing locomotives until 1894.

Beattie Locomotives
The first recorded South Western locomotive running west of Exeter appears to have been the 'Nelson' class 2-4-0WT No. 144 *Howe* which was derailed at Cowley Bridge Junction on 17th May 1862. This was only three months after South Western services to Crediton commenced. The numerous classes of Beattie's standard 2-4-0WTs took over many passenger duties in North Devon after 1863,

by sister locomotive No. 91 *Spitfire* in 1875-6. In the period of 1874-6 Exeter shed rostered all three members of the 'Eagle' class, Nos 27 *Eagle*, 28 *Hawk* and 30 *Vulture* to work on the North Devon line.

Several classes of 0-6-0 goods engine were used on the line, including the 'Lion' class which was introduced in 1863 and in 1877-8 included Nos 3 *Transit* and 54 *Medea*. Standard Beyer, Peacock goods engines also appeared including a double-framed locomotive photographed at Eggesford in mixed gauge days and a single-framed locomotive at Bideford in 1922.

When the broad gauge track was removed between Crediton and Bideford in 1877 the engineers department employed 0-6-0 Nos 201 *Harrison* and 202 *Bidder* on lifting the redundant rails and on ballast train duties. Quite possibly these locomotives were also involved in the doubling works between Cowley Bridge Junction and Coleford Junction from 1874 to 1877.

When Joseph Beattie died in 1871 he was succeeded as the LSWR's locomotive engineer by his son, William George and for the steeply graded and lightly constructed Barnstaple & Ilfracombe Railway he ordered eight small light 0-6-0s from Beyer, Peacock, known as the 'Ilfracombe Goods'. It seems that all members of the class spent some time in North Devon, but by 1881 Ilfracombe had Nos 282 and 283 and Barnstaple Nos 383, 394 and

Inside Barnstaple Junction shed in October 1907 was the old 0-6-0 Beyer, Peacock 'Ilfracombe Goods' 0-6-0 No. 0394, built in 1880, withdrawn in 1913 and subsequently sold to the East Kent Railway.

F. E. Box courtesy National Railway Museum

300 which at the time was receiving attention in Nine Elms works. They slowly drifted away, being sold off to light railways, with only No. 0394 remaining at Barnstaple by 1907.

For the opening of the Plymouth line in 1876 William Beattie again ordered a special class of locomotive from Beyer, Peacock - a class of six 4-4-0Ts known as the 'Plymouth' or 'Metropolitan' tanks, These were Nos 318-323 which were all based at Exeter. At speed the locomotives were very rough riding, to the extent that on one occasion a fireman was flung across the cab, knocked unconscious and suffered a broken collar bone and this on straight track near Yeoford. They were soon replaced by earlier Beattie 2-4-0s on the Plymouth line.

As the South Western system west of Exeter expanded the company replaced its small locomotive shed at Queen Street station with a large depot at Exmouth Junction which opened in 1880 and was rebuilt and enlarged by the Southern in 1927-8. The depot was extensively equipped and could handle all major repairs and maintenance for locomotives in the area, including those based at the North Devon sheds of Barnstaple, Ilfracombe and Torrington. Most North Devon line trains were handled by Exmouth Junction locomotives, but Torrington and Barnstaple locomotives covered some Exeter trains, together with local trains and yard shunting.

Barnstaple shed allocation – March 1878.

Well tanks	2-4-0WT	263, 298
Ilfracombe Goods	0-6-0	300, 301
Single-framed Goods	0-6-0	302

Adams Locomotives

Many South Western locomotives designed by William Adams worked in North Devon. The radial 4-4-2 tank engines were regular visitors from Exeter, and in April 1886 Nos 169, 170, 171, 480, 485, 491 and 493 were in use. No. 524 was photographed on the Torrington turntable about 1891 and in 1901 No. 489 of Exeter worked on a roster which took her to Torrington and Sidmouth on alternative days.

Most of the Adams 4-4-0 classes worked in North Devon at some time. In the late 1890s there were the mixed traffic 380 class, the "Steamrollers", Nos 384, 385, 386 and 391 shedded at Barnstaple and Exmouth Junction. By 1905 Exmouth Junction was using Nos 0381, 0383 and 0384 in North Devon, and they remained in use until 1925. The 460 class of passenger locomotives, built in 1884, appeared in North Devon in the next century, with Exmouth Junction having Nos 0460, 0461 and 0462 in 1912. In later South Western days one was photographed on a passenger train at Lapford and No. 526 was shedded at Torrington. In July and August of 1925 the Southern sent Nos 0460, 0462, 0468, 0470, 0473, 0475 and 0476 to Barnstaple shed for light duties, with several sub-shedded at Torrington for the new service to Halwill. Nos 526, 0474 and 478 were also seen and the class covered numerous light passenger and freight workings, together with X6 class No. 665 which was kept in immaculate condition at Barnstaple shed, and No. 658 was also photographed here early in Southern days. Earlier in the century T3 class locomotives Nos 564 and 567 were at Barnstaple in 1903, with Nos 571 and 575 at Torrington,

Shortly after the Grouping Adams 460 class 4-4-0 No. E0473 leaves Barnstaple Junction with an 'up' freight train.

A. Halls courtesy National Railway Museum

all working principal trains to Exeter, whilst X6 class locomotives worked on the Plymouth line.

The Adams light 0-6-0 goods engines of the 395 class were regular visitors for many years, Exmouth Junction having ten of them in 1890. No. 83 was photographed at Torrington about 1891, but their use on the Plymouth line was restricted to slow goods trains after No. 442 was derailed on the Great Western near Yelverton in 1885. In Southern days, No. 0163 was photographed on a passenger train at Torrington and No. 0397 at Barnstaple shed. Weight restrictions on the Torrington to Halwill line were severe, and so when a cattle special was run to Hatherleigh or Hole, Exmouth Junction shed rostered one of the class if available.

The numerous 'Jubilee' class of 0-4-2 mixed traffic loco-motives of the late 1880s soon appeared in North Devon, an early arrival being No. 539 photographed on a passenger train at Bideford in the early 1890s. In March and April of 1903 Nos 618, 634, 638, 640 and 641 were fitted with automatic tablet exchange equipment in conjunction with installations at Portsmouth Arms and South Molton Road stations, but the experiment was apparently short-lived. In the Southern period, Nos 628 and 637 were photographed at Barnstaple on goods trains, and another was seen banking a long passenger train up Morthoe bank on the Ilfracombe line.

Adams also produced two designs of 0-4-4 tank engine. T1 class Nos 1, 2, 4, 69 and 363 were shared between

Early in Southern days Adams X6 class 4-4-0 No. E665 on an 'up' goods at Barnstaple Junction. This locomotive was kept in immaculate condition by the staff at Barnstaple shed.

A. Halls courtesy National Railway Museum

Adams A12 class 0-4-2 No. 637 in Southern livery on a 'down' goods train passing Bishops Tawton carrying Exmouth Junction duty disc 532.

A. Halls courtesy R. J. Sellick

Barnstaple and Ilfracombe sheds in 1907 for the branch work, and the smaller O2 class also put in an appearance.

Barnstaple shed allocation – March 1892.

O2 class	0-4-4T	190, 197
Ilfracombe Goods	0-6-0	301, 324, 394
Well Tanks	2-4-0WT	209, 217
380 class	4-4-0	384, 391
0415 class	4-4-2T	483
A12 class	0-4-2	547 (on loan)

Drummond Locomotives

Many of Drummond's South Western locomotives worked in North Devon, some classes for as long as half a century. He designed the T9 class 4-4-0s, the "Greyhounds", one of the finest designs of its type ever built. In Southern days, Nos 283 and 733 were recorded at Yeoford, but although they were used much more on the Plymouth line the T9s were also occasional visitors to North Devon at this time. In early British Railway days they were used on North Devon line freight services, Nos 30717 and 30730 being

Adams standard goods, 0-6-0 No. E0397, takes water outside Barnstaple shed as driver, fireman, shunter and porter pose for the camera.

A. Halls courtesy National Railway Museum

Still in Southern livery on 20th June 1949, Drummond T9 class 4-4-0 No. 730 on a goods train in Barnstaple Junction yard.

S. C. Nash

amongst those in use. However it was the mixed traffic designs of 4-4-0 by Drummond which were widely used in North Devon over the years. These were the "Small Hopper" K10 class, "Large Hopper" L11 class and S11 class, all of which started work in North Devon in South Western days. The locomotives used here by the Southern Railway included K10 class Nos 142, 153, 384, 387, 389 and 392, L11 class Nos 134, 159, 170, 175 and 406 and S11 class Nos 396, 401 and 409. These three classes continued to be employed in the area until about 1950. All three types also worked on the Plymouth and North Cornwall lines. From time to time, when Yeoford yard

was congested with wagons bound for Exeter St Davids, it was not unknown for an 'up' freight hauled by an L11 to depart from Yeoford with some eighty wagons. Signalmen did not detain such a long train behind such a small locomotive and it soon reached Exeter!

The Drummond standard goods engine, the 700 class 0-6-0 of 1897 soon arrived at Exmouth Junction with Nos 690, 691, 692 and 694 being allocated there in 1898, and may then have worked into North Devon. In the 1920s Nos 306, 350 and 692 were photographed near Barnstaple on 'up' goods trains and in 1957 Exmouth Junction duty No. 532, covering a freight train to Barnstaple and back,

Drummond S11 class 4-4-0 No. 396 carrying Exmouth Junction duty disc 572 passes Bishops Tawton with an 'up' passenger train of South Western non-corridor stock.

A. Halls courtesy R. J. Sellick

Drummond S11 class 4-4-0 No. 401, still in LSWR livery, awaits the road at Barnstaple Junction with a freight for Torrington.

A. Halls courtesy National Railway Museum

was rostered for a 700 class, No. 30691 being recorded on one occasion at Copplestone and on another at Cowley Bridge Junction.

Perhaps the longest serving class of South Western locomotive in North Devon were the M7 class 0-4-4Ts. Barnstaple shed had them for half a century for duties on the Torrington and Ilfracombe lines, including local passenger, freight, banking and shunting work. Some were there in South Western days, including No. 22 and in December 1931 there were Nos 36, 242, 250, 256 and 668 present, During the 1950s, there were Nos 30247, 30250, 30251, 30252, 30253, 30254, 30255, 30256 and 30670, and in June 1962 the last surviving LSWR locomotives in North Devon were Nos 30251 and 30670. In 1957 M7 rosters included Torrington duty 588, Barnstaple duties 576, 577, 578 and 580, and Exeter duty 533, which

covered the Exeter to Eggesford goods.

None of the Drummond or Urie 4-6-0 locomotives ventured west of Exeter. Loads were usually too light to justify their use and in any case the bridges could not take their heavy weight.

Barnstaple shed allocation – March 1922:

Class	Type	Nos
T1	0-4-4T	68, 80
O2	0-4-4T	177, 216
A12	0-4-2	612, 616, 633
460	4-4-0	0460, 0472, 526
X2	4-4-0	586
T3	4-4-0	559
X6	4-4-0	658

Drummond 700 class 0-6-0 No. 692 heads an 'up' goods at Bishops Tawton in Southern days.

A. Halls courtesy R. J. Sellick

arr	EXMOUTH JCT DUTY 825	dep
	Exmouth Junction	5.35am
5.40am	Exeter	6.20
7.44	Barnstaple	8.13
8.53	Torrington	9.25
11.39	Exeter	11.45
11.50	Exmouth Junction	12.45pm
12.50pm	Exeter	1.15
3.55	Torrington	4.55
7.18	Exeter	7.25
7.30	Exmouth Junction	

arr	EXMOUTH JCT DUTY 827	dep
	Exmouth Junction	7.50am
7.55	Exeter	8.20
10.48	Torrington	12.00 noon
2.10	Exeter	2.05
2.10	Exmouth Jcn	

arr	EXMOUTH JCT DUTY 834	dep
	Exmouth Junction	2.05am
2.10	Exeter	2.35
8.15	Torrington	12.20pm
7.40	Exeter	7.45
7.50	Exmouth Junction	

arr	EXMOUTH JCN DUTY 836	dep
	Exmouth Junction	5.15am
5.20am	Exeter	5.40
12.47pm	Torrington	3.15
5.42	Exeter	5.50
5.55	Exmouth Junction	

arr	EXMOUTH JCN DUTY 837	dep
	Exmouth Junction	8.55am
9.00	Exeter	9.20
4.52pm	Barnstaple	7.00pm
10.05	Exeter	10.10
10.15	Exmouth Junction	

arr	EXMOUTH JCN DUTY 839	dep
	Exeter	11.55am
12.56pm	Crediton	4.00pm
4.49	Exeter	5.00
5.05	Exmouth Junction	

arr	TORRINGTON DUTY 897	dep
	Torrington	7.25am
9.38am	Exeter	11.17
1.32pm	Torrington	4.00
5.42	Barnstaple Junction	6.09
9.40	Torrington	

arr	TORRINGTON DUTY 898	dep
	Torrington	1.40pm
3.54pm	Exeter	5.48
7.58	Torrington	

arr	BARNSTAPLE DUTY 893	dep	
	Barnstaple Junction	5.30am	NF
11.57am	Crediton	2.15pm	NF
2.35pm	Exeter	4.15	NF
6.01	Barnstaple Junction		NF
	Shunt		
	Fridays Only		
	Barnstaple Junction	5.30am	FO
10.55am	Exeter	4.15pm	FO
6.01	Barnstaple Junction		FO
	Shunt		

Note. Ilfracombe duties 891, 896, Barnstaple duties 890, 892, 895 worked on the Ilfracombe and Torrington lines. Numerous other Exmouth Junction and Plymouth Friary duties worked along the Exeter - Coleford Junction section.

Maunsell Locomotives

Maunsell's N class 2-6-0 mixed traffic locomotives, known to the men as the "Woolworths", since they were constructed at Woolwich Arsenal, mainly in 1924-5, were one of the few classes to be sent brand new to the North Devon line. They could take a load of 180 tons, or seven coaches, over Morthoe bank unaided, and from the introduction of the new timetable on 12th July 1925 the principal through passenger services from Exeter ran to Ilfracombe instead of Torrington. Nos A839, A841, A849 and A857 were shedded at Barnstaple and almost forty more at Exmouth Junction, from where Nos 1406, 1407, 1408 and 1409 regularly worked to Ilfracombe. By August 1939 Barnstaple had Nos 1830, 1833, 1835, 1840 and 1848, which monopolised principal North Devon line passenger trains until the arrival of the Bulleid Pacifics. The Moguls continued to work local passenger and freight services, in June 1959 Barnstaple still having Nos 31842 and 31843, an N class covering duty 574 on a freight to Exeter in 1957. One of the last recorded was No. 31846 on a freight train at Barnstaple on 18th August 1964.

Several of Maunsell's U1 class 2-6-0s were also allocated to Exmouth Junction and occasionally worked into North Devon, particularly during the Second World War. A number of Maunsell rebuilds of old LBSCR E1 class 0-6-0Ts, the E1R class 0-6-2Ts were shedded at Exeter and Barnstaple, the former using them for banking and piloting, the latter for services to Torrington and Halwill Junction.

Barnstaple shed allocation – January 1947:

Class	Type	Nos
M7	0-4-4T	23, 36, 42, 44, 247, 250, 321, 670
E1R	0-6-2T	2094, 2095, 2096, 2608 2610, 2696

Bulleid Locomotives

In the summer of 1945 the Southern Railway advertised the first of Britain's post-war locomotives, the 'West Country' class 4-6-2s, which immediately took over the principal trains between Exeter and Ilfracombe. In August, Nos 21C101 *Exeter*, 21C102 *Salisbury* and 21C103 *Plymouth* started work, and were soon joined by many others of the class. Several others were named after local towns and villages including Nos 21C105 *Barnstaple*, 21C148 *Crediton* and 34102 *Lapford*, while 21C117 *Ilfracombe* was originally based at the resort and worked the "Devon Belle" to and from Exeter. The 'West Country' and 'Battle of Britain' light Pacifics almost monopolised passenger services on the North Devon and other Southern lines west of Exeter, but when some of the class were rebuilt at the cost of several extra tons in weight they were too heavy for the North Devon line, although eventually they worked on the Plymouth line. In 1957, 'West Country' class locomotives covered Barnstaple duty 572 to Yeovil and Ilfracombe, numerous Exmouth Junction duties and Wadebridge duty 603 which finished up at Ilfracombe. The 'West Countrys' regularly worked most services until the demise of steam in the autumn of 1964.

Barnstaple shed allocation – 1959:

Class	Type	Nos
M7	0-4-4T	30251, 30253, 30254, 30255, 30256, 30671
2	2-6-2T	41294, 41295, 41297, 41298, 41314

Ivatt Locomotives

An interesting feature in British Railways' days was the arrival in the 1950s of numerous Ivatt LMR 2-6-2Ts which eventually took over all tank engine duties in North Devon. They displaced first the E1R 0-6-2Ts and then the M7 0-4-4Ts. The following saw service from Barnstaple shed in the period 1953-1964; Nos 41214, 41216, 41248, 41283, 41290, 41294, 41295, 41297, 41298, 41310, 41312, 41313 and 41314. They also took over some duties in the Exeter area and could be seen shunting the yards at Yeoford and Crediton.

British Railways Locomotives

British Railways Standard classes rarely visited North Devon although Class 5 73xxx series 4-6-0s often worked to Plymouth. On one occasion 2-6-2T No. 84020 worked the Exeter to Eggesford goods. Occasionally the larger tank engines were seen, particularly east of Coleford Junction, and on 3rd October 1965 the last steam train to North Devon, the "Exeter Flyer" organised by the RCTS, was hauled by two 2-6-4Ts, Nos 80039 and 80043.

Great Western Locomotives

Ever since 1887 Great Western locomotives worked into Barnstaple Junction, and most types which worked from Taunton could be seen here from time to time, and these are summarised in brief as follows. For some forty years the 2-6-0s of the 43xx and 73xx series were the main type in use, those working through to Ilfracombe having their steps cut back to 8ft 4in width. Other types seen were 4-4-0s in earlier years, 2-6-2Ts and the odd 0-6-0 or 0-6-0PT. During the Second World War and again after Nationalization GWR locomotives were regularly rostered on the Southern line to Plymouth, the trains being the 11.47am and 6.47pm from Exeter Central and 2.25pm and 4.40pm from Plymouth Friary, motive power usually being a 2-6-0 of the 43xx or 63xx series, but a 'Hall' or 'Star' 4-6-0 was also in occasional use. In 1963-4, some GWR locomotives, including the 0-6-0 Collett goods, worked along the Exeter to Barnstaple line.

Diesel Locomotives and Multiple Units

By the late 1950s diesel locomotives began to work on the Plymouth line, for example on 18th July 1959 the 2.45pm from Plymouth to Exeter left Crediton hauled by two North British Type 2 diesels, Nos 6302 and 6303. However it was not until May and June of 1963 that diesel locomotives and multiple units appeared north of Coleford Junction, but change was then rapid and in the new timetable of 6th September 1964 most Exeter to Ilfracombe trains were provided by three-coach diesel multiple units, together with some trains hauled by diesel locomotives. Of the locomotives the North British Type 2 was the most popular, assisted by 'Hymeks' on the principal trains. On 10th November 1971 the Royal Train was hauled from Exeter to Barnstaple by 'Warship' Class 42 No. 818 *Glory* returning behind 'Western' Class 52 No. D1049 *Western Monarch*. 'Warships' and Brush Type 4s were also seen later, and for a time an 08 class shunter was employed at Barnstaple. After the closure of the Plymouth line beyond Okehampton the short-lived Exeter to Okehampton passenger service was operated by diesel multiple units, single car units often sufficing.

By about 1972, the North British Type 2s had been superseded by other classes, mainly Class 25s, but also some Class 31s. The Class 25s continued to operate until about 1980 when the Class 31s became dominant, later assisted by numerous Class 33s. By the mid 1970s the condition of Pill Bridge was such that the heavier classes were banned north of Eggesford. However, the Meldon Quarry line could accept almost any locomotive and Classes 40, 45, 46 and 47 were all in use, together with 31s and 33s. Class 50s were also seen occasionally, and all these locomotives could have been seen on the odd working to Lapford.

A pair of Class 20s appeared, one at each end of the Chipman's weedkilling train, and Class 37 No. 37167 came on an enthusiasts' special. 'Skipper' Class 142 units took over most services in 1986-7 but were soon found to be unsuitable and were replaced with conventional Class 101 and 108 dmus reduced to two cars. However the 07.05 Exeter and 08.50 Barnstaple departures were usually

N Class 2-6-0 No. A829 of Exmouth Junction shed accelerates the 'up' "Atlantic Coast Express" away from Pill Bridge.

A. Halls courtesy
R. J. Sellick

The 1.45pm Ilfracombe to Waterloo express approaches Cowley Bridge Junction behind Bulleid Pacific No. 34096 *Trevone* on 22nd August 1959.

S. C. Nash

Bulleid Pacific No. 34069 *Hawkinge* running tender first with a short 'down' passenger train at Barnstaple Junction, probably the 11.23am to Torrington, on 13th August 1962.

A. E. West

covered by a Class 155 'Sprinter'; Class 150s and 156s have appeared and No. 158714 carried out clearance tests on 13th September 1990.

In June 1989 the bar on larger locomotives north of Lapford was lifted and numerous trains of two or three coaches, or a failed dmu, have been hauled by Class 47 or 50 locomotives which had to run round at Barnstaple. For example on 31st August the 16.06pm Exeter consisted of No. 47451 and three Mk1 coaches. This practice reached a peak on Friday 15th June 1990 when the 17.08 Exeter and 16.14 Barnstaple services crossed at Eggesford, the trains being hauled by Nos 50015 *Valiant* and 50036 *Victorious*

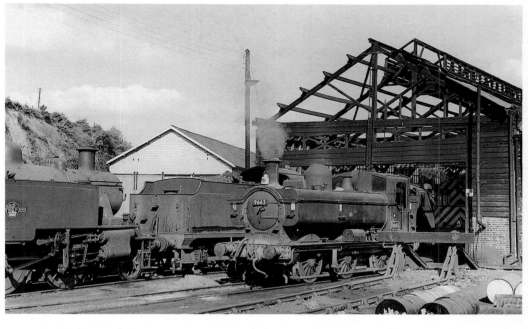

A variety of motive power at Barnstaple shed on 30th August 1964 including WR 0-6-0T No. 9663, two Ivatt 2-6-2Ts, an N class 2-6-0 and an 08 diesel shunter.

S. C. Nash

respectively. Enthusiasts' specials in 1990 included a High Speed Train from Paddington to Barnstaple on 18th March, and a 12-coach train from Manchester on 16th September hauled by Nos 50032 *Courageous* and 50031 *Hood*, with one at each end, the new loop being too short to allow the locomotives to run round the train.

Carriages and Wagons

From 1863 standard South Western standard gauge rolling stock of the period was used on the line, starting with four-wheel and six-wheel coaches in dark brown livery. For some years no brakes were provided on any coaches, trains being halted by locomotive brakes and by brake van or vans, the driver whistling to the guard for braking when required. Eventually continuous brakes operated by the driver came in, and by early 1890s, the first bogie carriages appeared on through workings from Waterloo. Corridor stock appeared in the early 1900s, now in the umber and salmon livery of the LSWR. In the summer of 1913 the 11.10am and 12.50pm North Devon expresses from Waterloo each comprised nine corridor coaches, being split at Barnstaple Junction into Torrington and Ilfracombe portions, the dining car working right through to Torrington. However some four and six-wheelers were still in use on local trains at this stage. In Southern days first Maunsell and then Bulleid coaches appeared in their distinctive green liveries, although some South Western stock, such as three-coach set No. 126 was still in use as late as 1954. Pullman stock appeared on the "Devon Belle", including the observation car which was turned on the Ilfracombe turntable. In the 1970s and '80s most locomotive hauled trains have consisted of rakes of BR Mk 1 coaches in blue and white livery.

A number of vehicles were supplied for the Post Office sorting train. In 1895 a 20ft vehicle, No. 3, was employed as the Barnstaple and Exeter Bag Tender, on the 3.10am 'down' from Exeter and the 8.24pm 'up' from Barnstaple mail trains, this being replaced later by 32ft vehicle No. 9. In 1903 the duty was extended to Torrington, the 'up' service becoming the 7.40pm from Torrington. In 1906, carriage No. 9 was used as a sorting carriage on the Exeter to Torrington mail services, the service ending in 1917.

For freight services the usual variety of wagons have been used. More unusual have been the milk tanker wagons serving depots at Torrington, Lapford and Crediton and flat wagons for the conveyance of meat containers. In the 1980s specialist wagons for traffic in steel plate, cement, grain, glue and fertilisers were used, all North Devon freight services of course, now being air-braked. For almost a century several generations of specialist ballast wagons have been used on the Meldon Quarry trains, these all being vacuum braked.

A Survey - August 1984

In August 1984 the author recorded 187 trains near Crediton on both the North Devon and Meldon lines. On the North Devon 98 trains were formed by a three-car diesel multiple unit, 20 trains hauled by Class 31s and 33 by Class 33s. On the Meldon line nine Class 31s and 17 Class 33s were recorded, in eight cases double headed, together with six Class 45s, two Class 46s, nine Class 47s and one Class 50.

On the North Devon line the weekday service of ten passenger trains was covered by eight diesel multiple units, and Class 33s hauling the 03.00 and 15.00 services from Exeter St Davids and 07.10 and 16.07 return from Barnstaple. A bogie mail van went down on the 03.00 from Exeter and a bogie newspaper van on the back of the 04.05 diesel multiple unit, both returning on the 07.10 which also comprised four, five or six Mk 1 coaches. The 16.07 was normally provided with four Mk 1 coaches, the train running to Post Office requirements. The 04.05 freight from Exeter and return 09.10 from Barnstaple was worked by a Class 31 hauling anything up to five wagons. Other workings included a ballast train and an engineers train, both hauled by Class 31s.

At weekends the pattern changed. On Saturdays most of the eleven trains were covered by two Class 33s hauling rakes of four or five coaches, with two or three provided by diesel multiple units. On Sundays the three services were provided by one Class 33 hauling a rake of four Mk 1 coaches.

Until the derailment on 21st August at Bow, which shut the Meldon line for almost a week, there was usually five daily stone trains to and from Meldon Quarry, on weekdays only. There were two to Bristol, one to Taunton and two to Salisbury, one of which, the 11.30 from Meldon ran direct up the South Western main line. The heavy stone trains consisted of a variety of types of wagon including 'Dogfish', 'Dace', 'Sealion', 'Sea Cow', and 'Grampus' and were booked to run from the 09.10 from Meldon to Bristol until the 21.10pm Meldon to Taunton.

Locomotives in use included Nos 31119, 31210 (usually working in multiple), 31231, 33014, 33015, 33019, 33037, 33038, 33052 *Ashford*, 33108, 33112, 33118 and 33203, together with 45012, 45120, 46026, 47240, 47282 and 50012 *Benbow*.

On 18th July 1959 the 2.45pm passenger train from Plymouth to Exeter departs from Crediton behind North British Type 2 locomotives Nos D6302 and D6303, whilst an N class 2-6-0 shunts the yard.
S. C. Nash

'Warship' class No. D803 *Albion* passes Yeoford hauling the 10.55am Plymouth to Brighton express on 3rd October 1964.
C. L. Caddy

Class 45 No. 45064 passes Crediton on 26th August 1981 with a train of ballast wagons bound for Meldon Quarry.
Author

Class 47 No. 47577 *Benjamin Gimbert GC* passes Cowley Bridge Junction with a train of loaded ballast wagons from Meldon Quarry on 4th June 1982.

Author

Saturday 23rd August 1980 sees the 12.00 train from Barnstaple to Exeter arriving at Eggesford consisting of five coaches hauled by Class 25 No. 25058.

Author

On 18th August 1981 the 17.59 train from Exeter St Davids to Barnstaple passes Umberleigh Gates. The train consists of five coaches hauled by Class 31 No. 31263.

Author

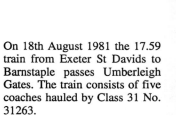

Imported grain is unloaded from a Grain Flow Polybulk wagon into a lorry at Lapford sidings Wednesday 13th August 1986. On the right of the lorry is timber to be forwarded by rail.
Author

ENGINE WORKINGS SUMMER 1957 – WEEKDAYS

Ex Jc Duty 527 7P5F (WC Class)

	Ex Jc Loco	1.53	(am)
1.57	Exeter Cent	2.6	F
4.55	Barn Jc	6.38	F
7.22	Ilfracombe		
	F Shunting 7.25-7.40		
		7.40	
7.45	Ilfracombe Loco yard	7.55	
8.00	Ilfracombe	8.10	P
10.11	Ex Cent	10.20	
10.24	Ex Jc Loco		
		12.41	(pm)
12.45	Ex Cent	1.28	P (9.00 Waterloo)
3.42	Ilfracombe	++	
++	Loco yard	4.25	
4.30	Ilfracombe	4.48	P
7.3	Exeter Cent	7.11	
7.14	Ex Jc Loco		

Ex Jc Duty 531 4P5F (N Class)

	Ex Jc	3.15	(am)
3.18	Ex Jc yard	3.30	F
4.37	Yeoford		
	F Shunting 4.45 – 6.55		
		7.9	F (6.00 Ex Jc)
8.35	Barnstaple Jc	++	
++	Barnstaple Loco		
		10.25	
++	Barnstaple Jc	10.45	F
12.36 (pm)	Ilfracombe		
	F Shunting 12.40 – 12.55		
	C Shunting 1.50 – 2.20		
		++	
++	Ilfracombe Loco yard		
		3.00	
++	Ilfracombe	3.14	F
4.38	Barnstaple Jc	4.48	
4.53	Barnstaple Loco	5.00	
5.5	Barnstaple Jc	5.15	P
5.56	Ilfracombe		
	C Shunting 6.00 – 6.20 and 6.40 – 6.55		
	Ilfracombe	7.0	
7.34	Barnstaple Loco		

Stable for Duty 573 next day

Ex Jc Duty 526 7P5F (WC Class)

	Ex Jc Loco	4.35	(am)
4.39	Exeter Cent	5 6	P (1.15 Waterloo)
6.50	Ilfracombe		
	C Shunting 7.00 – 7.25		

	7.45 – 8.30 & 8.50 – 9.15		
		9.15	
9.20	Ilfracombe Loco yard		
		10.00	
10.5	Ilfracombe	10.30	P
12.24 (pm)	Exeter Cent	1.10	P
2.46	Yeovil Jc		

Returning to Ex Jc Loco 8.52

Ex Jc Duty 528 7P5F (WC Class)

	Ex Jc Loco	4.35	(am)
4.39	Exeter Cent	5.21	P
7.41	Ilfracombe	7.51	
7.56	Ilfracombe Loco yard		
		8.40	
8.45	Ilfracombe	8.55	P
11.4	Exeter Cent	11.12	P
12.42 (pm)	Yeovil Jc		

Returning to Ex Jc Loco 7.45

Ex Jc Duty 540 7P5F (WC Class)

	Ex Jc Loco	5.40	(am)
5.43	Ex Jc yard	6.00	F
6.41	Yeoford		
	F Shunting 700 – 9.15		
		9.30	F
3.25 (pm)	Plymouth Friary		

Returning to Okehampton 11.35
(to Ex Jc 12.49 Fridays 28/6–23/8)

Ex Jc Duty 544 5F (N Class)

	Ex Jc Loco	4.35	(am)
5.7	Yeoford	6.0	F (3.30 Ex Jc)
11.00	Bude		

Returns (pm) on F to Okehampton
then Stone train to Exeter

Ex Jc Duty 532 3F (700 Class)

	Ex Jc Loco	6.10	(am)
6.13	Ex Jc yard	6.30	F
12.45 (pm)	Barnstaple Jc	1.00	
1.5	Barnstaple Loco		
		2.50	
2.55	Barnstaple Jc	3.20	F (12.45 Torrington)
6.38	Ex Jc yard	6.50	
6.53	Ex Jc Loco		

Ex Jc Duty 523 6MT (WC Class)

	Ex Jc Loco	1.1	(am)
1.4	Ex Jc yard	1.20	F (4.30 Wadebridge)
	to Yeovil Junc & Town	6.25	P
8.8	Exeter Cent	8.31	P
10.52	Ilfracombe		

	C Shunting 11.00 – 11.20			
11.25	Ilfracombe Loco			
		12.00 (noon)		
12.5	Ilfracombe	12.20	P	
2.23	Exeter Cent	2.25		
2.28	Ex Jc Loco			
		4.25		
4.29	Exeter Cent	5.5	P	(1.00 Waterloo)
7.17	Ilfracombe	7.37		
7.42	Ilfracombe Loco	8.10		
8.15	Ilfracombe	8.30	P	
9.9	Barnstaple Jc	9.30		
9.35	Barnstaple Loco			

Stable for Duty 572 (FX)
529 (FO)

Ex Jc Duty 543 5F (N Class)
(Morning F. Trip and F Shunting at Broad Clyst)

	Ex Jc Loco	6.40	(pm)	
6.43	Ex Jc yard	7.00	F	
8.19	Yeoford			
	F Shunting 8.20 – 9,35			
	Yeoford	9.35		
10.5	Okehampton Loco		(Q: if required for 11.27 Stone Train to Exeter)	
	or Yeoford	9.45	LE	
10.25	Ex Jc Loco			

Ex Jc Duty 533 2PT (M7 Class)
	Ex Jc Loco	8.40	(am)	
8.43	Ex Jc yard	9.15	F	
2.39 (pm)	Eggesford			
	F Shunting 2.40 – 3.15			
		3.17	F	
4.27	Crediton			
	C Shunting 5.00 – 5.30			
		5.36	M	
6.3	Exter Cent	6.22		
6.26	Ex Jc Loco			
		7.3		
++	Ex Jc yard	7.18	F	
7.35	Exeter St Davids	8.45	F	
9.13	Yeoford	10.11	F	
11.41	Ex Jc yard	12.1	(am)	
12.4	Ex Jc Loco			

Ex Jc Duty 524 7P (WC Class)
MO Stabled off duty 572 (Sat)
MX stabled off duty 507

	Yeovil Loco	5.15	am	
5.20	Yeovil Town			
	C Shunting 5.20 – 7.20			
		7.50	P	
9.29	Exeter Cent	9.40	P	
12.00 (noon)	Ilfracombe	12.10		
12.15	Ilfracombe Loco			
		2.5		
2.10	Ilfracombe	2.20	P	
4.24	Exeter Cent	4.26		
4.29	Ex Jc Loco			

Wadebridge Duty 603 7P5F (WC Class)
	Padstow	8.30	P	
11.58	Exeter Cent	12.00	(noon)	
12.4	Ex Jc Loco	1.49		
1.53	Exeter Cent	2.21	P	(11.00 Waterloo ACE)
4.11	Ilfracombe	++		
++	Ilfracombe Loco	5.30		
++	Ilfracombe	5.50	P	
6.28	Barnstaple Jc	6.41	F	(5.25 Torrington)
9.33	Exmouth Junc yard	9.53		
9.56	Ex Jc Loco			

Ex Jc Duty 525 7P (WC Class)
	Ex Jc Loco	6.25	am	
6.29	Exeter Cent	6.50	P	
	to Axminster & return			
8.49	Exeter Cent	8.57		
9.00	Ex Jc Loco			
		11.3		

11.7	Exeter Cent	11.27	P	(8.12 Salisbury)
1.48 (pm)	Ilfracombe	1.58		
2.3	Ilfracombe Loco			
		2.45		
2.50	Ilfracombe	3.00	P	
5.24	Exeter Cent	5.26		
5.29	Ex Jc Loco			
		6.6		
6.10	Exeter Cent	6.52	P	(3.00 Waterloo)
9.6	Ilfracombe			
	C Shunting 9.10 – 9.25			
		9.25		
9.30	Ilfracombe Loco			

Stable for Duty 529 (FX)
572 (FO)

Barnstaple Duty 574 MO 7P (WC Class)
MX 4P5F (N Class)
MO Stabled off duty 574 (Sun)
MX Stabled off duty 573

	Barnstaple Jc Loco	5.30	(am)	
++	Barnstaple Jc Loco	5.45	F	
11.33	Ex Jc yard	11.43		
11.46	Ex Jc Loco			
		3.3	(pm)	
3.7	Exeter Central	3.20	P	
4.59	Yeovil Jc			

Returning to Ex Jc loco 11.50

Ex Jc Duty 529 7P5F (WC Class)
MO Stabled off duty 529 (Sun)
MX Stabled off duty 525

	Ilfracombe Loco	6.20	(am)	
++	Ilfracombe Loco	6.50	P	
7.52	Kings Nympton	8.30	P	
8.52	Barnstaple Jc	++		
++	Barnstaple Loco			
		11.00		
++	Barnstaple Jc	11.23	P	(Tender First)
11.58	Torrington	12.45	F	
2.29	Barnstaple Jc	2.40		
2.45	Barnstaple Loco			
		4.50		
++	Barnstaple Jc	5.8	F	(4.15 Bideford)
7.4	Exeter Central Goods	7.11		
7.14	Ex Jc Loco			

Barnstaple Duty 572 7P (WC Class)
MO Stabled off duty 572 (Sun)
MX Stabled off duty 523

	Barnstaple Loco	7.30	(am)	
7.35	Barnstaple Jc	7.39	P	(7.5 Torrington)
8.58	Exeter Cent	9.38	P	
11.8	Yeovil Jc	11.10		
11.15	Yeovil Loco			
		1.31	(pm)	
1.36	Yeovil Jc (Turn)	2.20	P	(12.46 Salisbury)
3.35	Exeter Cent	4.21	P	
5.46	Barnstaple Jc	5.55	P	
6.37	Ilfracombe	6.52		
6.57	Ilfracombe Loco			
		7.25		
7.30	Ilfracombe	7.42	P	
10.7	Exeter Cent	10.36		
10.40	Ex Jc Loco			

Ex Jc Duty 548 4P5F (N Class)
(AM, works F to Okehampton & Bude the P to Halwill & return to Bude then F to)

2.14 (pm)	Okehampton	2.56	F	(11.5 Plymouth Fri)
4.8	Yeoford			
	F Shunting 5.15 – 6.45			
	Yeoford	7.11	F	
8.11	Exeter St Davids	8.30		
8.42	Ex Jc Loco			

Carriage Working Notice 13th June – 18th September 1955 (Incl) Weekdays

Train	Destination	Formation	Time	Previous Service From	Due

Barnstaple Junc

Train	Destination	Formation	Time	From	Due
7.30	King's Nympton	2 Lav Set (ECS)	–	Berth	–
8.56	Exeter Cent	1 3rd (M.O.til 18/7)			
		1 BK CPO	8.10	Ilfracombe	8.51
		2 3rds (MFO from 22/7)			
		3–Set (770)			
		2–Set (63–75) (MO)			
		1 3rd (MX)	8.10	Torrington (Front portion)	8.41
		1 BK CPO (MX)			
9.39	Salisbury	3–Set (770)	8.55	Ilfracombe	9.33
	Waterloo	2 News Vans B	8.53	Torrington	9.23
	Exeter Cent	1 Van B (Stove)		(Front Portion)	
11.18	Exeter Cent	1 3rd			
		1 3rd (MFO also T.W.TH 26/7 to 25/8)	10.30	Ilfracombe	11.13
		2 Set (63–75)			
	Waterloo	1 3rd			
		1 BK CPO (New)	10.30	Torrington	11.3
		2 News Vans B			
1.4	Exeter Cent	1 BK CPO (C.A.) (Fo, Comm 19/8)			
		2 3rds	12.20	Ilfracombe	12.59
	Waterloo	1 BK CPO (New)			
		1 3rd	12.18	Torrington (Front portion)	12.49
		1 BK CPO (New)			
3.5	Exeter Cent	3–Set (MO)			
		1 3rd (til 19/8)	2.20	Ilfracombe	2.58
	Waterloo	1 3rd (MX)			
		2–Set (63–75)			
		1 BK CPO (New)	2.15	Torrington	2.46
	Exeter St Davids	1 W.R. Stores Van (TuO)	Ex W.R.	(Front Portion) –	
5.35	Waterloo	1 PMV (4)			
		1 3rd	4.48	Ilfracombe	5.28
	Exeter Cent	3-Set			
		1 PMV (4)	4.38	Torrington (Rear portion)	5.10
8.30	Exeter Cent	2–Set (63–75) (FO)			
		3–Set (770)	7.42	Ilfracombe	8.21
		1 Van B			
		1 PMV (4)	7.38	Torrington (Front Portion)	8.10
	Paddington	WR 1 WR Van			

Torrington

Train	Destination	Formation	Time	From	Due
(AM)					
7.6	Exeter Cent	1 3rd (MO)			
		3–Set (770) (MO)	–	Berth	–
		3–Set (MX)			

Ilfracombe

Train	Destination	Formation	Time	From	Due
(PM)					
3.00	Waterloo	1 News Van B	5.21	Exeter Cent	7.42
		1 3rd (MFO)	–	Berth	–
		1 BK CPO (New) (MFX)	8.00	Barnstaple Jc	8.46
		1 BK CPO (FO, till 12/8)			
		1 BK CPO (New)	5.21	Exeter Cent	7.42

King's Nympton

Train	Destination	Formation	Time	From	Due
(AM)				(ECS)	
8.28	Barnstaple Jc	2 LAV Set	7.30	Barnstaple Jc	7.51

Exeter Central

Train	Destination	Formation	Time	From	Due
2.6(F)	Ex St Davids	1 BY			
	Ilfracombe	1 Van B			
	Barnstaple Jc	1 Van B			
	Torring ton	1 Van B (Stove)			
		1 PMV (4)			
	Plymouth Friary	1 BY (Stove)		Berth	
	Bude	1 BY		(Attached to 1.38 (F) Ex. Exmouth Junc Yard)	
	Padstow	1 Van B			

	Train	Destination	Formation	.Time	Previous Service From	Due
	5.6	Ilfracombe	1 3rd			
			1 BK CPO (New)	1.15	Waterloo	5.0
		Bideford	1 BK CPO (New)			
		Thence Torrington	1 News Van B			
	5.21	Ilfracombe	1 BK CPO (New)	(MO) 4.25	Exeter St Davids	4.28
				–	Berth (MX)	–
			1 News Van B	1.15	Waterloo	5.0
		Torrington	1 News Van B		(Rear portion)	
	8.20	Ilfracombe	1 3rd			
			3–Set	6.25	Yeovil Town	8.10
			1 PMV (4)			
	9.40	Ilfracombe	3–Set (770)	7.50	Yeovil Town	9.29
	11.27	Ilfracombe	1 3rd			
			3–Set (770)	8.12	Salisbury	11.19
	1.28	Ilfracombe	2–Set (63–75)	9.00	Waterloo	1.8
			1 3rd		(Mid portion)	
		Torrington	1 BK CPO (New)			
			1 3rd (FO 15/7 to 14/8)	10.30	Ilfracombe	12.24
		Lapford	Van B (FO)	–	Berth	–
MO (Also TWTh 26/7-25/8)	2.21	Ilfracombe	1 3rd	8.15	Plymouth Friary	10.23
			2 3rds			
			1 BK CPO (New)	11.5	Waterloo	2.15
		Torrington	1 BK CPO (New)			
TWT (until 21/7 and comm 31/8)	2.21	Ilfracombe	1 3rd	8.15	Plymouth Friary	10.23
			1 3rd			
			1 BK CPO (New)	11.0	Waterloo	2.5
		Torrington	1 BK CPO (New)			
FO	2.21	Ilfracombe	1 3rd	8.15	Plymouth Friary	10.23
			2 3rds			
			1 Kit Buff Car (3) 15/7 to 26/8			
			1 Refresh Sal 15/7 to 26/8	11.5	Waterloo	2.15
			1 BK CPO (New)		(Front portion)	
		Torrington	2–Set (63–75)			
	4.21		3–Set	12.46	Salisbury	3.27
		Torrington	1 3rd	8.12 (AM)	Salisbury (Front portion)	11.19
			1 BK CPO (C.A.) (MO)	1.25 (AM) (Vans)	Plymouth Friary	3.47
	5.5	Ilfracombe	3–Set (770)	1.0	Waterloo	4.41
		Torrington	1 BK CPO (New)		(Mid portion)	
	6.52			–	Berth (FO)	–
		Ilfracombe	1 3rd	10.30	Ilfracombe (FX)	12.24
			1 Rest Car (30) (FO)			
			1 Open 3rd (FO)			
			2 Set (63–75)	3.0	Waterloo	6.31
		Torrington	1 3rd		(Mid portion)	
			1 BK CPO (New)			
	–	Berth	1 3rd (MO til 18/7)	8.10	Ilfracombe	10.11
			1 BK CPO (MX)			
	–	Berth	1 BK CPO (FO Comm 19/8)	12.20	Ilfracombe	2.23
	–	Berth	3–Set (MO)	2.20	Ilfracombe	4.24
	–	Berth	1 3rd			
			3–Set	4.48	Ilfracombe	7.3
			1 PMV (4)			
	–	Berth	2–Set (63–75) (FO)			
			3–Set (770) (Not F. Comm 19/8)	7.42	Ilfracombe	10.7
			1 Van B			
			1 PMV (4)			

The 12.45 train from Exeter St Davids to Barnstaple on Saturday 18th August 1984 was formed of Class 33 No 33014 and four BR Mk 1 coaches, seen here at Crediton.
Author

A three-coach diesel multiple unit forms the 11.04 train from Exeter St Davids to Barnstaple, seen here leaving Crediton on Saturday 18th August 1984. Colour light signal CN 4 is in position ready to replace the semaphore signals then in use.
Author

A pair of Class 31 diesels, Nos 31210 and 31119, wait for the road at Crediton on 14th August 1984 after delivering a crane to the engineers siding in connection with forthcoming track alterations.
Author

Class 33 No. 33019 heads the 18.25 train from Exeter St Davids to Barnstaple, comprising of four BR Mk 1 coaches, past Salmon Pool Crossing on Sunday 12th August 1984.

Author

The 09.54 empty stone hopper train from Salisbury to Meldon Quarry crosses bridge No. 553, west of Crediton on 13th August 1984, the 'Sea Lion' wagons being hauled by Class 47 No. 47282.

Author

The 16.07 passenger train from Barnstaple to Paignton passes Salmon Pool Crossing on 13th August 1984, the train consisting of Class 33 No. 33019 and four BR Mk 1 coaches.

Author

Class 46 No. 46026 *Leicester-shire & Derbyshire Yeomanary* on 16th August 1984 with an 'up' train of twelve loaded 'Sea Cow' wagons. The 09.10 train, from Meldon Quarry to Exeter, it passes over bridge No. 554 and slows for Salmon Pool Crossing.

Author

The following day, Class 33 No. 33015 with a mixed train of loaded ballast wagons, forming the 11.30 from Meldon Quarry to Salisbury at the same location.

Author

Class 50 No. 50012 *Benbow* is in charge of a train ballasting new track work just east of Crediton on Sunday 19th August 1984.

Author

The first Class 158 dmu to visit Barnstaple was set No. 158714 on Thursday 13th September 1990 on gauging trials. Cameras and lights were mounted on the corners of the unit.

R. B. Dark

On Saturday 27th April 1991 Class 155 set No. 155334 forms the 14.14 service from Barnstaple to Exmouth. At this time these Cardiff-based 'Sprinters' were regularly scheduled for this service.

R. B. Dark

Two round trips on the North Devon line were operated on 24th May 1991 by Class 37 No. 37010 in 'Dutch' livery hauling a failed diesel multiple unit. Here, the driver hands over the single-line token to the signalman at Crediton.

Peter Knottley

Index

Class 47 No. 47361 is about to leave Lapford sidings with empty Kemira fertilizer vans - one of the last such workings before the demise of Speedlink. 22nd May 1991.

Peter Knottley